# URBAN LAND RENT

# Studies in Urban and Social Change

# URBAN LAND RENT

## SINGAPORE AS A PROPERTY STATE

Anne Haila

WILEY Blackwell

This edition first published 2016
© 2016 John Wiley & Sons Ltd

*Registered Office*
John Wiley & Sons Ltd, The Atrium, Southern Gate, Chichester, West Sussex, PO19 8SQ, UK

*Editorial Offices*
350 Main Street, Malden, MA 02148-5020, USA
9600 Garsington Road, Oxford, OX4 2DQ, UK
The Atrium, Southern Gate, Chichester, West Sussex, PO19 8SQ, UK

For details of our global editorial offices, for customer services, and for information about
how to apply for permission to reuse the copyright material in this book please see our
website at www.wiley.com/wiley-blackwell.

The right of Anne Haila to be identified as the author of this work has been asserted in
accordance with the UK Copyright, Designs and Patents Act 1988.

*Library of Congress Cataloging-in-Publication Data*

Haila, Anne.
  Urban land rent : Singapore as a property state / Anne Haila.
    pages cm
  Includes bibliographical references and index.
    ISBN 978-1-118-82768-0 (cloth) – ISBN 978-1-118-82767-3 (pbk.)   1. Land use,
Urban–Singapore.   2. Rent–Singapore.   3. Real property–Singapore.   4. Urban
policy–Singapore.   5. Real estate development–Singapore.   I. Title.
    HD890.67.Z63H35 2016
    333.5095957–dc23

                                                                    2015021548

A catalogue record for this book is available from the British Library.

Cover image: Skyline of Singapore business district © oksana.perkins / Shutterstock

Set in 10.5/12pt NewBaskervilleStd by Aptara Inc., New Delhi, India
Printed and bound in Malaysia by Vivar Printing Sdn Bhd

1   2016

# Contents

# Series Editors' Preface

The Wiley Blackwell *Studies in Urban and Social Change* series is published in association with the *International Journal of Urban and Regional Research*. It aims to advance theoretical debates and empirical analyses stimulated by changes in the fortunes of cities and regions across the world. Among topics taken up in past volumes and welcomed for future submissions are:

- Connections between economic restructuring and urban change
- Urban divisions, difference, and diversity
- Convergence and divergence among regions of east and west, north, and south
- Urban and environmental movements
- International migration and capital flows
- Trends in urban political economy
- Patterns of urban-based consumption

The series is explicitly interdisciplinary; the editors judge books by their contribution to intellectual solutions rather than according to disciplinary origin. Proposals may be submitted to members of the series Editorial Committee, and further information about the series can be found at www.suscbookseries.com:

Jenny Robinson
Manuel Aalbers
Dorothee Brantz
Patrick Le Galès
Chris Pickvance
Ananya Roy
Fulong Wu

# Acknowledgements

First and foremost, I would like to thank Robert Beauregard. Not only did he read my entire manuscript, he read it three times. Without Bob this book would have never been published. I am also grateful to my good Singaporean friend KC Ho, who has generously shared his knowledge of his exciting hometown. KC also read the manuscript several times and commented on it skillfully. Chua Beng Huat has always provided an intellectual conversation and great company, and his comments on the manuscript were extremely valuable as well.

The editors of Studies in Urban and Social Change book series – Jennifer Robinson, Patrick Le Galès, Chris Pickvance and Matthew Gandy – deserve thanks for accepting this book in the SUSC series and for their brilliant comments. I would also like to thank Rees Rhiannon, Jacqueline Scott and Allison Kostka at Wiley. I would like to thank the Academy of Finland first for giving me an opportunity to continue my PhD research at UCLA, and second for granting a one-year sabbatical to rewrite the manuscript. I thank Asla Fulbright for a travel grant to Los Angeles, and the SOAS, University of London, for a scholarship to do research in Hong Kong.

I am grateful to the late Matthew Edel for his lessons on rent theory during my one-year stay at the City University of New York, and to Allen Scott for hosting me at the Lewis Center, UCLA, and for his contribution to rent theory as well. I would like to thank Takashi Machimura for arranging excellent interviews for me in Los Angeles (with Mitsui, Mitsubishi and Nomura) and Ed Soja and Michael Storper for their excellent teaching.

I had the privilege to teach at the National University of Singapore for two years, and my colleagues at the Building and Real Estate (BEM) and other departments of the National University helped me to understand this unique Asian city-state. Thank you Robert Cooke, Rick Howard, Kwame Addae'dapaah, Kuniko Fujita, Ho Siew Lan, David Kim Hin Ho, Amy Lee, Lim Lan Yuan, Rashi Mohsini, Sim Loo Lee, Yu Shi Ming and Zhu Jieming.

I am indebted to Li Si Ming for hosting my several visits to Hong Kong. I would like to thank Tang Wing Shing and Ng Mee Kam for their critical comments on Hong Kong, and Tang Bo Sin for arranging several trips for me to China.

Colleagues at the Nordic Institute of Asian Studies (NIAS) in Copenhagen – Thommy Svensson, Stein Tönneson, Börge Bakken, Robert Cribb, Geir Helgesen and Ian Reader – taught me that it is possible to write about Asia, not just yearn for it.

A number of people have commented on various parts of the manuscript and inspired my thinking in several ways. Thank you Eric Clark for your encouraging comments on rent theory and Brett Christophers for your comments on finance. Thanks to Carolyn Cartier and Igal Charney for sharing an interest in real estate. Several people have invited me to give a talk on rent theory: Toshio Kamo in Fukuoka, Hyun Bang Shin in London School of Economics, Brett Christophers in Uppsala, Vandana Desai and Alex Loftus in London, Gilles Pinson in Saint-Etienne, Ben Teresa and Desiree Fields in Tampa, Ute Lehrer and Roger Keil in Toronto, Maros Krivy in Tallinn and Maria Kaika and Julie-Anne Boudreau in Yokohama.

I would like to thank NUS university librarian Tim Yap Fuan for searching for information about Singapore's land acquisition for me. In addition, Chong Shao Lun Cherie and Joannah Shane Bte Mohamed helped me search for information about Singapore's developers.

I am grateful to John Gray for revising my text into proper British English and to the members of Helsinki School of critical urban studies – Kevin Drain, Shin Bokyong, Chaitawat Boonjubun and Mika Hyötyläinen – for all their help and comments.

# List of Figures

# List of Tables

# List of tables

# List of Abbreviations

**ASEAN**  Association of Southeast Asian Nations

**CMIO**  Chinese, Malays, Indians and Others,

**CPF**  Central Provident Fund

**DBS**  Development Bank of Singapore

**DBSS**  Design, Built and Sell Scheme

**EDB**  Economic Development Board

**GIC**  Government Invest Corporation

**GLC**  Government-linked company

**HUDC**  Housing and Urban Development Company

**JTC**  Jurong Town Corporation

**HDB**  Housing Development Board

**MAS**  Monetary Authority of Singapore

**MND**  Ministry of National Development

**MTI**  Ministry of Trade and Industry

**NTUC**  National Trade Union Congress

**NUS**  National University of Singapore

**PAP**  People's Action Party

**PSA**   Port of Singapore Authority

**REDAS**   Real Estate Developers' Association of Singapore

**REIT**   Real Estate Investment Trust

**SGX**   Singapore Exchange

**SIT**   Singapore Improvement Trust

**SLA**   Singapore Land Authority

**SWF**   Sovereign Wealth Fund

**URA**   Urban Redevelopment Authority

# Glossary

**Absolute rent** the conditions are the barriers landownership makes to urban development (speculation, withholding, hoarding and land banking increasing the price of land).

**Actual rent** is the rent from the present use.

**Capitalization rate** property earnings divided by the property value.

**Density rent** the condition is the vertical mobilisation of land (the use of land is intensified, the density and plot ratio increased).

**Derivative rent** the yield from land titles that are securitised, packaged together with mortgages, and traded on the market as a financial instrument.

**Development charge** a payment that developers need to pay when they increase the building density or change the land use.

**Differential rent** the conditions are different qualities of land, for example location.

**Economic rent** earnings from productive factors in excess of the minimum payment needed to keep that factor in its present use.

**Extension rent** the condition is the horizontal mobilisation of land (extending land use, subdivisions, suburbanisation).

**Extensive margin** the last piece of land taken into use when land use is extended.

**Financial assets**   money, securities, bonds, shares.

**Financialisation**   a growing influence of financial markets in the economy. The yield of real estate compared to the yield of other investment options and financial institutions owning REITs.

**Fiscal rent**   public revenue from the use of state or municipality land.

**Global rent**   connected to global real estate investment flows.

**Intensive margin**   the last piece of land taken into use when the use of land is intensified (vertical mobilisation, increasing the plot ratio).

**Land rent**   paid to the landowner for the use of land. It represents a social relation, and is a basis for social control and power.

**Manipulated rent**   a payment received because of special privileges through political rent-seeking due to lobbying, bribery, favourable tax treatments and subsidies.

**Margin of transference**   the last piece of land taken into use when the use of the land is changed.

**Monopoly rent**   the conditions are monopoly price and excess demand.

**Physical assets**   land, buildings, equipment.

**Potential rent**   the rent from an alternative use of land.

**Real estate security**   a paper asset consisting of real property.

**Rent gap**   the difference between actual and potential rent.

**Rent-seeking** *(political)*   the use of resources to obtain, through political process, special privileges.

**Yield**   the income from a security related to its price.

# Preface

This book is about the difference that land makes. Land matters, yet it is all too often ignored in contemporary economic and social theories. Surprisingly, land and real estate are even ignored in disciplines that are supposed to take land seriously. Contemporary studies of architecture and town planning overlook real estate issues, although the garden-city builders and early modernists criticised land speculation and proposed reforming the land development processes that were producing cities. Land matters in the sense of an area and location, but land occupied by people matters also because land tenure makes land development processes social, political and cultural processes.

In contrast to some earlier approaches to the issues of land – like Allen Scott's urban land nexus, David Harvey's production of the built environment and John Logan and Harvey Molotch's political economy of place – I am interested in forms of landownership (private, collective, common, shared, state and municipal) and the use, management and revenue of land. I am not interested in land as a physical thing or land use as a planning problem. Nor I am interested in the landed society of the eighteenth century in which landowners had economic, social and political power. Rather, what intrigues me are the institutions and actors, landownership forms and social relations in which land is embedded. Land in this study is not another name for nature, to paraphrase Karl Polanyi ([1944] 2001), but a social relation affected by laws and customs. Land is used and owned, its ownership is justified with stories, and people are emotionally attached to land. Every now and then land ownership and land use become a social problem as their forms and policies are debated, fought over, and transformed.

The theory of land rent explains the relationship between the use and price of land, and is a significant part of this book. It is an old economic theory that has sometimes been at the core of economics; at other times few economists have taken any interest in it. The theory of land rent, however, is an amazingly persistent one. Like the title character in Virginia Woolf's novel *Orlando,* it wanders through centuries and takes on different disguises. Rent theory started its journey in the eighteenth century, reached maturity in the nineteenth century and has since been applied to various questions, ranging from the price of corn and taxes to house prices and the construction industry. Land rent theory continues to live because it explains essential relations between labour, capital and land.

The theory of land rent was originally developed in connection to agriculture. This book, however, is not about agriculture or rural land, but about urban land. The aim of this inquiry is to elaborate urban land rent theory from its agricultural origins to explain contemporary problems of urban real estate. Because this is an urban studies book, it needs a real city as its object of research. The city that is used as a case to apply, test and elaborate land rent theory is the city-state of Singapore.

For two years in the 1990s, I taught urban economics at the National University of Singapore. I had moved there from Los Angeles (UCLA) where I had gone to analyse global real estate investments (especially by the Japanese) after finishing my PhD on land rent theory in Helsinki. Finland was about to join the European Union, and the EU demanded that Finland open its real estate market for foreign investors. I thought Los Angeles was a good place to study global real estate investments, and I arrived there in 1993 (one year after the riots), just in time to discover that big Japanese investors were reconsidering their investments in Los Angeles.

Soon after moving to Singapore, I began to think of the city as a laboratory for testing land rent theory. Singapore is a city-state, without rural landowners and rural land interests. Land is under government ownership and is leased at auctions. Despite this, Singaporean development companies are global actors. Paradoxes seemed to abound, and from the beginning several things puzzled me. I read advertisements of properties being sold in Australia and London in the local newspaper, *The Straits Times,* and I could not understand why Singaporeans would buy properties there. Such advertisements in Finnish newspapers would have made no sense. I read stories about the 'property lobby' and was unable to comprehend what this might be. Slowly I solved these puzzles, thanks to the theory of land rent.

Urban scholars have debated whether any particular city can be a representative, typical, ideal or exemplary case (Brenner 2003). I am not claiming that what happens in Singapore happens, or should happen, in other cities. But I am arguing that what happens in Singapore has a lot to do with land, and understanding this will help us understand and explain the land question in other cities. For me, Singapore is a case with which to compare and make understandable the land development processes that occur in other cities. Singapore is the protagonist of my story. It is a case and a comparison, but it also (like the case of Dora for Sigmund Freud) enables me to generalize. My generalisations concern land, property and land rent.

Singapore became my story's protagonist by accident; I happened to read of a job opportunity in Singapore (in the Association of American Geographers' newsletter), applied for the job, was hired, and moved there. It was an accident, like cycling across the Low Countries was a happy accident for China historian Timothy Brook (2009), leading him to write his book *Vermeer's Hat*. He chose Delft as the place from which to begin his story about the dawn of the global world, because he happened to fall off his bike in Delft, because Vermeer happened to have lived there, and because he enjoyed looking at Vermeer's paintings. He later asked himself to what extent choosing Shanghai over Delft might have changed the story. His answer was that it would not have changed it a great deal. In my case, Singapore changed the story from what it might have been if I had written about the theory of land rent through the lens of Helsinki.

In Los Angeles, the urban scholar Edward Soja taught me that an image of a city can be more real than the city itself. This is as true for Singapore as it is for Los Angeles. The global image of Singapore is both complicated and nurtured by an ideological battle. As a European scholar talking and writing about Singapore, I have encountered ignorance about and prejudices towards this city-state. The Western media likes to mock the rules and regulations in Singapore, as if banning chewing gum is a significant social problem. After the collapse of the Soviet Union, Singapore was assigned the role of antagonist in the ideological battle between the free and democratic West and the authoritarian East. And what has been particularly intolerable, in the mind of neoliberals, is the heavy involvement of the state in Singapore.

In addition to prejudices towards Singapore, the second challenge I face when writing about land rent (especially its political applications) are the prejudices against Henry George (1839–1897), the great American land reformer who proposed taxing land rent. In his 1879 bestseller, *Progress and Poverty*, George proposed taxing land rent as a remedy to the problem of poverty. George inspired reformers around the world: the Fabian socialists in Britain, Sun Yat-sen in China and Leo Tolstoy in Russia, for example. His legacy is still alive in Georgist organisations in the United States. George, however, is also a disputed character in economics, a self-educated man who preferred common sense to economic textbooks, and who managed to stir up a heated single tax debate still remembered decades later. He figures prominently in what I have to say about land reforms.

The third prejudice I have to overcome is that against land rent theory. Today the theory of land rent sits outside mainstream economic theory and barely features in the curriculum of economics departments. Land rent theory is regarded as outdated, its applicability narrow. One popular claim against it is to say that, because land rent theory was developed as a theory of agriculture, it is inapplicable in urban situations. A similar claim could be made against John Locke's theory that justified private property with farmers' labour: such a claim, though, is not made.

The main thrust of this book is that the theory of land rent is a useful one for urban scholars. It concerns the relationship between land use and value, and makes understandable the production process of the built environment. It explains the effects of landownership on housing prices. And still only a small coterie of urban scholars talks about land rent, the importance of which, however, is not denied. Peter Saunders once told me how he (in Sussex, UK) discussed rent theories in his urban sociology class, after which the class 'returned to the main topic of urban sociology'. Unlike Saunders, I believe rent theory belongs not as a footnote, but among the main topics of urban sociology.

In addition to rent theory, there is also another theory in my story, a story within my story. In *Ulysses*, James Joyce introduced the adventure of the soap called Soapinades (Riikonen 1985). The story begins when Leopold Bloom buys soap, then puts it in his pocket and in the end uses the soap for washing his hands. It is a sub-story. My sub-story is the theory of property rights. It is introduced in the third chapter, and will appear later in my discussion of landownership forms, planning, developers and real estate markets. I will compare property rights theory to rent theory: the first invites us to define property rights and let the market allocate land; the second calls us to analyse the historical relationships between social classes, the social and political conditions and consequences of using land, and to interrogate the origin of rent.

This book is about land. Talking about the importance of land easily invokes physiocratic ideas that land is the source of all wealth, or risks seeming like a yearning after an older landed society where landlords and farmers knew their place. Such prejudices point to a change in the meaning of land and landed property. Centuries ago land was understood as part of nature, then (after Jean-Jacques Rousseau) nature came to mean that part of the environment least altered by human beings (Dambrosch 2005: 321). The arrival of the market economy further transformed the meaning of land. Instead of customs regulating its use, land became treated as a commodity. Recently, old ideas of common property have been revived, for example in claims of the environmental movement and claims for urban commons. Thus it is time to update the theory that elucidates the transformations and meanings of land and property.

This inquiry into land, property and rent in Singapore has taught me a lot about my hometown Helsinki. I hope this book will also give the readers tools to analyse landed property, housing, developer interests and public space in their own hometowns.

# 1

# Introduction
## *Singapore as a Case and Comparison*

This is a book about land, rent and state in Singapore. Singapore is
an island city-state in Southeast Asia, situated between Malaysia and
Indonesia. Its population in 2013 was 5.4 million; its landed area was
716.1 square kilometres and population density 7540 persons per square
km (Yearbook of Statistics 2014). It became independent in 1965 after
140 years as a British colony (some colonial-time buildings still remind
us of its colonial past, see Figure 1.1). In 1819 Sir Thomas Stamford
Raffles, working for the East India Company, landed in Singapore and
decided to develop what was a tiny fishing village lying on the sea route
from The Spice Islands to Europe into a port city. After the opening
of the Suez Canal in 1869, ships between Europe and East Asia sailed
through the Singapore Straits, making Singapore an important node in
the maritime economy.

Unlike prominent port cities that lost their role as trade routes shifted
(places like Calicut, Alexandria, Goa and Malacca), Singapore was able
to keep its place in international networks and grew into a prosperous
world city. An often-cited reason for this has been Singapore's good leadership. Stan Sesser (1994: 12), for example, compared Lee Kuan Yew, the
first and long-serving prime minister (1959–1990) and founding father
of modern Singapore, to Mao Tse-tung, Pandit Jawaharlal Nehru, Ho
Chi Minh and Sukarno, all of whom failed in the transition from revolutionary to ruler and left disorder in their wake. Lee was followed
by Goh Chok Tong (1990–2004) and Lee Hsien Loong, the present
prime minister.[1] Their party, the People's Action Party (PAP), has been

*Urban Land Rent: Singapore as a Property State*, First Edition. Anne Haila.
© 2016 John Wiley & Sons, Ltd. Published 2016 by John Wiley & Sons, Ltd.

**Figure 1.1**  Colonial Singapore. Photo: Anne Haila.

in power since 1959. Unlike in countries where elections change political programmes, Singapore has built itself step by step, as if there has
been a logical plan. This makes Singapore function almost as a laboratory for a social scientist.

As is often the case with port cities, Singapore is an ethnically diverse
city composed of Chinese migrants, immigrant labour transplanted by
colonialists, and Western expatriates brought in by recent waves of globalisation. The first census in 1871 showed that there were already Malays,
Javanese, Bugis, Boyanese, Chinese, Burmese, Indians, Klings, Bengalis,
Europeans, Americans, Eurasians and Arabs (Chiew 1985). Today the
census differentiates four groups: Chinese, Malays, Indians and Others
(known as the CMIO classification). In 2012, there were 74 per cent
Chinese, 13 per cent Malays and 9 per cent Indians. The rest were classified as Others.

Today Singapore is a cosmopolitan city where Chinese, Malay, Indian
and European populations speak different languages and live close
to each other. Its cosmopolitan atmosphere contradicts the image of
Singapore as a boring and sterile place. Hawkers cook Chinese, Indian,
Thai and Indonesian food on the street. Unlike in Helsinki, street walk-
ers are tolerated in the main shopping street, Orchard Road, and, not so

long ago, transvestites, depicted by James Eckardt (2006: 55) in his memoir *Singapore Girl,* made Bugis Street an 'eternal theatre with actress and spectator the same person'.

When Singapore gained independence in 1965, it was poor and underdeveloped. The prospects of a tiny city-state with a Chinese majority situated between two Muslim majority nations and without a hinterland, resources or industries were so poor that imagining Singapore as an independent polity was deemed inconceivable (Chua 1995; Leifer 2000). Contrary to pessimistic expectations, Singapore's economic rise since the 1960s has been astonishing and, together with Korea, Taiwan and Hong Kong, Singapore became renowned as one of the rapidly growing Asian 'tigers'. Figure 1.2 shows Singapore's economic growth since 1988.

Economic growth until the 1997 Asian crisis was high and stable (between 6.5 and 11.5 per cent). Singapore became a favoured location for transnational companies thanks to its rule of law, predictable government institutions and good business environment. Singapore's domestic economy is small but it has a role in the global economy as a financial centre. For several years Singapore has been ranked as one of the world's most competitive economies. In 2013 the World Economic Forum ranked Singapore second after Switzerland. Year after year, the World Bank has ranked Singapore as the easiest place to do business. Among the criteria used by the World Bank are government regulations and protecting investors' rights.

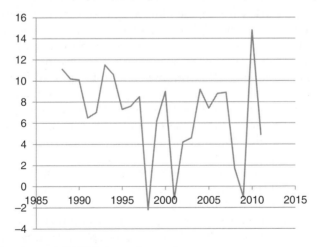

**Figure 1.2** Singapore's GDP. Annual growth.
Source: The World Bank.

After the Asian crisis, economic growth became unpredictable and less stable. To cope in the new global environment, Singapore introduced several new laws and began to change. Figure 1.2 shows three troughs: the 1997 Asian crisis, the burst of the dotcom bubble in the early 2000s and the 2008 subprime crisis. The 1997 Asian crisis was a turning point after which Singapore started liberalising its economy. Although there was a rapid recovery soon after the Asian crisis, there was a sharp recession in 2001 due to the downturn in the global electronics market. Singapore is not just a service economy, it has a significant manufacturing sector as well. In 2001, manufacturing formed 23 per cent of Singapore's economy, of which electronics was 36 per cent (financial and business services was 28 per cent) (Economic Review Committee Report 2003, MTI). The Gulf war and a SARS (severe acute respiratory syndrome) outbreak at the beginning of the twenty-first century worsened the situation. The third trough was in 2009. The subprime crisis in the USA and the global financial market turmoil affected Singapore's economy. The crisis in the Western financial market made speculative money flow into Singapore, increasing property prices and necessitating government intervention (see Figure 8.3).

Singapore is dependent on foreign labour. In 2013, the total population was 5.4 million, of which 1.5 million were foreign workers, expatriates or students. A white paper on population released in 2013 projected that the population could rise to 6.9 million by 2030, and the number of foreigners to 2.5 million. The white paper anticipates Singaporeans becoming more educated, taking managerial, executive and professional jobs. Hence foreign workers are needed to provide healthcare, domestic work, care for the elderly and construction work.

Compared to its Asian neighbours, who from time to time close their doors and isolate themselves from the world, Singapore consistently attracts foreign talent, is open to imported influences and adapts quickly to new trends. Occasionally, foreigners taking the jobs of Singaporeans (and simultaneously escalating housing prices) have stirred up discussions and led to tighter employment regulations, but foreign workers have been welcomed and leaders defend Singapore's open door policy. In 1997 Deputy Prime Minister Lee Hsien Loong said: 'Let's say, for the sake of argument, you bring in Bill Gates. Will he take away the job from a Singaporean entrepreneur? I don't think so. He will bring in his business. If Microsoft starts up here with 2,000 employees, that's 2,000 extra jobs created' (Chua M H 1997: 39).

Singapore's economic development has been complemented by social development. Slums were demolished and people were moved to public housing. In 2012, 82 per cent of the population lived in public housing, 12 per cent in condominiums and other apartments and 6 per cent in landed properties (resident households by type of dwellings, Yearbook of Statistics 2013). The state appropriated and reclaimed land and established a powerful housing authority, the Housing Development Board (HDB), to develop public housing (which also benefitted transnational companies locating in Singapore). A compulsory savings scheme, the Central Provident Fund (CPF), offered a generous savings rate and gave the government revenue for investment in infrastructure and public goods, explaining an astonishingly high homeownership rate of 90.1 per cent in 2012 (people were allowed to use their pension savings to buy housing). A staggering 82 per cent of the resident population lives in public housing and 90.1 per cent are homeowners: this book explains this paradox that contradicts Western scholars' image of public housing.

Singapore's built environment is as amazing as its economic rise (see Figure 1.3 of one of the imaginative new buildings). It is a collage of modernist housing estates, iconic office skyscrapers, luxurious shopping malls, five-star hotels, industrial estates and conserved shop houses. The government, advertising its land sales in newspapers abroad, has invited foreign developers and architects to build Singapore. Since the mid 1970s, Singapore's architecture has been dominated by foreign architects (Powell 1989: 13). World famous architects such as Moshe Safdie,

**Figure 1.3** The durian-shaped opera house. Photo: Anne Haila.

I. M. Pei, Kenzo Tange, John Portman, Paul Rudolf,and Zaza Hadid have designed their signature buildings in Singapore. Among its eye-catching buildings is the durian-shaped opera house and three skyscrapers topped by a ship-shaped structure.

The government has an important role in Singapore's economic and social development. Government expenditure relative to gross domestic product (GDP), however, is low in Singapore compared to other countries. Between 2000 and 2009, total government expenditure was about 16 per cent of GDP, which is low compared to OECD countries (from 30 per cent to 50 per cent) (Tan et al. 2009: 18). Yet the government is present in other ways. It intervenes and regulates, issues comprehensive plans, and its investment corporations and companies are globally operating companies bringing revenue to Singapore. The state owns 90 per cent of the land and produces public housing and industrial space. Government expenditure on healthcare is low (3.5 percent of GDP in 2005,Tan et al. 2009). This low figure does not, however, give a fair picture of Singapore's welfare policy, because healthcare is covered by a compulsory individual savings system (Medisave), while extensive public housing provides a safety net.

High economic growth, a competitive economy, a majority of people living in public housing and being homeowners, a cosmopolitan atmosphere, a futuristic built environment and the omnipresent government make Singapore a distinctive city that defies easy categorisations. Some studies, such as Peter Rowe's (2005) *East Asian Modern*, group Singapore together with East Asian cities in China, Japan, Korea and Taiwan, even though Singapore is located in Southeast Asia. Some other studies, such as Malcolm McKinnon's (2011) *Asian Cities*, exclude Singapore explicitly because it differs from other Asian cities. How to make sense of such a unique city? There are four traditions from which Singapore could be approached: comparison from the point of view of the West; Asian studies seeing Singapore from the perspective of Asian cultures; urban studies comparing Singapore to other global cities; and Singapore as a developmental state.

## European Classics and Western Theories

European classics used Asia in order to understand Europe. Max Weber compared Asian and European cities, and through this comparison formulated his definition of the city: an urban community has a fortification, a market, a court of its own (and at least partially autonomous law), associations of urbanites, and an administration by authorities whose election involved the burghers (Weber 1966: 81). By contrast, Chinese

cities were, in Weber's imagination, the seats of central imperial authorities where urban dwellers belonged to their families, native villages and
temples. Weber concluded that an urban community, in the full meaning of the word, appears as a general phenomenon only in the Occi-
dent. Another European scholar, Fernand Braudel, asked why change
was a striking feature of European cities, whereas cities elsewhere in the
world had no history and were like clocks endlessly repeating themselves
(Braudel 1973: 396).

Weber and Braudel praised the superiority of European cities over
Asian cities. The glorification of Europe was even more obvious in the
theories of oriental despotism invented to showcase European democracy. Montesquieu, who in *The Spirit of the Laws* (1748) introduced three
types of government – republic, monarchy and despotism – presented
'oriental despotism as an ideal type that had fear as its key value, in
which there was no secure private property, the ruler relied upon religion rather than law, and the entire system was essentially static because
of the dominant role of custom and taboos' (Pye 1985: 8). Karl Wittfogel
(1957) further developed Montesquieu's idea and connected despotic
state power in Asia to the necessity of controlling floods and arranging
irrigation, along with the absence of private property and civil society.

Empirical research in the wake of Weber, Braudel and Wittfogel has
tested the speculative ideas of these European classics. Historians of
China have found evidence, some to support Weber's speculations, some
to disprove them. Faure (2002), for example, explained why cities were
less autonomous in China by referring to the imperial examinations system that sent literati around the country spreading the influence and
control of the central state, and to the Chinese way of organising the
community around the family temple rather than forming an urban
community. As to Southeast Asia, Weber was right. Fortifications were
needed in Europe to protect towns from pillage by marauding bands
of Vikings, Moslems, Magyars, pirates and brigands (North and Thomas
[1973] 1999: 19); in Southeast Asia cities began building walls when they
needed defence against the Europeans. Aytthaya built its walls in 1550
and Makassar erected fortifications in 1634 to protect itself from Dutch
attack (Reid 1993: 88). Wittfogel's ideas of oriental despotism have been
criticised (Hindess and Hirst 1975: 213) and Edward Said (1978) challenged Western conceptions about Asia in general as a social construction of the Orient.

Following the legacy of European classics, Asian cities were studied using Western theories and analysed as colonial, modernising and
developing Third World cities. Studies of colonial Singapore (Yeoh
1996) analysed the land-use planning system brought by British colonial administrators. Studies of modern Singapore focused on the

consequences of modernisation, industrialisation and urbanisation on culture and social institutions (Khondker 2002: 35). The development studies perspective was popular in Singapore, and until the 1980s much of the social science research was practically oriented and developed 'in close association with development and policy agendas, specifically engaged in questions about the social conditions for and impact of economic modernization' (Yee and Chua 1999: 229).

There was also criticism of the use of Western theories. Syed Hussein Alatas (1974) challenged uncritical imitations of Western studies, calling those whose thinking was dominated by Western thought in an imitative and uncritical manner 'captive minds'. Despite criticism, the Eurocentric look is still alive. One Western theory in particular has been popular in analysing Asian cities. This is the theory of property rights. Chapter 2 dwells upon Europe's history to show the Western roots of this theory.

### Asian Studies: A Focus on Villages

Singapore is in Southeast Asia; hence, it is tempting to approach it from the perspective of Asian studies. Three characteristics of Asian studies, however, make it less applicable to the case of Singapore: its village bias, normative approach and cultural explanation. Covering a vast and heterogeneous area (starting from Turkey, continuing through Tibet and Cambodia, before reaching Korea and Japan), Asian studies' research topics include economic, cultural, religious, social, environmental and technological issues. Encompassing the Indian and Chinese cultures, and religions like Buddhism and Shintoism, Asian studies is an inconceivably broad discipline. Until recently, Asian studies has not been particularly interested in cities. Asian scholars were more interested in studying villages than cities and Asian studies journals seldom included articles on cities.

A popular method to study villages was fieldwork, gathering information directly thus privileging empirical research. Anthropologists such as Margaret Mead, Bronislaw Malinowski and Clifford Geertz immersed themselves in villages in Samoa, New Guinea and Java, and their followers preferred the exoticness of the jungle to Western-looking cities. The focus on villages, though, produced an odd picture of Asia where the rate of urbanisation is high, mega-cities grow rapidly, and the density of urban population is higher than in the West. As O'Connor (1995: 30) remarked: 'while Southeast Asia revolves around its cities, scholarship spins off into disciplines that ignore this fact. In a region that has known cities for two millennia, where even remote peoples have shaped themselves to or against urban rule, research goes on as if the city were an alien entity, easily factored out and best forgotten.'

Importantly, the village focus affected how cities in Asia were later studied and described. Asian cities were analysed as influenced by external forces (colonialism and modernisation), and described not as cities (Evers 1984) but as social networks (Nas 1989), 'ruralopolises', village-like settlements ('kotadesasi' – kota is town and desa is village) (McGee 1989), a mix of royal and rural cultures, with villagers retaining their peasant practices even after migrating to cities (Pasuk and Baker 1998).

Proper fieldwork entails not just visiting a village but living in the place for a long time. Studies on Asia often begin with a detailed account of the places visited and duration of time spent with the natives. For example, Li (1998: 5) writes: 'I spent over 18 months travelling the length and breadth of China to assemble the data for this book. I visited Beijing, Shanghai, Guangzhou, Harbin, Urumqi, Kunming, Chengdu and Dalian, among other far flung cities to gather first-hand accounts from the instigators of China's fast-changing economic revolution.' Such introductions, repeated frequently, suggest that Asianists believe that living in a place gives a scholar a better understanding and makes the resultant study more credible. Because I write about Singapore, I have been asked several times how long I lived in Singapore. I do not know whether my two years living there qualifies me to write about it in the minds of my Asian colleagues. Asked frequently, this question suggests that Asian scholars share a concept of knowledge that questions the interpretations of foreigners, prefers stories to explanations and privileges the voices of locals.

But there is danger in living too long in a village. Anthropological literature is full of stories illustrating the perils of 'going native'. In the epistemological sense, the danger lies in becoming embedded in one's research object and developing attachment to the site. Western Asianists often have a personal story to tell of how they became obsessed with Asia. Usually it is love or politics. Alex Kerr (1996: 106–108), who studied both Japanese at Yale and Chinese at Oxford, described the difference between scholars of China and Japan: 'Lovers of China are thinkers; lovers of Japan sensuous. People drawn to China are restless, adventurous types, with critical minds … Japanologists tend to abandon their critical faculties and "convert" to Japan … Sometimes I think "Japanese studies" would be more accurately described as "Japan worship".' More prosaically, I am attracted to Singapore as a strong state that regulates its real estate market.

An attachment to a research object can easily morph into a normative approach. A popular normative perspective on Asia in the 1990s was that of human rights. Asianists criticised the Washington consensus,[2] and questioned the structural programmes of the World Bank and the International Monetary Fund. Instead, they looked at Asia from a humanist point of view and, following the tradition of Montesquieu and Wittfogel, Asian authoritarian regimes were criticised for their lack of democracy and violations of human rights.

Approaching Singapore from the perspective of Asian cultures is no less problematic than that of village studies-based Asian studies or analysing Singapore from a normative perspective. Singapore is a Chinese majority city in Southeast Asia. Southeast Asia, with its bewildering variety of languages (Austronesian, Mon-Khmer, Tai, Vietnamese and Burmese) and religions (Buddhism, Muslim and Christian) 'appear(s) at first glance to defy any attempts at generalization' (Reid 1988: 3). The names 'Mediterranean Asia' and 'region in between' (Widodo 2009) describe Southeast Asia as open to trade, exchange and communication. The region comprises numerous countries: Burma, Thailand, Malaysia, Singapore, Indonesia, Philippines, Brunei, Cambodia, Laos and Vietnam. For Malay speakers, the region was the land 'below the winds', 'in distinction to the world of outsiders (especially Indians, Arabs, and Europeans) who came from "above the winds" by taking advantage of the prevailing Indian Ocean monsoon' (Reid 1999: 5). The Japanese and Chinese called the region the 'South Seas'. Reid (1999) regarded the defining characteristics of Southeast Asia to be its diversity and openness to outside influences brought by Arab and European trade. Reid (1988) suggested that a common physical environment and maritime connection linked the peoples of Southeast Asia to one another, explaining common cultural features: eating rice, fermented fish, coconut and sugar palms, using wood, palm and bamboo as construction materials, chewing betel, cockfighting and bronze gong music. Some of these we still find in Singapore, others we do not.

## Urban Studies

In recent years, urban scholars have paid more attention to non-Western cities. The urbanisation of China in particular has fascinated both Chinese and Western scholars (for example Logan 2002; Friedmann 2005; Wu 2005; Wu and Webster 2010), continuing a tradition of studies by archaeologists, art historians and architects on Chinese Imperial cities (Skinner 1977; Steinhardt 1990; Heng 1999) and by social scientists on Chinese cities in the Maoist era (Chan 1994).

Compared to Chinese cities, Southeast Asian cities have been little studied. In *The Indianized States of Southeast Asia*, G. Coedes (1968) analysed the close relationship between India and Southeast Asia, and introduced the concept of Indianised languages, scripts, texts and practices in Thai, Khmer, Burmese, Javanese, Prambanam and Borobudur cultures. The idea of fusing cultures is also present in Peter Nas' (1986) four stages in the historical development of Indonesian settlements: the early Indonesian, the Indische (mixing Indonesian and Dutch cultures), the colonial and the modern town. Terry McGee's (1967) seminal study *The Southeast Asian City* described 'a mosaic of cultural and racial worlds each involving the memory of other lands and other people' (McGee 1967: 24). In the search for specification, Southeast Asian cities have been classified as port cities distinct from old inland administrative and cultural centres along the Silk Road (Baghdad, Bokhara, Kaefeng) (Ness and Tawlar 2005), as commercial and inland sacred cities (Evers and Korf 2000), and as indigenous cities (market cities and sacred cities) and colonial cities (Forbes 1996). Such variety makes the concept of the Asian or Southeast Asian city as amorphous as the concepts of the American city (as segregated city) or the European city (characterised by public landownership, historic city centres and the strong role of the state and town planning). Consequently, some scholars have given up attempting to define and talk about the city in Southeast Asia rather than 'the Southeast Asian city' (Bunnell et al. 2002). And indeed, the richness of Southeast Asia is its cities: royal and religious Bangkok, Kuala Lumpur with its Moorish skyline and the feeling of Arabian nights (Sardar 2000), Yangoon with its everyday life on the muddy roads, Jakarta with its monuments, Ho Chi Minh City with its motor cycles, and the city-state of Singapore with its ubiquitous public housing estates.

The commensurability and comparisons (both among Asian cities and between Asian and Western cities) were increased after John Friedmann (Friedmann and Goetz 1982) and Saskia Sassen (1991) presented the globalisation thesis. Sassen's inclusion of one Asian city – Tokyo – broke the dichotomy between Western and Asian cities, and began undermining urban studies' Western-centred focus. Several empirical studies were carried out to find out the role of Asian cities in the globalising world (e.g. Lo and Yeung 1996). The city-state of Singapore, with its myriad international relations, has since become a popular subject for globalisation studies (see e.g. Chang 2000; Yeoh and Chang 2001).

Criticism of the global city paradigm reinforced the criticism of 'Western' theories in general. 'Western' urban studies have been criticised for focusing exclusively on certain large Western cities, leaving ordinary cities 'off the map' (Robinson 2002) and ignoring several important issues like informality, peripheries, illegal activities and everyday life (Simone 2010; Roy 2005; MacFarlane 2012). Calls for alternative approaches, 'beyond the West' (Edensor and Jayne 2012), invite urban scholars to investigate cities in the global south and a broader range of topics. Another type of criticism questioned comparisons of cities as 'bounded and discrete units' (Ward 2008: 406) and called for 'transnational examinations' (Smith 2001; Roy 2003) in which cities are understood through their relations to other cities. Such an approach will offer an appropriate method to analyse the Asian city-state of Singapore, not only its maritime past but its present cross-border interconnections.

### The Developmental State, Asian Values and Rent-seeking

In the 1990s, it became popular to analyse Singapore together with other rapidly growing Asian economies as a 'developmental state'. The term 'developmental state' was invented to solve the puzzle of why Asian economies were growing while Western economies were stagnating. First there was Japan, then the four Asian tigers (Korea, Taiwan, Hong Kong and Singapore), and now China and India. At first, economists questioned the reliability of the statistics showing high economic growth in Asia or, like Paul Krugman (1994), suggested that the whole Asian miracle was a myth – the growth was just a temporary result of the mobilisation of more resources. Other economists asked whether the rise of Asian capitalism was due solely to injections of foreign investment and transfers of foreign technology.[3]

The most disturbing question for Western economists was the role of the state, so obvious in Asia. The economic rise of East Asian countries challenged the Western doctrine of *laissez faire* and free markets as conditions for economic growth. In fact, the term 'developmental state' was introduced to explain the peculiar Asian economic model. Developmental states intervene, draw up programmes for economic development and have a relative autonomy from social classes and specific private economic interests. In this regard, Singapore differs from its Southeast Asian neighbours and resembles instead countries in East Asia. In Southeast Asia, state agencies are weaker than in Northeast Asia. Southeast Asian countries such as Thailand have been compared to the city-state of Genoa, with weak governments changing frequently, whereas Singapore has been likened to the city-state of Venice, with effective regulation, political stability and rule of law (Unger 1998: 182).

The ubiquitous presence of its government makes Singapore difficult to classify. My American colleagues in Singapore regarded it as a socialist economy, while Finnish businessmen regarded it as a free market economy. This difficulty in categorising Asian economies is also observed by scholars such as Jomo (1997), who suggested that the successful industrial policy experiences of Northeast Asia and Singapore were obscured from international attention by their political alignment with the West (particularly with the USA) and consequent political pariah status in some circles, their continued reliance on market signals (including international markets), export orientation, and greater tolerance for state intervention (Jomo 1997: 156).

The Singapore developmental state emerged after independence from Britain. The colonial government in the Straits Settlement[4] did not interfere with the economy. Its main task was enforcing law and order. Taxes were low and 'the largest single source of revenue came from the monopoly sale of opium to the Chinese' (Huff 1994: 168). The People's Action Party (PAP) that had come into power in 1959 called for a forward-looking and problem-solving programme aimed at economic growth and building a national identity founded on pragmatic values (Chan and Evers 1978: 317). Several studies, such as Raj Vasil's (2000), have pointed out the emphasis of the first-generation PAP rulers on social and economic policies. With its economic focus, the state of Singapore seems more the heir of the British East India Company – a joint-stock company (bringing together private merchant capital with a royal charter from the sovereign and a monopoly to trade goods) (Ogborn 2007) – than the successor to the colonial government.

Another argument that became popular in the 1990s was to explain Asia's economic rise by reference to culture. Western values of individualism, liberalism and welfarism, and Eastern values of family, collectivism and discipline, were compared to explain economic growth in Asia. Joel Kotkin (1993), for example, introduced the concept of a global tribe, sharing the same origins with strong ethnic identity and solidarity, that has dispersed around the world without forgetting its original values. Those superior Asian values of collectivism, discipline, hard work, education, family, tribe and ethnic kin perceived to generate economic growth are East Asian Confucian values, as distinct from the softer values of inner peace and harmony which are associated with Southeast Asian Buddhist countries.

In the political arena, the proponents of Asian values included Senior Minister Lee Kuan Yew from Singapore and Dr Datuk Mahathir Mohamed from Malaysia. Singapore's first finance minister, Goh Keng Swee (1994: viii–ix), saw Confucian values behind Singapore's economic growth and found the missing link to support Max Weber's theories on capitalism among overseas Chinese entrepreneurs. He wrote:

It is a strange irony that supporting evidence of the moral basis of entrepreneurial behaviour had been gathered in Singapore some eighty years after Weber's exposition. Further, the moral basis was founded on the Confucian ethic, not Protestant ethic. Confucianism, Weber believed, lacked the essential elements present in the more austere forms of the Protestant faith such as Calvinism, and therefore could not promote the kind of entrepreneurial behaviour required in the early stage of state capitalism. How wrong he turned out to be in this respect.

Promoting Asian collective values created a problem for the *laissez faire* capitalist city-states of Hong Kong and Singapore. In the case of Hong Kong, the term 'positive non-interventionism' was introduced to find a compromise between traditional Chinese values and *laissez faire*, and allowed government intervention in social welfare, public services and public housing (Lau 2003: 379). In Singapore, pragmatic politics and the construction of what are called shared values solved the dilemma between Confucian and liberal values. Concerned about the erosion of traditional Eastern values as a result of Singapore's Westernisation, in the late 1980s Prime Minister Goh Chok Tong called for a discussion about national ideology. He referred to the book by George Lodge and Ezra Vogel (1987), *Ideology and National Competiveness: A Study of Nine Countries*, which argued that economic competitiveness is affected by whether people are communitarian or individualistic. In 1988, a government committee was appointed to develop a national ideology, and in 1991 a *White Paper on Shared Values* was introduced. These shared values are: 'Nation before community and society above self. Family as the basic unit of society. Community support and respect for individual. Consensus, not conflict. Racial and religious harmony.' Chua Beng Huat (1995: 27–38) claimed that by introducing shared values, the PAP government replaced its earlier ideas with a new ideology. In the early years of industrialisation, the time of the first-generation PAP leaders, the individualism of entrepreneurial migrants was seen as positive, and the extended family system an obstacle to economic growth. Now the latter values are embraced. This emphasis on values by the leaders of Singapore shows that, despite its rapidly growing economy and business-friendly environment, Singapore's economy has a moral side. This book analyses the use of the state land, not only for economic growth but for the public good as well.

There was also criticism of the whole idea of Asian values. Critics pointed out that there are several cultural traditions in Asia,[5] and there is no empirical evidence showing that Asian values contribute to economic growth.[6] The 1997 Asian financial crisis terminated the debate about Asian values and identified a new explanation for the decline of Asian economies. Ironically, in an attempt to find a scapegoat for the crisis, Asian cultural values of favouring one's own ethnic tribe in business dealings and giving *guanxi*[7] business presents were now turned against

Asian countries, and interpreted as the 'cronyism' and rent-seeking (discussed in Chapter 6) that created the crisis.

## Singapore as a Property State

Weber, Braudel and Wittfogel were purely interested in understanding Europe, and only used Asia as a mirror. Asian area studies seeking to understand cities embedded in their regional cultures faces a problem in Singapore: Confucian values. Singapore is unlike its Southeast Asian neighbours and resembles more developmental states of East Asia. Urban studies comparing cities as discrete units is not the best method for analysing places like Singapore that are hubs made of their relations to the world. Further, the topics of the agenda in the global south cities – informal and illegal activities – are not relevant in Singapore, which is a modern and well-ordered city. Seeing Singapore as a developmental state captures one essential feature of Singapore: the presence of the state. However, explanations of Asia's economic rise and decline ranging from the developmental state to Asian values and rent-seeking, show the ad hoc nature and poverty of such cultural explanations.

My approach differs from these attempts to understand Asia. First, this is an inquiry into the political economy of land and urban development in Singapore. The political economy approach implies analysing Singapore's land regime using the concepts of rent (introduced in Chapter 3) and paying attention to ideological justifications (Chapter 2) and political reforms to change land tenure (Chapter 4). Second, land, or more precisely the form of land tenure analysed in this book, namely the public or state ownership of land, forms only a condition. State ownership as such is not decisive. Governments can use their land bank for the public good or maximise revenue from their land assets. So, this is also an inquiry into the state of Singapore.

In contrast to studies by archaeologists, architects and development scholars, and macro-level comparisons and ethnographies, my study focuses on one causal factor, land, and attempts to explain urban development from this perspective. One study akin to my aspiration is *The Shek Kip Mei Syndrome* by Manuel Castells, L. Goh and R. Y-W Kwok (1990). They investigated the relationship between economic development and public housing in Singapore and Hong Kong. One of the most striking paradoxes, they noted, is that these two market economies with the highest rates of economic growth also have the largest public housing programmes in the capitalist world (in terms of proportion of the population directly housed by the government). In their thorough analysis, they show that the public housing programmes in Hong Kong and

Singapore facilitate economic growth by lowering reproduction costs of labour, subsidising wages, reinforcing social stability, increasing security, socialising immigrants and creating a safety net.

I have previously called Singapore and Hong Kong *property states* (Haila 2000). In a property state, real estate plays an important role in the economy, public revenue and the wealth of people. Patsy Healey and Susan Fainstein (see, e.g., Healey 1994 and Fainstein 1994) have analysed the relation of planning and property development. In this book, the institutions, actors and policies of property states are analysed in detail and in a systematic way drawing the whole argument together in the conclusion (Chapter 9). I analyse the legitimacy (philosophies of property, Chapter 2), preconditions (the gradual accumulation of state landed property, Chapter 4), measures and outcomes of Singapore's property state model. The following questions are asked. What is Singapore's land regime? What kind of land, housing and real estate policies has Singapore practised? How did Singapore accumulate its land bank? What kind of ideological and political controversies did the process generate? How does the government use and benefit from its land bank? What are the conditions for producing affordable housing? How did Singapore solve the housing question? Why have Singaporean development companies become large and successful despite state landownership? Are Singaporeans asset investors concerned with property prices? What are the effects of Singapore's status as a financial centre on housing and real estate prices and policies? How has the government intervened in order to strike a balance between rising real estate prices and affordable public housing?

There are seven reasons why Singapore was selected as a case to study the difference that land makes and to elaborate an urban land rent theory. First, in this small city-state without a hinterland, land is scarce. This scarcity of land has caused Singapore to use its land resources in the most efficient way possible. Since Lionel Robbins (1932) defined economics as the science of human behaviour involving the relationship between ends and scarce means with alternative uses (Hodgson 2001: 233), scarcity has been defined as an economic problem.[8]

This book will show how Singapore has used its scarce land resources to balance between maximising rent revenue and using its landed property for public good, to provide public housing for the majority of its population and public industrial space for the transnational companies locating in Singapore. The state land in Singapore is treated as a use value (public housing and industrial space), as an exchange value (leased for private developers) and as a source of public revenue (land leases and property tax). This triple way of using public land has caused Singapore's economy to grow and, paradoxically, Singapore's development companies to prosper. The book will show the dangers of creating liquid international markets for real estate price risk and of drawing real estate deeper into real estate speculation: land and houses as visible forms of wealth are rendered invisible and real estate investment trusts as landlords think only about yield not use value.

Second, land is publicly owned. The government owns 90 per cent of the land in Singapore and leases the land to developers through land auctions. At a time when European cities are privatising their public land, the exceptional case of Singapore offers a real-world alternative showing the benefits of land as a public good. At the outset of town planning, Thomas More and Tomaso Campanella sketched utopian visions that posited land as a public trust. These models were never realised, and prevailing wisdom deems individualised private ownership as necessary for economic growth. Singapore offers an alternative model, not merely a utopian ideal but a practice that works and has even been exported to China and Africa. Nevertheless, I am not suggesting that Singapore is a model for a good or just city. Rather, following Amartya Sen (2009), who argued for removing injustices rather than trying to achieve a perfectly just world, I want to show that by analysing Singapore's land regime we can understand and explain land-related problems and injustices in other cities.

Contrasting with historical-ideal types of land regimes, the book will identify Singapore's land regime as one of regulating public land. The debated concept of public space is ambiguous, and instead of analysing public land from the point of view of users, this book examines the ownership and management of public land. The Singapore case brings a new twist to the popular story of connecting private ownership with efficient economy and democracy. The book will show how Singapore strikes a balance between individual development rights and collective urban development rights. This challenges today's popular idea of bundling all kinds of rights together: development rights are very special kind of rights.

Third, Singapore has managed to produce affordable owner-occupied public housing for the majority of its population. We can say that Singapore has solved the 'housing question'. The first-generation leaders realised the importance of solving the housing question for the urban working class. The urban working class received the right to the city. Further, housing in Singapore is not just housing. It has been important in nation building, was a great success story for the first-generation PAP leaders, has facilitated economic growth, created wealth for Singaporeans and been a prominent issue in elections.

The book will show how Singapore, inspired by Fabian socialists, solved the 'housing question' and made urban workers homeowners, and how Singapore is trying to solve the current housing crisis. After accommodating the urban working class, the public housing option was offered to the middle classes and the majority of the population became asset holders. The book will discuss irrational overpricing of real estate and show how the property state of Singapore has intervened in the market for the benefit of homebuyers, enterprises and Singapore's economy.

Fourth, because there has been no change in the political regime since the PAP came to power in 1959, the government of Singapore has been able to follow a consequential regulatory policy aimed at the most efficient use of land. In countries where elections change political regimes, policies change abruptly and do not follow any 'land logic'. In Singapore, there is a thoroughly planned web of government institutions, statutory boards, government-linked companies, and government investment corporations that develop, manage and invest in land and real estate developments as if there has been an 'invisible hand' at work.

This book will introduce Singapore's consistent land policy and examine the effects and possibilities of long-term land policy. Singapore's development shows the benefits of keeping land-development power in the hands of the state. In Singapore, land-development power is exercised by what I call the state land institutions, the most important of which are the Singapore Land Authority, the Housing Development Board, the Urban Redevelopment Authority and Jurong Town Corporation. The book shows how these land institutions form a dynamic web of regulating institutions controlling and balancing each other, without concentrating too much power in one office. The book will show how Singapore gradually accumulated its public land bank, checked land speculation and used its land assets in a prudential way. An important element of this prudent land policy is regulating the land and real estate market. The book will show how Singapore's central bank, the Monetary Authority of Singapore, has regulated the real estate and housing market for the benefit of the economy and homeowners. Today, when financial and real estate sectors are intertwined in complicated ways, crises spread from one sector to another and real estate investment trusts own an increasing number of properties that they seek to use in the most efficient way, Singapore's way of connecting monetary, fiscal, real estate and housing policies deserves proper analysis. In the neoliberal era when free market and competition are the highest values, Singapore's regulatory land regime offers an alternative model to strike a balance between allowing the free flow of investment and containing the harmful effects of globalisation.

The fifth reason is that Singapore is urban. It has no farmers, countryside, or need to redistribute a surplus to undeveloped regions. For an urban scholar, Singapore provides an opportunity to find out the difference that urban makes. Several conceptions explicitly or implicitly depend on dichotomies between urban and rural. For example the Malays in Malaysia, living close to the land and being exposed to the erratic forces of nature, have been characterised as rural, whereas the Chinese, with their predictable habits and routines, were seen as urban people (Pye 1985: 259). Communal rights are usually associated with rural villages and less-developed economies. Studying Singapore's land policy will show that they are crucial in cities as well, and that in cities land can effectively be used for the benefit of all. The land question is not only a question in informal economies, but absolutely crucial in developed economies as well (where it calls for the regulation of real estate market). Singapore's urban character influences its pace of development and sense of history. Nostalgia and longing for the pastoral way of life can disrupt urbanisation, but Singapore, without a hinterland and with a short history, can draw upon global city strategies in full without the need to accommodate regional development.

Land acquisition, or eminent domain, is a controversial issue. Justification, valuation, compensation and the accommodation of evicted persons are difficult problems authorities must solve. Today, when land grabbing is a global problem, urbanising China seeks a solution to its land question and governments are tempted to sell their landed properties and deliberate on the value of urban land, Singapore offers a unique and guiding example. The book will show how Singapore values its land and legitimated its land acquisitions, how it accommodated evicted slum dwellers in public housing (making them homeowners) and, after the initial settlement was completed and more land was needed to accommodate the growing population, how it incentivised people to sell their condominium buildings to developers to build higher buildings. The experience of Singapore raises questions about the nature and value of urban land in general. These topics and more will be discussed in the book.

Sixth, without a rural landowner class and its interests, Singapore provides a laboratory case to test and elaborate the theory of land rent. Classical economists observed the conservative and parasitic nature of the landowner class, who were protected by monopolies and spent their revenues on luxuries instead of investing. The great puzzle of Singapore is why, despite state landownership, successful development companies prosper there. This book will solve this puzzle, and explain the division of land rent between the government and the real estate sector in Singapore.

This book will show how Singapore's real estate market is shared between private and government developers, how the land-owning government of Singapore appropriates land for private developers, allocates land to developers in fair land auctions (making developers compete and hone their competitiveness) and intervenes in the real estate market to prevent speculation, to cool or stimulate the property market.

Seventh, Singapore compels us to rethink the role the state. British historian David Cannadine (2002) commented that the British Empire had difficulty exporting its paternalistic, hierarchical and rural domestic social structures and social perceptions to Singapore. The reason for this was that this small colony was urban and working class with communist sympathies. Singapore is known for its liberal business climate and as a financial centre, but its policies are inspired by socialist ideas, and its land and housing policies in particular can be said to be radical.

This book distinguishes between the municipality and the state as landowners. This distinction is important and ignored by urban scholars. Singapore, where 90 per cent of the land is owned by the state and used for the benefit of the municipality, offers a model of allocating land that is worth examining in more detail in our time when governments face pressure to cut their expenses, find new sources of revenue and are tempted to sell off the properties they own for short-term gain.

Although Singapore is my focus, this is not only a case study of a single city. I will compare Singapore to Hong Kong, other Asian cities, and Western cities. I am convinced that urban studies is always comparative, in the sense that a scholar will have a city or cities in mind when studying one city; this may be a specific city or the city of the scholar's childhood (as in the case of Walter Benjamin). My comparisons differ from those of European classics who defined the European city by comparing Eastern and Western cities. In the case of Singapore, I am interested in understanding how land and real estate policies produce cities. I discuss Singapore's relationship to East Asia and Southeast Asia, with Hong Kong featuring as an especially appropriate comparison. As in Singapore, land in Hong Kong is owned by the government and allocated to developers through land auctions. Despite these similarities, the policies in Singapore and Hong Kong diverge. One significant difference concerns state intervention and regulation. Hong Kong is embedded in an impermeable ideology of *laissez faire*, whereas Singapore is a planned city par excellence, constantly introducing new programmes to make the city-state even better. I once asked a Singaporean friend where the more imaginative social regulations, like banning chewing gum or punishing people for being naked at home, come from. 'They are the result of too much planning,' he replied.

A few words about the language of this treatise are also needed. The words referring to landownership and urban development differ from culture to culture and time to time. Some words are neutral, such as 'plot ratio', whereas some words in some cultures can be pejorative, like the neologism 'developata' in Finnish. Further, different theoretical approaches use the same terms differently. A good example is the term 'rent', and therefore Chapter 3 clarifies different meanings of rent. In his book on customary Chinese land law, Patrick Hase (2013: 1) noted that writing in English was a problem. 'English has a rich legal vocabulary, but that vocabulary is a Common law vocabulary.' In my case, writing about Singapore in English is not a problem, because documents and laws in this former British colony are written in English. However, English is problematic because I am interested in comparing different land tenure systems that express their rights and duties with different terms having different meanings to English common law. To render commensurable this variety of land rights and duties a vocabulary of the concepts of rent theory is helpful, hence my dwelling upon the genealogy of the rent concepts in Chapter 3. A simple glossary is added in the beginning. I have written this study for an international audience, and made efforts to use the terms in an intercultural, neutral and general sense. This made my study also an inquiry into land vocabulary. I hope the result is not a new *Finnegans Wake*, no matter how great a book it is.

## The Chapters

This book is an analysis of land, land ownership, land tenure, land use, allocation mechanisms of land, land development processes, the real estate sector and its developers. The land question is analysed in its various dimensions: as resource, ideologies, intervention, actors, regional reach, investment flows and finance. Each topic is addressed in a separate chapter. Land is not analysed as 'original and indestructible powers of the soil', but mobilization of the land (to use this phrase of Polanyi 1944) is analysed in five dimensions: horizontal (extending the use of land, subdivision and suburbanisation), vertical (intensive use of land and erecting high-rise buildings), global (international flows), redevelopment (densification) and valorisation (financialisation and securitisation). The main message of the book is that land matters, and urban studies should pay attention to land development processes. Following the vocabulary of Henri Lefebvre, the analysis is divided into two parts. The first, representations of land (Chapters 2–4), discusses land in economic theories, ideologies of land and land reforms. The second (Chapters 5–8) analyses development practices: land institutions, actors, globalisation of real estate investment and financing of development projects. Chapter 9 concludes matters, discussing the difference land makes, contrasting rent theory and property rights approaches, and summarising what this study of Singapore can offer to other cities.

Chapter 2 looks at various philosophies, ideologies and stories that have been presented to justify landownership. There is one puzzle that has disturbed me for a long time. This is the origin and truthfulness of the taken-for-granted idea that private property creates economic wealth and democracy. This puzzle will be solved, and the relativity and historical nature of land claims demonstrated. The chapter introduces historical land regimes and begins revealing Singapore's as one without an indigenous land question and with a unique frontier and homeownership myth.

Chapter 3 dwells upon the puzzle of the dominance in our time of the economic argument. It introduces the theories – rent theory and property rights – and the main concepts used in this study: land rent, property rights and rent-seeking. Recent writings on rent theory have been rare contributions. For this reason, this chapter introduces a systematic history of rent debates. Throughout this study, rent theory and property rights theory are contrasted and the implications of these alternative approaches are shown. This chapter discusses the methodological difference between these theories and defines the concepts of rent used in this study: differential rent, absolute rent, monopoly rent, manipulated rent, fiscal rent, global rent and derived rent. While Chapter 2 discusses justification of landownership and rent, the chapters following Chapter 3 analyse political programmes to capture rent (Chapter 4), state-created conditions to affect rent (Chapter 5), actors and owners who compete for rent (Chapter 6), effects of globalisation on rent (Chapter 7), and fusion between interest and rent, finance and real estate (Chapter 8).

In Chapter 4, political implications of rent theory and property rights theory are analysed. I discuss political programmes and social movements that have sought to resolve the land question and change land tenure institutions. I differentiate between radical, moral, modern and neoliberal land reforms, and introduce land reformers ranging from romantics to technocrats. After discussing the ideas of Henry George and China's land reforms, I analyse Singapore's modern and pragmatic land reform that gradually expanded the state's land bank and created conditions for economic growth and affordable housing.

Chapter 5 begins discussing development practices by analysing the institutions, rules and policies of using land. The resolution of the housing question is analysed, particularly the role of state landownership in solving it. Public housing, with its rules and regulations, is introduced and contrasted to private housing. The fiscalisation of rent (that is, rent as the source of public revenue that I call fiscal rent) is investigated. Instead of analysing state intervention in general terms, I look at various methods of controlling urban development, and trace the gradual evolution and functions of various land institutions: land leases, auctions and public housing. Using Singapore as an example, questions concerning the functions of the state and the municipality and the value of public land are discussed.

Chapter 6 investigates the players in the real estate market: tycoons, landlords and companies. Singaporean construction and development companies are contrasted with those in Japan, the United States, Europe and Hong Kong. Rent theory explanation is contrasted with explanations that refer to political rent-seeking, and concepts of manipulated rent and absolute rent are discussed. The chapter solves the puzzle of why private development companies can prosper under state landownership, and analyses land speculation. This chapter also introduces Singapore's production of public industrial space, a topic that has not received the attention it deserves.

Chapter 7 examines international diversification of real estate portfolios, global real estate investment flows and the global real estate market. Overseas property companies, investors receiving rent from abroad (global rent), and the effects of modern absentee landlordism are analysed. Government, with its laws and physical renewal programmes, has made Singapore an attractive and safe investment haven. This has led to a rise in real estate prices. The price increase is, however, mitigated because part of the surplus produced in Singapore is invested in real estate abroad by Singaporean companies, sovereign wealth funds and Singaporean individual investors. The chapter discusses real estate investment trusts that have made it possible for small investors to invest in real estate, and the racial discrimination and nationalist sentiments provoked by global property investment flows.

Chapter 8 explains the relationships between land and money, property and finance, and the financial market and the real estate market, analysing the role of land in an age when the role of financial instruments is in the ascendant. Singapore's position as a financial centre brings advantages but also harmful effects to its real estate market. Among the harmful effects are the financial crises discussed in this chapter. The government's measures to check the harmful effects of financial crises are analysed using the concept of derivative rent: a payment for a security derived from real estate as an underlying asset and packed together with other assets into marketable bundles. The chapter also discusses the puzzle of why money and interest have become privileged in economic explanations and policies.

Chapter 9 summarises Singapore's land regime as introduced in the previous chapters, and discusses what the analysis of Singapore can bring to understanding the land, urban and rent 'questions'. Among the main conclusions of this study are that: affordable housing for the majority of people is feasible; preventing land speculation is possible and the key to successful housing and urban policy; a city can simultaneously have government intervention and a successful private development industry; and real world alternatives for urban development (not just utopias) exist.

## Notes

1  Singapore recycles ministers. For example, Lee Hsien Loong was deputy prime minister and Monetary Authority of Singapore chairman before he became prime minister. The titles also change. After 1990 Lee Kuan Yew was called senior minister, and after that minister mentor. I use the title that was applied at the time.

2  Krugman (1999: 42) defined the Washington consensus as the belief that growth could be best achieved via sound budgets, low inflation, deregulated markets and free trade. Today, some scholars argue that it has been substituted by the post-Washington consensus or the Beijing consensus (Halper 2010).

3  See debate: Riggs 1996; Yoshihara 1988; Deyo 1987; Robinson R 1986; Jomo 1986; Searle 1999.

4  In 1826 the East India Company united Singapore with Penang and Malacca to form the Straits Settlements. From 1830 it was governed by British India and in 1867 the Straits Settlements became a Crown Colony run by the Colonial Office in London (Perry et al. 1997).

5  Amartya Sen (1997) claimed that in Asia there exist traditions emphasising freedom, tolerance and equality. The Emperor Ashoka in the third century BC championed equalitarian and universal tolerance, and a Bengali poet praised dialogue thus: 'Just imagine how terrible it will be on the day you die. Others will go on speaking, but you will not be able to respond.'

6  There are cases showing the opposite. In Korea, Confucianism had existed for centuries, yet mass education was institutionalised rather recently by the US military government and the Syngman Rhee regime (1948–1960). As late as 1960, literacy rates in Thailand and the Philippines (countries not influenced by Confucianism) were as high as in South Korea. Confucianism, argued Lie (1998: 79), could even have hindered modernisation in cultivating an authoritative and bureaucratic spirit. A study by Christine Dobbin (1996) showed that it was not inherited values but colonial powers which strengthened the economic capabilities of some ethnic groups. In order to establish their regimes and hegemony, colonialists used as collaborators local minorities who were ethnically different from the majority population. A Spanish expedition to Manila in 1570 collaborated with the Chinese, the Dutch in Batavia in the seventeenth century collaborated with the Chinese, and the British in Burma collaborated with Indians. These collaborations between ethnic minorities and colonial powers strengthened the economic

role of minorities, especially the Chinese, who still play a role in the Indonesian, Thai, Malaysian and Singaporean economies.

7   *Guanxi* is a Chinese word used to refer to business favours based on personal connection.

8   Today when another natural resource, the ubiquitous air, has become less clean, it too has become a scarce commodity, a traded good and of interest to economists.

# 2

# Ideologies of Land

*The Orang Laut[1] of the Singapore River – the original inhabitants of the island. But the growth of trade meant that the Orang Laut community became a hindrance to the increasing River traffic. The government eventually forced their dispersal: some joined similar communities in the Riau islands, while others were absorbed in the mainstream Malay population. By end of the 19th century, 'Orang Laut' was no longer a term of meaningful distinction. Their traditional water-based lifestyle having given way to the pressures of commercial development.* (Asian Civilization Museum, Singapore, 14 February 2009)

In contrast to this Singaporean story of assimilation of an indigenous population thanks to growth in trade, European history is filled with forced evictions, violence and a variety of justification stories. This chapter investigates such stories and the evolution of land ownership. The argument is simple: there is not just one form of land tenure or one justification story. The point of this enquiry for the history of land tenure is: first to show the embeddedness of today's dominant justification story (John Locke justifying private ownership of land and Douglas North on the efficiency of private property) in European history and European philosophies; and second to introduce alternative stories. Why one European story is taken for granted and as evidence of superiority of one form of tenure is a great puzzle of our time. This chapter attempts to solve this puzzle. In the first part, I introduce a framework of ideal types of historical land regimes. These types function as a comparison in my

*Urban Land Rent: Singapore as a Property State*, First Edition. Anne Haila.
© 2016 John Wiley & Sons, Ltd. Published 2016 by John Wiley & Sons, Ltd.

search for Singapore's land regime and various mobilisations of land. In the second section I present debates on property, concerning the origin of property, the relationship between property and democracy, and efficient ways of using property. The third section discusses philosopher John Locke, who is still referred to in attempts to justify private property. This is followed by a discussion of two Lockean myths, the frontier and homeownership, popular in novels and the media. In urban Singapore, the ideas of the frontier and homeownership have distinctive meanings. Lastly, the chapter ends with a comparison between the landownership conception behind rent theory and property rights theory.

## Land Regimes

Forms of landownership are many and have changed through history, from being common, then enclosed, commodified, privatised and securitised. From time to time, landownership becomes a social issue and is debated: in John Stuart Mill's day in the nineteenth century the issue was inheritance, whereas today's debates revolve around whether real estate derivatives are good investment options compared to other financial instruments. Table 2.1 differentiates four historical land regimes. These are ideal types in the Weberian sense and are thus aimed at differentiating systems of land governance. They do not describe the richness of real-world landed property relations. The table identifies four historical periods (indigenous, feudal, capitalism and financialisation), specifies how land is treated, and the forms of property and relationships in these periods. It then introduces how use or ownership is justified, the forms of rent transferred (a payment to the landowner for use of the land), and, in the last column, modes for development. The point of the table is to show various mobilisations of land, and that land regimes do not just constitute land use but also affect social relations and need justification. The table also guides the topics analysed in this book. While this chapter briefly illustrates the indigenous and feudal phases, the following chapters discuss the capitalist and financial phases.

The first of these land regimes I call the indigenous phase. Land equates to nature and the focus is on its sustainable use. Before enclosure, farmers and indigenous people used land jointly, shared the produce of land and were stewards of natural resources. There were obligations and duties connected to the use of land, and land resources were to be preserved for future generations. Using land was not exploitation of nature, but made the user a member of the community, as was the case for the native people of Ninnimissinouk in New England in the sixteenth century (Bragdon 1996). To be denied the privilege of consuming the

**Table 2.1** Land regimes.

| Land regimes | Land treated as | Form of property | Relationship | Justification | Rent | Development modes |
| --- | --- | --- | --- | --- | --- | --- |
| indigenous | nature | shared and common | man & nature | use | no | sustainable |
| feudal | social relation | leased | landlord & tenant | power | feudal rent | municipal land for public good |
| capitalism | commodity | private | production & built environment | market | differential, absolute, monopoly, fiscal & global | uncontrolled development suburbs & gated communities |
| financialisation | asset | investment object | real estate & other investments | speculation | derivative | corporatisation and selling municipal lands |

produce of land was to be a 'non-member' or servant – one without a name. For indigenous peoples, private and exclusive ownership was incomprehensible and land had no boundaries. Today, the Yukon First Nation people in Canada speak of land in terms of travel, and understand 'landownership' without boundaries. 'How can you own a piece of land? It's like saying you can own a cloud!', says a Yukon woman (Cruikshank 1998: 16–17).

Whether indigenous peoples used land in a sustainable way or wasted natural resources is a contested issue. For example, were American Indians, represented as 'truly people of the land'[2] who respect Mother Earth, really ecologists and conservationists? Shepard Krech III (1999) challenged the use of such Western concepts. Many native people, according to Krech III, believed that herds of animals returned again and again to be killed as long as hunters demonstrated proper respect. The Cheyenne, Arapahoe and other Indians 'believed that the buffalo were produced in countless numbers in a country under the ground' (Dodge 1882/1970, cited in Krech III 1999: 148). Krech III (1999: 149) concludes that, in order to call these Indians ecologists or conservationists, one must allow for the presence of lakes into which buffaloes disappeared, and to accept that what might have been most important to conserve was not a herd of buffaloes but a ritually expressed relationship with the buffalo.

The second type of land regime, the feudal system (prevalent in Europe between 900 and 1500), was based on a lease relationship between a landlord and a tenant. European feudalism was a complicated and hierarchical system. There were two types of ownership: *dominium directum* (proprietorial status pertaining to the lord) and *dominium utile* (the use-right of a peasant). Tenants paid feudal rent (in the form of work or produce) to the landlord. Property was a right and a relationship. The king owned the land, subdivided it among his lords, who granted it to tenants, who let labourers cultivate the land.[3] Douglas North and Robert Thomas ([1973] 1999: 28) identified five tenure types: tenure by knights' service (granted in return for the provision of knights), tenure in free and common socage (a grant of land in return for specified services such as money, produce, labour and attendance at the lord's court), tenure in serjeanty (granted in return for the provision of military services), tenure in frankalmoign (a grant of land to a man providing religious services) and tenure in villeinage (unfree land that could not be returned to the lord and required a villein to remain on the land). The forms of tenure and the duties connected to use rights varied between European countries, and were often a source of conflict. For example, incumbent upon to peasants in Finland[4] was a duty to provide quarters and food for the king's soldiers. Resistance

against this led to the 1597 peasant uprising known as the Cudgel War
(Ylikangas 1977).

In addition to lords' and peasants' land, there were also the commons. Common rights and commoning varied from country to country.
In England, cottagers and day labourers without arable land were able
to use the commons for pigs, poultry and cows (Linebaugh 2008: 50).
Among the various rights commoners had were herbage, agistment and
pannage (Linebaugh 2008: 42). As a result, commoners had rights to
the same piece of land as the king, lords and tenants: ownership was
overlapping. The commons was not just accessible land, it also affected
people's relationships and mentalities. Peter Linebaugh (2008: 51), following England's influential social historian R. H. Tawney (1880–1962),
talks about cooperation, the fellowship of mutual aid and hospitality created by the commons. In *The Country and the City*, Raymond Williams
(1975: 134) suggested that rights to grazing and fuel on common pas-
tures created a breathing space, a fortunate distance from immediate
and visible control.

The relationship to land was important in feudal times. A man's condition, as Henri Pirenne ([1936] 1972: 12) wrote, was 'determined by his
relation to the land ... To possess land was at the same time to possess
freedom and power.' There were several overlapping rights to a piece
of land. This led to conflict, but also strengthened community ties. In
village communities, customary rights were seldom written down. There
was no need for written contracts because people in communities knew
and agreed upon the use of land. The need for a written deed emerged
only when land was sold. This was the case, for example, in Hong Kong's
New Territories, where customary rights were enforced by village public opinion (Hase 2013: 178), implying a different model for deciding local affairs rather than voting rights based on landed property as
in Europe.

Municipal landownership started to develop in this pre-commodity
era in European towns. In the case of Helsinki, the City received land as
a donation from the king upon its foundation in 1550. The king confiscated peasants' land and handed it to the City to be used for the common
good of the citizens. For the City of Helsinki this was a long-term endowment that later made possible an urban policy immune from speculation
by private developers.

The third type of regime, capitalism, developed when the parcelling
up of land and enclosure practices commodified land in the early modern ages. This was a crucial change in Europe: a market for land developed, prices were attached to land, and the built environment became
subordinated to production. Enclosure and parcelling changed the
nature of land from a source of livelihood to a commodity, an object to

be bought and sold. With this process the meaning of land also changed: land came to mean a thing, while previously it had been understood as a right (Macpherson 1978). This transformation affected class relations. Polanyi (1944) deplored the disruption of the fabric of society by the enclosers, initially the aristocracy and then wealthy country gentlemen and merchants. The emerging bourgeoisie struggled against the feudal rule of property. As Thomas Grey (1969: 73–74) (cited in Heller 1998: 661) wrote, for 'the rising bourgeoisie, property conceived as a web of relations among persons meant the system of lord, vassal, and serf from which they were struggling to free themselves. On the other hand, property conceived as the control of a piece of the material world by a single individual meant freedom and equality of status.'

Enclosure and the parcelling up of land did not only happen in England, but all over Europe. In Finland, these processes began in the middle of the eighteenth century and followed the English model. The arguments presented then sound familiar, and could have been taken from one of Douglas North's books: the appeal was to efficiency and incentives. In a 1746 debate in the Finnish Parliament, the Mayor of Vaasa said that 'Joint ownership of forest and land and the open field system of arable land and meadows considerably restrain agriculture. Everyone can with a little thought realize the inconvenience an ignorant and lazy farmer can cause a wise and hard-working farmer who uses the same open field or owns forests jointly with him' (Jutikkala 1958: 247).

The commodity phase and the development of the land market meant a new type of urban development. Differential, absolute and monopoly rent began to affect the form of cities as a real estate industry developed, and town planners and real estate brokers established themselves as urban development professionals. Uncontrolled squatting, private subdivisions and suburbs were things that happened beyond the city limits. By the twentieth century, gated communities were developed as private commodified developments on private land, and changed the meaning of private and public land.

Outside Europe, a comparable process to enclosure was colonialism. 'Much colonialism,' commented Margaret Davies (2007: 65) 'rested on the concept of *terra nullius* as an inherently but not-yet-appropriated resource.' When European colonialists landed in new territories they did not, with the odd exception like the Spanish Salamancan School (Mäkinen 2008), respect the customary ownership of land (land as something non-alienable to be used by the community). Colonialists brought with them the idea of enclosure and private ownership. One example is provided by the Dutch when they landed in what is today called Manhattan in the seventeenth century. They first shared the land

with the Lenape people, the original inhabitants of the island, but soon
walled themselves in and blocked Lenape use of the area (Pritchard
2007: 134).

When Europeans arrived, Southeast Asia was not *terra nullius*. Early
kingdoms like Funan, Champa, Kambuja, Nan Chao, Srivijaya and
Sailendras had produced magnificent cities and monuments like Vyad-
hapura, Angkor, Pagan, Palembang, Borobudur and Prambanan (see
SarDesai 1994). Temasek (today's Singapore) was a cosmopolitan urban
community in the fourteenth century (Miksic 2013). How did the colonialists treat land in Southeast Asia, and what were the land tenure systems in the Malay world to which Temasek belonged?

In Malaya, before the colonialists arrived, there was an abundance of
land and, through the clearing of land from jungle, people had a right to
land as long as they occupied it (Ooi 1959: 192). When the British came
to Singapore in 1819, the Malay chiefs permitted them to set up a trading
post. Colonel William Farquhar,[5] 'following Malay custom, believed that
this did not confer ownership of land or rights to make laws' (Turnbull
1982: 23). Sir Thomas Stamford Raffles,[6] though, had different ideas,
and in 1823 'he made an agreement to buy out their [the Malay chiefs']
judicial powers and rights to land, except the areas specifically reserved
for them' (Turnbull 1982). Raffles made an agreement with the local
chieftain, Temenggong Abdur-Ranman of Johor, to establish a trading
post and for the island to be ceded to the East India Company. The
treaty was problematic because of a dispute over the succession of the
Johor Sultanate and because of the conflicting interests of the Dutch
and the British. The Treaty of London in 1824, signed by the Dutch and
the British, recognised the latter's claim to Singapore. The same year
a treaty with Sultan Hussein and Temenggong Abdur-Rahman of Johor
consolidated the British position, thereby ceding the entire island to
Britain forever, in full sovereignty and property (Wake 1975; Dale 1999:
3; SarDesai 1994: 86–87).

British common law was introduced to Singapore and still defines
landownership there today. All land belongs to the state and there are
four kinds of estate in land: 'the freehold fee simple estate, the freehold
life estate, the estate in perpetuity created by the State Lands Act and
the leasehold estate' (Tan S Y 1998: 5). 'The concept of estate is derived
from the feudal law which permitted a man to hold a parcel of land
belonging to his lord for a given period of time (estate) in return for
the performance of services (tenure)' (Tan S Y 1998: 5). This concept
of estate, as a man holding a piece of land for a given period of time after
which the land returns to the state, is still the basis of Singapore's land
tenure relations (the modernisation of this feudal thinking is discussed
in Chapter 4).

In our current time of financialisation – the fourth type of land regime, characterised by the increased importance of the global finance market and financial instruments – land has come to be treated as an asset and object of speculative investment. The real estate market has become intertwined with the financial market and investment in land assessed from the point of view of the yield from other assets. Land titles together with mortgages have been securitised, making it possible to buy and sell real estate shares on the stock market. I call the yield from such sophisticated real estate instruments *derivative rent*. Investors speculate, comparing the yield of real estate options and shares to the yield of other financial instruments. The real estate sector develops logics of its own, making public policies difficult to implement because the external forces of the global financial market and the built environment are vulnerable to crises (global rent is discussed in Chapter 7 and derivative rent in Chapter 8).

For urban development, the treatment of land as a financial asset, and determining the value of land after comparisons with the yields of other investment instruments, means further submission of the built environment to market forces and financial speculation. Urban development becomes dependent on the external forces of debt crisis, bank defaults, sovereign debt and lending by banks. Vacancies follow booms, and prices of real estate and housing become difficult to control. In this phase, it becomes tempting for states and municipalities to sell and corporatise the land they own, using it as an instrument for fiscal revenue (fiscal rent).

The concept of land regime elucidates the point that the treatment of land in a society is not only about choices concerning economically efficient use of land, as property rights theorists assume, but also requires justification of ownership, affects social relations and defines the mode of urban development. In debates concerning the origin, evolution and effects of landed property, genetic (relating to origin), consequential (referring to consequences such as efficiency and democracy) and moral (fairness and justness) arguments have been presented and confused.

## Debates on Genealogies

Historians have debated whether the original form of land governance was private or shared use. Based on Lewis Morgan's (1877) classification of epochs of savagery, barbarism and civilization in the human history, Friedrich Engels (1884) in *The Origin of the Family, Private Property, and the State* explained the primitive community and how it disintegrated after the emergence of private property. Engels believed that private ownership of land emerged together with money and commodity production. In *The Evolution of Property from Savagery to Civilization* (1890), Karl Marx's son-in-law Paul Lafargue traced the history of property from common, tribal and village property to family, feudal and bourgeois property. These ideas that the original form of ownership was common were not accepted by Fustel de Coulanges (1891) who argued that there was private ownership of land in Ancient Greece, and Moses Finley (1981) who presented the Homeric poems as evidence of private ownership.

Another debate has concerned the evolution of property, in particular whether changing forms of ownership imply progress and civilisation, leading eventually to the highest level of civilisation – democracy and liberty. Karl Marx connected the evolution of property rights to social and economic development (Pejovic 1982), distinguishing modes of production (tribal, ancient, feudal and capitalist) with different types of ownership and use of land (communal, state, feudal and private property). Alexis de Tocqueville (1805–59) connected small-scale ownership to democracy and Thomas Jefferson (1743–1826) believed in farmers' democracy (White and White 1962; Luria 2006). From these ideas developed the popular contemporary idea of connecting landownership with democracy and liberty. Property in land, as Polanyi ([1944] 2001: 189) wrote, 'formed an essential part of the Benthamite conception of individual liberty'. Following similar reasoning, authoritarian government in Russia (where all landed property was under the tsar, who not only ruled the realm and its inhabitants, but owned them) has been explained by referring to the absence of property rights, and contrasted to England where parliamentary democracy developed as the result of secure property rights (Pipes 1999). As we saw in the first chapter, Karl Wittfogel (1957) characterised oriental despotic Asia as lacking private property and civil society, and Nial Ferguson (2011) even offered property rights as one reason for the ascendency and supremacy of the West.

A third debate concerns the transition from feudalism to capitalism. From this has evolved an important pillar of property rights theory: assumed economic efficiency. Scholars have debated whether feudalism's decline was on account of an external reason (namely that trade dissolved feudalism) (Pirenne 1936; Sweezy 1950), whether the reason was within the feudal system itself (Dobb 1946), or whether the reason was class conflict and the resistance of peasants (Merrington 1975; Brenner R 1977). Europe on the threshold of capitalism revolved around the question of property; land was enclosed and parcelled up, and properties concentrated. Even the seventeenth-century witchcraft trials were about property: 'improper' female owners who got into disputes with neighbouring farmers could be burnt as witches (Karlsen 1989; Rose 1994: 288–289). Nobel laureate Douglas North suggested a solution to the debate concerning property rights and economic efficiency: exclusive property rights increase efficiency and are the key to capitalism. Together with Robert Thomas (North and Thomas 1973), North argued that the elimination of common ownership of land, the establishment of property rights and enclosures created incentives to economic growth, improved efficiency of markets and led to an expanded market economy. Later, North (2005: 1–2) clarified: 'well-developed property rights that encourage productivity will increase market efficiency'. This interpretation became accepted by property rights scholars, and is used to justify titling programmes suggested by the World Bank and Hernando de Soto (discussed in Chapter 4).

Despite its popularity, North's explanation is questionable. First, if property was in individual ownership by the end of the thirteenth century, as for example Alan MacFarlane (1978) has argued, several hundred years before the rise of 'efficient' capitalism, why the delay? Another problem is that not even in the West are property rights secure and permanent. They are changing and overlapping, and the ambiguity of property rights is acknowledged – for example, in the legal concept 'the usage from time immemorial'.[7] The third problem – and this is relevant in the urban context and will be discussed later – is the fallacy of generalisation. The argument that 'well developed property rights increase market efficiency' assumes the tragedy of the commons[8] – namely that if resources are available for free use (that is, there are no property rights over them) they become over-exploited. This assumption (used as evidence against common ownership) is an attempt by property rights theorists to demonstrate collective behaviour on an individual basis. But the argument that 'an individual takes care of what he/she owns' cannot be generalised to the urban scale, where externalities and public goods affect people's behaviour.

A fourth problem with North's explanation is that it is specifically based on the history of England. Elsewhere in Europe, development followed different paths, and even more markedly so outside Europe. In Asia, forms of tenure were and still are various. In the Tai world,[9] for example, community rights included use rights granted temporarily to community members for their productive activities, and 'natural rights' included rights to resources provided free by nature (such as mushroom or ants' eggs) (Anan 2001, cited in Walker 2009b: 16). In Sarawak (Borneo, now part of Malaysia), longhouse communities owned communal land and individual families had usufruct rights to the lands held by consent of the whole community (Colchester 1989). In Hong Kong's New Territories, British colonialism[10] is to thank for the preservation of the ancestral Chinese estate system which remains in force today (Watson and Watson 2011b: 11). In one New Territories village – Ha Tsuen, studied by Rubie Watson (2011) – an ancestral hall was established in 1749 and endowed with land that has subsequently been held corporately by those Teng males whose forebears had participated in the initial temple subscription. In another village – San Tin, studied by James Watson (2011b: 56) – the Man lineage 'still retains many of its traditional functions, including the management of commonly owned property, maintenance of five ancestral halls, and support of the village school'.

The origin, evolution and efficiency of landed property are contentious issues and differ from country to country. In the case of Singapore the Orang Laut people were in the remote past and the British introduced common law and the practice of agreements.[11] The state began regulating land use and the state land regime is legitimised by using an economic argument; economic benefits, however, are not understood in the way as Locke and North understood them.

## Philosophies of Property

The enclosure and parceling of land in Europe and colonial possessions in the New World were traumatic and violent events that needed justification. The most influential justification story was told by John Locke, who suggested that by ploughing, sowing and reaping a man can take land into his possession. Other philosophers (Hume, Pufendorf, Rousseau and Kant) told different stories and, instead of focusing on individual possession, paid attention to the consent of others and contingent development of property relations as a response to social problems.

John Locke (1632–1704) is acknowledged as the theorist of the dominant concept of private property, and is used as the authority to justify private ownership of land. Locke presented arguments to justify initial acquisition (both in the colonies and Europe) at the time of enclosure. In the *Second Treatise of Government* (1689), Locke wrote:

> God, who hath also given the World to Men in common, hath also given them reason to make use of it to the best advantage of Life, and convenience ... Though the Earth, and all inferior Creatures be common to all Men, yet every Man has a *Property* in his own *Person* ... The *Labour* of his Body, and the *Work* of his Hands, we may say, are properly his. Whatsoever then he removes out of the State that Nature hath provided, and left it in, he hath mixed his *Labour* with, and joyned to it something that is his own, and thereby makes it his

*Property*… The same *measures* governed the *possession* of *Land* too: Whatsoever he tilled and reaped laid up and made use of, before it spoiled, that was his peculiar Right; whatsoever he enclosed, and could fence, and make use of, the cattle and Product was also his. (Cited in Macpherson 1978: 17–22.)

Locke wrote his treatise at the time when England was establishing colonies in America and competing with the Dutch, French and Spanish for ownership of the New World. His theory, as shown by Barbara Arneil (1994, 1996), has its historical roots in English colonisation. Locke defended English colonial policy; his theory enabled the English to justify the taking of land used by Indians. Locke argued that people had a natural right to property through their labour, but only a certain type of labour created ownership. The natural right to property excluded Spanish conquistadors who were interested in gold and silver, and Native Americans who were hunters. Mining and hunting did not create ownership. Only an English (and Protestant) farmer, by ploughing, sowing and reaping, could be a legitimate proprietor and citizen. Only mixing labour with the soil created a right to own land.

Locke's ideas were contested. John Stuart Mill remarked that, as long as your labour is no loss to you, why should you care (Becker 1977: 44)? Pierre-Joseph Proudhon scoffed at Locke's idea and wrote: 'The rich have the arrogance to say. "I built this wall, I earned this land with my labour." Who set you the tasks? We may reply, and by what right do you demand payment from us for labour which we did not impose on you?' (Cited in Becker 1977: 41.) Robert Nozick turned Locke's labour argument the other way round: 'why anyone should think that mixing one's labour with a thing is a way of making the thing one's own rather than a way of losing one's labour' (cited in Becker 1977: 34).

Other philosophers wrote different stories. They paid attention to the other side of the property relationship: the acknowledgement of others. David Hume thought that there was nothing natural about private property; property depends on the laws of society. In *A Treatise of Human Nature* (1739), he wrote: 'our property is nothing but those goods, whose constant possession is established by the laws of society… This relation is not natural, but moral, and founded on justice.' (Cited in Selby-Bigge and Nidditch 1978: 491.) In the seventeenth century, Samuel von Pufendorf criticised the aggressive expansionary policies of the commercial powers, arguing that property rights are founded on agreements and contracts with obligations and duties. Men, according to Pufendorf, need to live together with other men, and because men, unlike beasts, have passions and desires (avarice, desire of glory, envy,

rivalry and intellectual strife), they need contracts to obey (see Gaertner 2005). In *Discourse on the Origin of Inequality* (1755), Jean-Jacques
Rousseau noted the necessity of the consent of others. He wrote: 'The
true founder of civil society was the first man who, having enclosed a
piece of land, thought of saying, "This is mine," and came across people
simple enough to believe him' (Rousseau [1755] 1994: 54). Immanuel
Kant (1724–1804) extended Rousseau's idea of consent of others to the
community. Kant recognised that individual claims negate the interests
of others, and that 'an individual cannot of himself establish a right to
a thing, because a right consists of the public recognition of an existing
or desired future state of affairs' (Williams 1977: 34).

   Why did Locke's interpretation become dominant, despite alternative justification stories and criticism of it? Two aspects of Locke's theory have made it look natural and explain its popularity. The first is its
possessive individualism, and the second is his labour theory of property. Possession has been regarded as natural, not only among humans
but even among animals (see e.g. Pipes 1999 on possessiveness among
animals). Social theorists like Anthony Giddens (1984) and Peter Saunders (1990) talk about ontological security, the feeling of security that
property (especially homeownership) brings to an individual. Few social
understandings, remarks Michael Heller (1998: 660), are more deeply
intuited than core private property rights of 'my land' and 'your land'.

   Another appealing character of Locke's theory is its labour theory of
property. It appeals directly to people's sense of justice. It allows people to own what they produce. 'Most people, since Locke have said,
assumed, or implied', wrote Lawrence Becker (1977: 41), that people
are entitled to the products of their labour. Locke's justification became
so persuasive because it was based on man's natural right to his own
labour, wrote Macpherson (1978: 15). This 'natural' sense of owning
the products of one's labour has been one obstacle to implementation
of land reforms (discussed in Chapter 4).

   The popularity of the Locke's story, however, cannot be explained
solely by referring to the texts and debates of philosophers and
economists. The story is disseminated, reinforced and popularised by
myths, popular novels and the media, making it seem to be common
sense. As narrative research argues, tales have persuasive power.

## Myths of Frontier and Homeownership

Two Lockean myths found in several cultures are those of the frontier
and homeownership. The frontier myth tells of the relationship between
the man and land, and varies from country to country. In the United

States, Fredrik Jackson Turner (1861–1932) tells of a man who, by mixing his labour with the soil, brought civilization to the wilderness. In Finland, the first Finnish-language novel, *Seitsemän veljestä* by Aleksis Kivi (1870), recounts a frontier story about seven wild brothers who settled in the wilderness, cleared a forest for cultivation and in the process turned themselves into civil members of society. At the national level, we can see the influence of the frontier myth and the Lockean idea of privileging farmers' labour in Finland's borderland policy after the 1917 Russian Revolution. The lands along the border were settled with farmers, because it was thought that only farmers were reliable enough to resist the temptations of socialism. Canada has its own version of the frontier story: brave men went into the wilderness, tested their manhood in the harsh conditions, showed their endurance and survived, but then returned to civilisation (Shields 1992). The frontier myth is still alive in justifying gentrification, the conversion of working-class neighbourhoods into middle-class enclaves. In a modern frontier story, urban 'pioneers' conquer dangerous urban neighbourhoods; the social meaning of gentrification, as Neil Smith (1992: 69) wrote, 'is increasingly constructed through the vocabulary of the frontier myth'.

Locke's justification story is based on an assumption that unoccupied land to exploit must exist, that there is a frontier. To use the rent theory vocabulary, there exists an extensive margin. In Singapore this is not the case, and the frontier has a unique meaning. Singapore is a small Chinese-majority city-state, surrounded by the populous Muslim states of Malaysia and Indonesia in Southeast Asia. As an urban city-state without a hinterland, Singapore is dependent on its neighbours: water from Malaysia, sand from Indonesia and air space (for its air force's training flights) from Thailand. This isolation on the one hand and dependency on the other can be read in explanations of Singapore's vulnerability (Chua 1995; Leifer 2000). To understand the unique meaning of the frontier in Singapore, it is helpful to identify two meanings of the frontier, following Janet Sturgeon (2005): frontier as margin and as dividing line.

First, the frontier as margin is manifest as Singaporeans' anxiety of being left out: as individuals, as a nation and as members of the community. At the individual level, the *kiasu*[12] mentality is fear of losing. At the national level, a series of strategic programmes to position Singapore globally (discussed in Chapter 7) have been introduced to develop Singapore as the Switzerland or Monaco of Asia in order to keep Singapore in the race for global city status. At the neighbourhood level, the frontier mentality seeks quality improvements. Upgrade programmes have been implemented to improve housing estates. Instead of an extensive margin, the margin is intensive: 'mixing labour' to improve quality and build

**Figure 2.1**   Public housing. Photo: Anne Haila.

taller buildings. In the 1990s, a key word in the media was 'upgrading'. The television news began with news of upgrade projects on public housing estates. The front pages of *The Straits Times* had 'upgrading news'. Walking around housing estates, one could frequently see signs with phrases like 'again another upgrading project'. Upgrade projects were not just about improving the quality of housing and living conditions, they also fuelled optimism and the modernist spirit, creating what Benedict Anderson (1983) has called an 'imagined community'. Upgrade programmes were a manifestation of the aims of the benevolent government, maintaining Singaporeans' trust in the system by promising a better future. Modest public housing flats were replaced with executive public housing flats (see Figures 2.1 and 5.5, p. 110), culminating with the development of Punggol, the latest new town, mixing the middle and working classes (these issues are discussed in Chapter 5).

Second, the frontier as dividing line links Singaporeans with Southeast Asian cultures. Simultaneously, however, it separates Singapore (as a modern Chinese-majority city) from its neighbours. Some of the common cultural features of Southeast Asia mentioned by Anthony Reid (see p. 10), such as eating rice, fermented fish, coconut and sugar palms, we find in Singapore; others, such as chewing betel and cockfighting, we do not. But beyond the borders of Singapore we can still find the exoticism of Southeast Asia. There is the liminal space for occasional visits. Johan Lindqvist (2010), in his case study of Batam (Indonesia, close to Singapore and formerly part of the Malay world), writes about ethnically Malay Singaporean working-class men who travel to Batam at the weekend to have fun, meet their girlfriends and escape the stress of modern Singapore. One of them, Pak Haji, a retired Singaporean customs officer, has built a house there and compares it to Singapore 30 years ago, offering a nostalgic sense of the kampong life of his childhood.

In Singapore, Chinese, Malays, Indians and others live together, and the Housing Development Board (HDB), with its racial quota system (discussed in Chapter 5), prevents racial segregation. The dividing line is between cosmopolitans and 'heartlanders',[13] working-class residents living in public housing. In his novel *Heartland*, Daren Shiau (2002: 38–39) identifies their distinctiveness, characterising the life of heartlanders as moving, buying, eating and talking:

> The heartlanders of the east in Marine Parade and Bedok always prided themselves in having a unique character. They called it the cooler side of the island. Though mocked at whenever they proclaimed their individuality, the truth was that there was a difference to the ubiquitous heartlands which no one could deny. The southern estates, like Queenstown and Tanglin Halt, had a dour austerity that came with age. Quiet and peaceful, most were results of the first phase of high-rise developments after the HDB took over from the SIT in the sixties. They were now populated with old, conservative residents … The heart of the heartlands had to be the big, landlocked, densely populated regions of Ang Mo Kio and Toa Payoh, where through its arteries of bus interchanges and hawker centres, the crowds flowed and interacted incessantly. Moving. Buying. Eating. Talking.

Another persistent and universal Lockean myth is the homeownership myth. In the United States, 'the myth of the American dream' connects owning a house to becoming a full member of society (Cullen 2003). Ananya Roy (2003) has called this the American paradigm of propertied citizenship. It embodies private ownership as a value, defines existence through homeownership, and excludes the homeless. The World Bank even ascribes individual virtues to ownership: 'People who own their house or have secure tenure have a larger stake in their community and thus are more likely to lobby for less crime, stronger governance, and better local environmental conditions' (World Development

**Figure 2.2**   Private housing. Photo: Anne Haila.

Report 2009: 206). In novels, the idea of ownership's existential meaning is popular. Daniel Defoe's *Robinson Crusoe* – influenced by Locke – has been interpreted as a story of possessive individualism. Honore de Balzac's *Colonel Chabert* (1832) connected property to a person's name, fame, status and power (see Caruth 2002).

In Singapore, where 90 per cent of people are homeowners and the state owns 90 per cent of the land, the homeownership myth is different. The 'Singaporean dream' is to own landed property (see Figures 2.2 and 4.3, p. 84). Singaporean economist Linda Low (1998: 184) suggested that, at its worst, the Singaporean dream leads to 'the speculative mentality, that because land is finite commodity, the present generation tries to secure more properties and assets for their children and even grand children'. Only a few can realise the dream of landed property. For the rest there is a substitution, namely the asset value of home. In Simon Tay's (2009: 16) novel *City of Small Blessings*, a Singaporean returns from Canada and finds that a developer has built a condo on the site of his former home. The sojourner remembers selling his house in Singapore before leaving and contemplates the tripling of property prices.

> Ours was a nice house, but it was just a place where I lived. I had never really thought about it as anything special. So when the

estimate came back from the valuers, I had to take a good, hard look. We sold it for $ 5 million. A pretty sum then … I suppose I should have hung on for more money but then, who knew? Anyway, I had already got more money than I ever imagined possible. Of course, I lost the house.

Frontier and homeownership myths are not just entertaining bed-time stories –they have the effect of depoliticising, simplifying, purifying and giving contingent events a natural and eternal justification, to use Roland Barthes' ([1956] 1989: 130) definition of myth. Homeowner-ship looks natural, and people forget that it is a result of deliberate poli-tics of land and housing. The homeownership myth and the practice of defining existence through homeownership make understandable the irrational belief that house prices will always go up. Economists George Akerlof and Robert Shiller (2009) have, with good reason, called such irrational belief and the behaviour based on it 'animal spirit'.

Frontier and homeownership myths can change, however, and a look at the history of land regimes and varying justification stories shows the fragility of the concept of private property. What was just at one time became unjust in another, as when legal privateering turned into ille-gal piracy after the European colonial powers united against the Asian maritime cities (Reid 2010). Turbulent financial times today have even managed to crack the sacred homeownership myth and shown its con-structed nature. When the subprime crisis in 2008 led to foreclosures and negative equity, some extreme libertarians in the United States recommended giving up on homeownership by walking away (French 2010), and people realized that there were fewer narratives to help them understand downward mobility (Jefferson 2011).

## The Economic, Moral and Political Land Question

Locke claimed that by mixing labour with the land, a man created a right to own land. Land became a thing to be privately owned and the owner has the right to the land's produce (thus the category of rent as unearned becomes unnecessary). This is the justification of private landownership behind property rights theory. Today, the justification story does not apply to ploughing, sowing and reaping, as in Locke's time, but basically the story remains the same as in the days of enclosure and colonialism. Following North and Coase, it states that ambiguous property rights lead to waste and inefficient use of valuable resources. To enable the economy to grow, cities to prosper, and people's wellbeing to increase (so the contemporary justification story goes) necessitates

**Figure 2.3**   Statues of traders to commemorating the city-state's early history. Photo: Anne Haila.

defining ambiguous property rights and letting the market decide. This ownership myth does not only concern land; it is extended to all sorts of alienable things and universalised as a hegemonic ideology. Companies have tried to obtain patents for native plants, basmati rice, yoga positions, traditional knowledge, traditional medicine and genes. Countries like Italy, Turkey and China defend cultural patrimony, and are in conflict with countries that have developed markets for looted cultural artifacts. In addition, products of intellectual labour, body parts, children, indeed everything can be commodified and sold in the market.

To appeal to the act of mixing labour with land, or economically efficient use of land as the legitimation of property, is to forget that possession requires the consent of others, as Hume, Pufendorf, Rousseau and Kant showed in questioning the solitary declaration of possession. The treaty Raffles made with the local chieftain of Johor required the consent of others, and was recognised by the Dutch and the British (Figure 2.3 Singapore remembering its past). The land question is not only an economic question but also a moral, social and political question as rent theory sees it. Questions concerning justification or distributional effect are not separate from the question of economic efficiency.

It was the fallacy of Adam Smith, argued Duncan Foley (2006), to distinguish an economic sphere of life from the rest of social life. This fallacy was continued in Douglas North's formulation of the economic argument: exclusive property rights increase efficiency. To understand the economic argument and why it has become dominant, the next chapter dwells on the theories of rent and property rights.

## Notes

1   Orang Laut means the people of the sea (indigenous people of Malaya).
2   David Lester, executive director of the council of Energy Resources Tribes, cited in Krech III 1999: 302.
3   This system is not very different from that in ancient China, although the hierarchy is simpler. Since the Southern Song Dynasty (AD 1127–1279) ultimate ownership was vested in the Emperor and subject to the payment of land tax (Palmer 1987: 4).
4   Finland was not, of course, a nation station state until 1917. I will, however, call the territory in question, part of Sweden until 1809 and of Russia between 1809 and 1917, Finland because in both these periods Finland had certain specific rules and privileges.
5   Colonel William Farquhar (1774–1839) worked for the East India Company and was the first Resident of colonial Singapore.
6   Clerk in the East India Company, Lieutenant-Governor of Java (1811–1816) and Lieutenant-Governor of Bencoolen.
7   If nobody remembers how a person has acquired the property, he is the legitimate owner of that property.
8   Originally presented by Garrett Harding (1968), referring to the danger of overexploitation of resources in the absence of property rights upon them.
9   The Tai world is made up of those populations who speak Tai languages, living in Thailand, Burma, Laos and China (Walker 2009a).
10  Hong Kong became a British colony in three phases: Hong Kong Island after the First Anglo-Chinese War (1840–42), the Kowloon Peninsula after the Second Anglo-Chinese War (1858–60) and the New Territories were leased in 1899.
11  Unlike the British colonialists, the Spaniards and the Portuguese did not feel they needed to sign treatises with the natives. Their possessions had the backing of God and the Pope (as God's spokesman) (Weatherford 1997: 96).
12  *Kiasu* is a Hokkien word meaning 'fear of losing'. The word is common parlance, showing the multilingual character of Singapore.
13  Heartlanders are residents of public housing estates, contrasted to cosmopolitans (who are more internationally oriented).

# 3

# Economic Arguments
## *Rent Theory and Property Rights Theory*

*Rent is that portion of the produce of the earth which is paid to the land-
lord for the use of the original and indestructible powers of the soil.* (David
Ricardo, *The Principles of Political Economy and Taxation* 1817)

In contrast to single-city ethnographies and comparisons between
cities – the two typical approaches in urban studies – my approach is to
analyse land and landownership, and explain urban development processes. The two theories that anchor my study are property rights theory and rent theory. Property rights theory assumes a world of atomistic
individuals in an ahistorical market. The main idea of rent theory is to
see rent as a social relation between landlord and tenant. This relation
changes with time. Rent is a payment made to the landlord for the right
to use land. In recent years, property rights theory has become a popular ideology, and even rent theory has been reformulated to suit this
ideology. This chapter focuses on these theories, introduces the main
concepts and discusses the dominance of the economic argument.

## Concepts and Forms of Rent

In colloquial language, the term 'rent' means payment for use of a
house, an apartment, or a piece of land, without distinguishing between
payments for improvements to the land and the underlying land itself.

*Urban Land Rent: Singapore as a Property State*, First Edition. Anne Haila.
© 2016 John Wiley & Sons, Ltd. Published 2016 by John Wiley & Sons, Ltd.

The theoretical meaning of rent is different and has changed over the years. Classical economists Adam Smith and David Ricardo connected rent to land. Modern economic theory defines rent as a payment made for factors of production that are in *imperfectly elastic supply*,[1] with land as the main example (Stonier and Hague 1967: 273). Sometimes the prefix 'land' or 'ground' is used to distinguish land rent. Other concepts of rent have been introduced, such as economic rent (which refers to earnings from any factor of production) and scarcity rent (emphasising the scarcity of land or other resources). The commonest forms of rent are differential rent, absolute rent and monopoly rent.

The source of *differential rent* lies in the difference in quality between land parcels. Differential rent is the difference between what a certain piece of land produces compared to the least productive piece of land barely worth using (called the marginal land). For example, a shop located at a subway station attracts more customers than a peripherally located store, and produces more profit that can be paid as rent. Two forms of differential rent are differential rent I that is produced when the land use is extended (the extensive margin), and differential rent II that is produced when the land use is intensified (the intensive margin) (Figure 3.1). The concept of *absolute rent* was originally introduced as a

**Figure 3.1** Extending and intensifying land use. Photo: Anne Haila.

criticism of or extension to the theory of differential rent. In differential rent theory, the least productive (marginal) parcel of land is used to measure difference in productivity and define the market price. As a pure benchmark it does not produce rent, but private landlords are not going to give up any land for free and will demand some payment. The rental payment for the worst parcel of land was called absolute rent, and can be understood as the minimum amount for which landowners lease their land to tenants. *Monopoly rent* is based on monopoly prices. When demand exceeds supply or when consumers are willing to pay more for special goods (for example, housing in better neighbourhoods), the increase in prices creates an opportunity for monopoly rents. Thus monopoly rent is dependent on market conditions.

In addition to these three commonest forms of rent, several other concepts have been introduced. David Harvey (1974) has used the concept of *class-monopoly rent* to explain differentiated housing prices caused by discrimination in the housing market. *Redistributive rent* is the rent that has been redistributed by the state (Walker 1974). The concept of *potential rent* (Behnke et al. 1976) is the rent that a parcel of land could produce if used in an alternative way, and the concept of *rent gap* (the difference between actual and potential rent) builds on potential rent to explain land-use change and gentrification (Smith 1984, 1987, 1996; Ley 1987; Badcock 1989, 1990; Bourassa 1993; Clark 1987, 1988, 1995; Clark and Gullberg 1991; Hammel 1999). The concepts of *bid rent* and *rent gradient* are used in urban economics to explain the allocation of land. These different concepts make sense when understood in the context of different intellectual traditions. Before exploring these, a brief look at the history of rent, and the close connection between each elaboration of rent theory and social problems, would be useful.

### Rent and Social Problems

The theory of land rent is an old economic theory. Its origins are usually traced to the works of David Ricardo (1815, 1817), although economists before him (e.g. Petty 1662 and Anderson 1777) and other classical economists (Smith 1776 and Malthus 1815) already had their versions of the theory of land rent. Classical economists included a chapter on rent in their treatises, whereas modern textbooks do not. Economists like John Stuart Mill, Stanley Jevons, Alfred Marshall, Joan Robinson, Henry George, Karl Marx, Johann Heinrich von Thünen and William Alonso all developed versions of a theory of land rent.

The history of this theory is not a story of progress towards a better understanding of land rent but rather an adaptation to emerging social problems, like poverty, taxes, speculation, or high land prices. When such social phenomena became an object for political debate, scholars turned to the theory of land rent to explain them and legitimate political programmes.

When Thomas Malthus, Edward West, David Ricardo and Robert Torrens published their pamphlets on rent in 1815, the social problem of the moment was corn duties. Oser (1970) regards the coincidence that these four scholars published their pamphlets at the same time as an example of 'how a pressing contemporary issue can call forth a theory developed independently by different people' (Oser 1970: 88). This pressing contemporary issue was the Corn Laws being debated in the British Parliament. British landowners wanted tariffs on grain imports to protect their production. Industrialists, on the other hand, wanted to remove the tariffs, because their interests lay in importing cheap grain for workers. In order to participate in this public political debate, the four economists introduced their versions of the theory of rent. All argued that tariffs are harmful, and used the theory of rent to justify this claim. In his important conclusion, Ricardo wrote: 'Corn is not high because a rent is paid, but a rent is paid because corn is high' (Ricardo [1817] 1974: 38).

The second time scholars looked for help from land rent theory was in the latter part of the nineteenth century, when urban poverty was recognised as a social problem. In 1848, J.S. Mill published *Principles of Political Economy*. Unlike Smith and Ricardo, Mill did not regard property rights as perpetual or universal like natural laws, but as mutable. American economist Henry George took Mill's idea, developed Ricardo's theory further, and initiated a worldwide land reform movement. At the core of George's social reform was the theory of land rent. He used rent theory to explain why people lived in poverty and to legitimate his reform programme. His simple solution – to tax rent – was presented as a panacea to remove all social problems. It was the only social reform needed, hence the name 'single tax'. Using commonsense arguments, George declared that rent is 'unearned' and therefore it would be legitimate to confiscate it (George 1879).

Marx and Engels disagreed with George, both with his social programme and with his explanation for poverty. For Marx, the solution was not taxing rent but nationalising land and his social reform concerned not only land but more importantly labour. However, Marx paid a great deal of attention to rent. He did not manage to finish his theory of rent, and he changed his ideas on rent and landownership (see Vygodski 1976; Rosdolsky 1968). In the third volume of *Capital*, edited and interpreted by Friedrich Engels, Marx ([1894] 1981) defined rent as the sum of money the user pays the owner of the land. Rent is a social relation between landlord and tenant, and is the form in which property in land is realised economically. Land rent is also a historical, not universal, phenomenon – different in feudal times and the capitalist era.

In the twentieth century, the efficient use of land became a problem in modern cities, and economists developed a new version of rent theory to analyse land use. Starting from the works of Johann Heinrich von Thünen (1826), Lowdon Wingo (1960) developed a model of land market and commuting costs, Richard Muth (1969) a model of housing and residential land and William Alonso (1960 and 1964) a theory of the urban land market. Their work started a new subdiscipline in economics called urban economics.

The next time the theory of land rent was debated was during the 1970s, as Western countries faced rapid increases in land and housing prices. The question at the time was how to explain the housing boom, and the theory of land rent seemed to offer an answer. High land and housing prices were regarded as a social problem, and rent analysis seemed to offer a fruitful method for exploring conflicts and struggles over land use and housing provision (see, for example, Edel 1976; Clarke and Ginsburg 1976; Katz 1986). In *Land Rent, Housing and Urban Planning. A European Perspective*, Michael Ball, Vincenzo Bentivegna, Michael Edwards and Marino Folin (1985) expressed optimism about the power of rent theory. They thought that postwar housing booms, property speculation and office development showed that landed property 'has come into stark contradiction with rest of capitalist society, and land rent seemed to hold the key to understand why' (Ball et al. 1985: 7). In Germany, there was a lively debate concerning rent in the 1970s, continuing earlier German discussions on rent theory.[2] German scholars were particularly interested in rent in the case of housing and the construction industry (Neef 1974; Brede et al. 1975, 1976; Frank and Joeres 1973).

In the 1980s, a new economic boom hit the Western world. This time the issue was speculation and the casino economy. Rent scholars saw real estate as having an important role in this boom, and connected land as a financial asset to fictitious capital (Harvey 1982; Haila 1990). Speculation, boom, globalisation and the increase of foreign real estate investment were issues calling for a new application of land rent theory (Krätke 1992; Luithlen 1994).

Throughout its history, starting from the works of Adam Smith and David Ricardo to those of Jevons, Marshall, William Alonso and David Harvey, rent theory and the concept of rent have changed, and the ensuing controversies split scholars into different schools. Classical economists regarded rent as a separate and important concept, whereas neoclassical economists generalised the concept of rent. Urban economics later modified the concept of rent and connected it to individual utility. To understand the concept of rent within property rights theory, I now turn to examine how the concept of rent was extended and generalised in mainstream economics.

## Extending the Rent Concept

David Ricardo defined rent as 'that portion of the produce of the earth which is paid to the landlord for the use of the original and indestructible powers of the soil' (Ricardo [1817] 1974: 33). This definition comprises three parts: rent is the produce of the earth, is paid for the use of the earth, and is paid to the landlord. Three rent theory traditions can be identified on the basis of these three aspects of rent: mainstream economics focusing on land as a resource, urban economics on land use, and the Marxist tradition of the landlord–tenant relation.

Ricardo's definition that rent is the produce of the earth implies that land is unique, that land has special characteristics. This became a divisive issue among economists. On the one hand, land economists (Richard Ely) and urban economists (Edwin Mills and William Alonso) regarded land as unique and special. Among the special characteristics of land are immobility, fixity in place, possibility for alternative uses, and land as a necessary condition for all activities. On the other hand, there gradually developed the idea that there is nothing special about land. Land is simply one factor of production along with labour and capital. The concept of rent then became extended (to other factors of production) and generalised (capital and labour can also produce rent). Rent became understood simply as surplus produced under certain market conditions. There is nothing unearned or immoral in rent and, most importantly, rent from an alternative use came to be regarded as a cost.

The extended and generalised concept of rent developed gradually. Ricardo's rent theory was further elaborated by J.S. Mill, Stanley Jevons, Alfred Marshall, Joan Robinson and Paul Samuelson. John Stuart Mill ([1848] 1909: Book III, Chapter 6, paragraph 10) took into account the possibility of alternative uses of land and wrote: 'when land capable of yielding rent in agriculture is applied to some other purpose, the rent which it would have yielded is an element in cost of production of the commodity which it is employed to produce'. Stanley Jevons (1871) introduced the marginalist conceptualisation of diminishing returns, and marginalists (Jevons, Menger and Walras) shifted the point of view from supply to demand and the individual. For an individual buying land, the price of land is a cost, no different from other costs. A more radical step was taken when it was proposed to count costs not in terms of money you pay, but in terms of losing something you could have bought. This is the concept of opportunity costs: goods, products or income which could have been obtained if the money or resources had been used to buy or produce other goods. By introducing the concept of opportunity costs, Friedrich von Wieser (1851–1926) made costs calculated into subjective psychological costs based on sacrifice (Oser 1970: 223).

The last nail in the coffin of land rent was hammered in by Joan Robinson. She developed the ideas of Hubert Henderson (1921), who in *Supply and Demand* discussed the variety of purposes for which a piece of land may be used, and introduced the concept of a margin of transference between any two occupations of land. In defining the concept of differential rent, I referred to the concepts of extensive and intensive margin. The third margin concept, a margin of transference, is now applied to situations of changing land use. A site that is on the margin of transference is just worth transforming, for example, from housing to office use. 'The marginal sites for shops are the sites for which it is only just worth while to pay rents sufficient to entice them away from houses' (Henderson [1921] 1947: 96). This idea was further developed by Joan Robinson (1933) in her book *Economics of Imperfect Competition*. Robinson defined rent as a surplus earned by a factor of production over and above the minimum earnings necessary to induce it to do its work (Robinson [1933] 1959: 102). Land can be transferred from one use to another. The price which is necessary to retain a given unit of a factor in a certain industry is called transfer earnings (or transfer price), since reducing payment made for it to below this price would cause it to be transferred elsewhere. Robinson thus defined rent as the difference between the actual earnings of the factor and its transfer earnings (Robinson [1933] 1959: 105). In Robinson's rent theory, earnings from use of land are compared to earnings from alternative uses. Rent is that amount in excess of the earnings from the next most advantageous use of land. Robinson connected rent to the margin of transference and differentiated various points of view. From the point of view of society, land is provided free and the whole rent is a surplus. From the point of view of a particular industry, transfer payments are a part of supply price. From the point of view of an individual competitive producer, the whole rent is a cost of production.

This new conceptualisation of rent was consolidated as a textbook concept by Alfred Marshall and Paul Samuelson. In *Principles of Economics*, Alfred Marshall (1890) connected classical themes of supply and real costs to novel marginalist theories of demand and opportunity costs. With this integration, rent became dependent on supply and demand – the market situation. The same principles of supply and demand affect all factors of production; for example, quasi-rent is a reward produced by factors of production whose supply is fixed in the short term. In his textbook, *Economics* (1970), Paul Samuelson developed the market approach further and connected pure economic rent to the notion of inelastic supply. Thus emerges the peculiarity of land and why it is interesting to economists: its total supply is relatively fixed by nature and cannot be augmented in response to a higher price for it or diminished in response to lower land rentals (Samuelson 1970: 537). Expressed in the language of economics, land's supply curve is vertical and its price is determined from the intersection of supply and demand. Other resources, such as oil and mines (whose supply is inelastic), also produce rent.

The concept of rent was thereby disconnected from land, generalised and extended, and explained as simply one market situation. An example of this type of generalised concept is Baumol and Blinder's (1985: 664) analysis of the salary of Lee Iacocca, former CEO of Chrysler. There is only one Lee Iacocca and therefore he is a scarce commodity whose supply is fixed. Because of this, the price of his services is determined in a similar way to determination of land rent. Iacocca's salary is a reward that exceeds the minimum amount necessary to keep Iacocca in his present employment. Such an extended and generalised concept of rent is applied in property rights theory.

### Property Rights Theory

The University of Chicago has been home to several famous schools of thought, including the disciplines of urban sociology and pragmatic philosophy. Among the most distinguished of the contemporary Chicago schools is the university's economics department. Several well-known and Nobel Prize-winning economists have worked here: Frank Knight, Jacob Viner, Oscar Lange, Friedrich Hayek, Milton Friedman, Georg Stigler, Ronald Coase, Gary Becker and Robert Lucas. Chicago school economists are commonly associated with belief in the *laissez faire* market, the price mechanism, the quantity theory of money, monetary policy, and criticism of government intervention and Keynesian policies.

One subfield of the Chicago school of economics is the property rights school (known also as law and economics). The main ideas constituting property rights theory are that property rights are important (Alchian 1961), have a function in guiding incentives to achieve greater internalization of externalities[3] (Demsetz 1967) and play a role in economic growth (North and Thomas 1973) (see Chapter 2). In addition to property rights, another important concept is transaction costs. These comprise costs of acquiring information, negotiating costs, monitoring costs and enforcing costs. The particular form of property rights arrangements affects transaction costs, which individuals are assumed to seek to minimise (Furuboth and Richter 1991: 11).

The most important figure in the development of property rights theory is Ronald Coase, who received the Nobel Prize for economics in 1991. Coase criticised Pigou's idea that government intervention is needed to restrain externalities, suggesting instead that rights to perform certain actions should be assigned to those able to use resources most productively. Coase transformed the entire nature of the externality problem by arguing for the *reciprocal nature of harm* (Medema 2009: 106). Negative externalities like pollution can be understood in two ways: either harmful to citizens, or (if production is restricted) harmful to industrialists. Coase influenced several economists and, in his Alfred Nobel memorial Prize lecture, said that his approach 'will ultimately transform the structure of microeconomics' (Coase 1991). Steven Medema (2009: 102) credits Coase for changing economic thinking on externalities and government intervention, and Marc Blaug (2001: 156) regarded the Coase theorem as 'the very centrepiece of the modern law and economics movement'.

Formulated in its textbook version, the Coase theorem runs as follows: 'if costless negotiation is possible, rights are well-specified, and redistribution does not affect marginal values, then the allocation of resources will be identical, whatever the allocation of legal rights and the allocation will be efficient, so there is no problem of externality. Furthermore, if a tax is imposed in such a situation, efficiency will be lost' (Layard and Walters 1978: 192). Efficiency is gained if the partners negotiate freely and the initial entitlement of property rights does not matter. However, what the government can do is to assign initial rights to those parties most willing to negotiate.

The Coase theorem has been criticised from various perspectives. Economists have criticised it for its unrealistic assumptions. Steven Medema (2009: 187) called it 'a useful fiction' because no proof of it exists. Cass Sunstein (1997: 1179) argued that it is wrong to assume that the initial entitlement of rights does not matter: people have an aversion to loss, and therefore they are likely to value their initial entitlement more than that of others. Philosophers have criticised the assumption of *the tragedy of the commons* (see Chapter 2), often resorted to by property rights theorists when defending the necessity of secure property rights. Carol Rose (1994: 147) has argued that the commons was not tragic at all: the comedy of the commons is that a resource becomes more valuable the more people use it. Examples Rose mentioned were commerce, education and good manners. A happy outcome of the commons in Europe's medieval village communities was increased interaction, cooperation and sociability.

Chicago economists have expanded the boundaries of economics as a discipline. Public and social policies have been evaluated from an economic point of view, and economic efficiency has become a natural (and the most important) criterion. The word 'economic imperialism' has been used to refer to the extension of economics to topics that go beyond consumer choice, theory of the firm, markets and macroeconomics into new areas like democracy, discrimination, social interaction, religion, law and health (Lazear 2000; Medema 2009: 125). One such extension is public choice analysis. Before Ronald Coase moved to Chicago, he was at the University of Virginia, where his colleagues were James Buchanan (a founder of the public choice school of economics who received the Nobel Prize in 1986) and Gordon Tullock, one of the originators of the theory of rent-seeking (i.e. lobbying the government to change rules to help make businesses more profitable) (see Chapter 6). Public choice analysis questions the Pigouvian and Keynesian ideas of government intervention. Keynes' mistake, argue public choice theorists, was that he did not question the activities of politicians and bureaucrats, and did not see the dangers of totalitarian government. Keynes never asked 'who will guard the guardians' (Buchholz 1989: 258). Such a question is the concern of the public choice analyst. Friedrich Hayek (1945), for example, questioned the ability of planners to know enough to plan: market mechanisms are better than planning, and prices carry necessary information.

The concept of rent used by property rights and public choice theorists is the concept of 'rent-seeking'. The term 'rent-seeking' was invented by Anne Krueger (1974), with early contributors including Jagdish Bhagwati and Gordon Tullock. Rent-seeking is defined as the use of resources to obtain, through the political process, special privileges whereby the injury to others is greater than the gain to those who obtain rents (Tullock 2005: 28). Tullock gave the following example: if a person invests resources in lobbying for legislation prohibiting the import of a newly devised cure for cancer (because he is a manufacturer of an older and less effective medicine), then that person might gain but others would lose. Tullock suggested using the term solely for cases in which whatever is proposed has a negative social impact. Another example Tullock (2005: 104–107) gave was the state examination system in Imperial China. The highest status and greatest wealth in Imperial China were held by senior bureaucrats who had passed a very difficult competitive examination. More people failed than passed and, as a result, immense resources were invested in preparation for examinations, reading poetry and practising calligraphy. For those who passed, the reward was a return on talents and work invested long before. The problem of this recruiting system for those who failed, thinks Tullock, was that they were unable to transfer the resources invested (i.e. learning) to other uses. If the benefit to Chinese society is greater than the cost, then this activity is not rent-seeking, although it would resemble it. If the cost, the waste, is greater than the benefit, then this is rent-seeking.

The theory of rent-seeking has been used to explain the backward nature of Asian economies: Asian entrepreneurs were seen not as proper entrepreneurs but only as adept manipulators of the law or government authority, generating economic rent and obtaining special privileges and monopolies. This rent-seeking explanation (together with Asian entrepreneurs) is discussed in Chapter 6. Because I use the concept of rent connected to land, I suggest using the term manipulated rent when referring to rent received from political rent-seeking.

### Ambiguous Property Rights and the Market for Development Rights

Economic thinking has penetrated other social sciences, and a call for economic efficiency has become the norm in evaluating projects. Ben Fine (2002) described the colonisation of the other social sciences by economics as 'economics imperialism', and Edward Lazear (2000) explained the 'imperialism of economic' by referring to the qualities of economics: it is a genuine science that constructs rational individuals who engage in maximising behaviour, is interested in equilibrium and offers social scientists an opportunity to talk about efficiency.

Economic imperialism of the property rights doctrine has already reached the field of planning and urban research. William Fischel (1987) applied the Coase theorem in dealing with zoning and land-use controversies, attempting to show that 'the initial distribution of entitlements will not alter the final allocation of resources' (Fischel 1987: 82). Following Hayek, some planning theorists have questioned the capability of planners to have enough information to plan, criticising regulatory planning as unfair and having unwanted side effects. They see land-use planning as the ordering of the market (Buitelaar and Needham 2007), affecting property rights of landowners (Krabben 2009). Instead of regulatory planning, they recommend defining and assigning rights over negative external effects and free negotiations for compensation. Krabben (2009: 2872) illustrated the use of the property rights approach in solving land conflicts with a plan to build an airport. He assumed that:

> it may be more efficient to assign property rights to the inconvenience caused by an airport and leave the solution to negotiations

between airport and its neighbours, than to regulate this by some kind of government intervention. In the case of well-assigned property rights to such a nuisance, the airport can negotiate with its neighbours about, for example, the financial compensation and the reduction of nuisance or, in an extreme situation, it can decide to move to another location if the size of the financial compensation would be insurmountable. If the negotiations do not lead to an agreement, the partners involved can go to the court. (Krabben 2009: 2874)

The perception of the individual in these applications of property rights theory is that of someone who can tolerate nuisance if compensated for it.

Property rights theory directs planning and planning research to new domains: seeing town planning as a contractual relationship between government and individuals (Lai 1998), regarding development rights as commodities sold in the market (Renard 2007), favouring club goods (privately produced goods consumed by a group of people, for example services in gated communities) instead of public goods (Webster 2007), and focusing on transactions costs (Hong 1998). Those urban scholars influenced by property rights doctrine recommend abolishing what they call 'ambiguous property rights', seen by them as causing urban problems: 'vaguely defined property rights over urban land will leave valued assets in the public domain for competitive access, and inefficient land development due to externalities will be exacerbated as a result' (Zhu 2002: 43). Relying on recommendations of the World Bank, Douglas North's interpretation of European development (see Chapter 2) and the assumed tragedy of the commons, they advocate expanding market allocation instead of regulatory planning (Kung 2002).

### Rent as a Social Relation

The rise of property rights theory and the generalisation of the rent concept left rent theory in the shadows. One reason why rent theory has been marginalised is that the term rent is applied using different meanings. People talk about different things when they talk about rent, and therefore cannot understand each other. Too often, actual rental payment is confused with rent as a theoretical concept. Further, different rent concepts are embedded in different theoretical approaches, and thus have different meanings depending on the school of thought. A good example is the concept of 'rent-seeking' that is often used as and confused (even by rent scholars) with 'rent-maximizing'. Rent-seeking means manipulation of the law or government in order to obtain profit. The rent concept in this is the extended and generalised concept of rent, economic rent. In order to avoid misunderstandings I propose to call this 'political rent-seeking', and the form of rent it creates 'manipulated rent' created by lobbying, bribery, favourable tax treatments and subsidies. Rent-maximising, on the other hand, describes the behaviour that uses land to produce the highest rent.

The difference between rent theory and property rights theory, however, is not merely nominal, and cannot be solved simply by defining rent concepts. The difference is methodological. Property rights theory is based on methodological individualism, and assumes a world consisting of individuals making contracts in self-regulating markets. There is no community or society with communal rights. What matters, according to property rights economists, are incentives making the owner of property (understood as a thing) use it in the most efficient way. Such reification of the concept of rent into a material thing, rather than seeing it as a social relation, downplays the fact that the institution of property also involves social relations, necessitates acknowledging others, and is backed up by customs and legal sanctions (Hodgson 2001: 250). Possession is not a solitary declaration but demands the consent of others, as Hume, Pufendorf, Rousseau and Kant argued (see Chapter 2).

Generalising and extending the concept of rent to all factors of production, fusing rent and yield of financial instruments (discussed in Chapter 8) and regarding landed property as a thing that owners put to use as they like – all obfuscate landed property relations. By ascertaining the source of rent, who receives it, and why, land rent theory points out that rent as a social relation involves a power relationship and social control. These can be arranged in different ways: land can be private, common, public, collective, state, municipal and shared. Different arrangements have different consequences. Property relations create inequalities and need justification, and differ among different cultures.

The theory of land rent concerns the relationship between owners and users of land. It explains allocation of land and land-use changes, but also concerns incentives and conflicts. Land rent theory gives us concepts to understand and explain urban development processes. It explains the price of land as the claim for future rent, helps us understand the behaviour of landowners and developers, and redefines with theoretical concepts the production of the built environment and the social and power relations within it. It is important to differentiate the levels of abstraction. I differentiate the conditions from the cause of rent. The cause of land rent is landownership, and the conditions are different for different forms of rent. For example, we can explain why housing is more expensive on the seaside by referring to location (differential rent) and excessive demand (monopoly rent) as conditions, and the power of property owners or developers to charge the extra profit as cause. Borrowing the realist vocabulary of Sayer (1992: 104) to illustrate the difference between rent as a theoretical concept and an actual rental payment, we can say that landlords have causal powers to extract rent, but whether a landlord or developer maximises rent depends on their strategies and special conditions. The effects of landlords' causal powers are contingent.

### Urban Land Rent

Land rent theory originally concerned agriculture, and the price and value of a product. Scholars debated the question of whether the theory of land rent as developed for agriculture was applicable to the urban situation (Harvey 1973; Ball 1977, 1985a, 1985b; Lipietz 1985). Matthew Edel (1976: 108) mentioned Friedrich Engels' discussion in *The Housing Question* in 1887 as the first important application of land rent theory in the urban context. Engels argued that if workers own their little houses, the sum saved on rent allows employers to pay lower wages. This is the same argument as that presented by industrialists in the British Parliament during the Corn Laws debate: the cheap price of grain gave capitalists an opportunity to pay lower wages (see p. 49). The same argument has also been used to explain the lower wages that transnational companies locating to Singapore need to pay thanks to state-subsidised public housing (see p. 16 and a more detailed discussion in Chapter 5).

Starting with Thünen and his agricultural rent theory, urban economists have developed the theory of land rent as the theory of urban land market equilibrium, introducing two concepts of rent: the concept of bid rent (based on users' rent-paying ability and utility, and expressing the 'willingness' of firms, households and farmers to pay for land in different locations), and the concept of market rent (that is the highest bid). The market mechanism is assumed to allocate land to different users. One basic assumption of urban economic models has been that the residential rent gradient is negative; that is, rents decrease with distance from the city centre. Several empirical studies have attempted to show a negative rent–distance function. However, empirical research has neither verified nor disproved this. The assumption of a declining rent gradient resists refutation. When empirical research found that rents increase with distance, this was explained by referring to quality of the environment and the neighbourhood (Richardson et al. 1974; Richardson 1977: 239).

Urban scholars have been divided as to the question of land rent.
Mark Gottdiener (1985: 193–194) regarded theories of rent and location as providing 'only limited ways of understanding the articulation of
capital and space', seeing it as 'more fruitful to study the role of the secondary circuit and its array of institutions and individuals involved in the
turnover of real estate for profit than it is to analyse ground rent within
an urban context using nineteenth-century concepts derived from agricultural production'. Bandyopadhyay (1982: 177), on the other hand,
preferred David Harvey over Manuel Castells 'because of his focus on
two basic problems in urban analysis; the necessary unification of spatial
and social relations with land and its material base, and the inescapable
analytic priority of a rational theory of rent and land-values'. David
Harvey is of course the rent theorist par excellence. He has constantly
returned to the rent question. In *Social Justice and the City*, Harvey (1973)
connected rent to three aspects of space (absolute, relative and rela-
tional) and subsequently (Harvey 1974; Harvey and Chatterjee 1974)
used rent theory in empirical analysis of the Baltimore housing market,
paying attention to the role of financial institutions in creating conditions for monopoly rents. In *The Limits to Capital*, Harvey (1982) introduced the ideas of land as a financial asset and fictitious capital (a claim
over future revenue), and in *Spaces of Capital* (2001) he applied the concept of monopoly rent to analyse culture and collective symbolic capital.
In *Rebel Cities*, Harvey (2012: 112) showed the cunning nature of rent:
'By seeking to trade on values of authenticity, locality, history, culture,
collective memories, and tradition they [capitalists] open a space for
political thought and action within which socialist alternatives can be
both devised and pursued.'

To summarise, the concepts of rent I use are as follows. *Land rent* is
a payment to the landowner for the right to use land. The conditions
for *differential rent* are the different qualities of land. The theory of differential rent implies the concepts of extensive (the last unit – piece of
land – taken into use when use is extended) and intensive margin (the
last unit in which new capital is invested when use is intensified). Based
on the theory of differential rent I distinguish two mobilisations of the
land: horizontal (a subdivision and extended use of land) and vertical
(intensified use of land) (see Chapter 1). Following the vocabulary of
Jäger (2003), I call the first *extension rent* and the second *density rent*.
The conditions of *absolute rent* are the barriers landowners make to land
supply. Following Evans (1999) and Jäger (2003), I connect the concept
of absolute rent to speculative land-holding and hoarding. Landowners
can withdraw land from the market in order to get absolute rent. However, the success of this strategy depends on whether others are willing to
pay for it. The conditions of *monopoly rent* are demand exceeding supply,

and monopoly prices. *Fiscal rent* is revenue the state or municipalities receive from their landed property. *Global rent* emerges when global flows raise real estate prices. *Derivative rent* refers to financial speculation and is a yield from land titles that is securitised together with mortgages. The concepts of potential rent and the rent gap refer to alternative uses of land. The concept of rent-seeking used in property rights theory I suggest calling *political rent-seeking*, and the rent that lobbying behaviour creates *manipulated rent*. The point of differentiating these rent concepts is not to suggest calculating the shares of various forms of rent in prices or rental payments, but to pay attention to different conditions of these forms of rent, and hence the different policies seeking to affect them.

The cause of all forms of rent is landownership, the monopoly of landowners. Land tenure relations and conditions for using land and paying rent have changed. Chapter 2 discussed John Locke, who justi-fied ownership by arguing that, in mixing labour with the land, a man created a right to own land. But Locke also thought that men must leave land for others. To use the vocabulary of rent theory, Locke assumed that there was an extensive margin (or frontier) to exploit. What happens when there is no land left for others, when all land is occupied? If Locke's theory concerns initial acquisition, does it also justify ownership when conditions change? Different answers have been given. Modern prag-matists like Daniel Bromley (2006: 190) allude to Immanuel Kant rather than Locke, arguing that when conditions change, land justly acquired may evolve into land unjustly held. Some others think that when use of land ceases, property should revert to the commons. Land reformers like Henry George thought that the long history of private ownership in Western societies makes it too difficult to confiscate land (although it would be just), so it is better only to confiscate rent. These answers lead to the discussions in the next chapter, which analyses practical and polit-ical programmes to change landed property relations. I examine how genetic, consequential and moral arguments have been translated into political programmes, and what kinds of reforms have been suggested to the conditions of vested property rights. This discussion again shows the peculiarity of Singapore, and how the Singaporean government solved the land question in a peaceful way.

## Notes

1   If an increase in price increases supply, the supply is elastic. The total amount of land is fixed and therefore its supply cannot be increased.
2   Oppenheimer 1909; Diehl 1921; Wagner 1926; Wieser 1929; Carell 1948; Müller 1933; Müller 1952; Ischboldin 1957.

3   Externality is the positive (benefit) or negative (cost) effect of an activity
    that is unintended and not paid for in the market; for example, a rise in
    land value because of a beautiful new house on the neighbouring site, or a
    decrease in value because of pollution from a nearby factory. Internalisation
    of externalities means that they are paid for in the market (for example,
    through emissions trading).

# 4

# Land Reforms
## *Practical Solutions and Politics of Land*

*In considering the institutions of property as a question in social philosophy, we must leave out of consideration its actual origin.* (John Stuart Mill 1848: *The Principles of Political Economy*)

John Stuart Mill came to the conclusion that, given the history of centuries of vested property rights, it would be more reasonable to try to redress future injustices rather than engage in dispute as to the origin of property. Mill's solution to the debate about the origin of property (discussed in Chapter 2) was practical. This chapter investigates other practical programmes and how ethical arguments concerning justification and consequential arguments concerning beneficial effects of property have been translated into political programmes. Property rights theorists justify neoliberal proposals and global land-grabs with economic arguments, whereas rent theorists pay attention to social causes and consequences of land reforms.

Land regimes have been changed using different strategia. I divide land reforms into radical, modern and neoliberal types. Henry George is an example of a radical reformist, and Singapore exhibits examples of modern land reform. Singapore's powerful land acquisition laws created conditions for its economic growth and production of public housing. Gradually, the state's land bank was accumulated and the people that were displaced were settled in public housing.

*Urban Land Rent: Singapore as a Property State*, First Edition. Anne Haila.
© 2016 John Wiley & Sons, Ltd. Published 2016 by John Wiley & Sons, Ltd.

## Radicals and Moralists

Many countries have their social reformers believing that land reform is the way to a better society. In the United States it was Henry George; in England Thomas Paine, Thomas Spence, James and John Stuart Mill, and Alfred Russel Wallace; in China Sun Yat-sen; in Russia Leo Tolstoy; and in Finland Arvid Järnefelt. Land reformers have combined moral and economic arguments, and mixed these with theories like the physiocratic ideas of land as the basis for all subsistence. The measures that land reformers have proposed contradict those of mainstream economists, who have tended to regard land reformers as heretics.

In the eighteenth century, Adam Smith famously stated that 'as soon as the land of any country has all become private property, the landlords, like all other men, love to reap where they never sowed' (Smith [1776] 1904: I.6.8). John Stuart Mill in the nineteenth century was not so polite, suggesting that 'landed proprietors are the only class ... who have a claim to a share in the distribution of the produce, through their ownership of something which neither they nor any one else have produced' (Mill [1848] 1909: II.16.1). Unlike Adam Smith and David Ricardo, who regarded economic laws as natural laws, Mill regarded the laws of distribution as manmade and therefore changeable. One of those laws concerned land. 'No man made the land', Mill declared in *Principles of Political Economy* (Mill [1848] 1909: II.2.26), stating: 'It is the original inheritance of the whole species. Its appropriation is wholly a question of general expediency. When private property is not expedient, it is unjust.'[1] Mill, however, did not propose confiscating land but rather taxing the future increase of the value of land and, if landlords were to be dispossessed, he advocated that they should be entitled to full compensation (Martin 1981: 32). Mill's solution was thus a concession to vested injustices and an attempt to correct future injustices. Other land reformers were not so diplomatic.

In *What is Property? Or an Inquiry into the Principle of Right and Government* (1840), Pierre-Joseph Proudhon asked about the nature of property, and came up with the answer that 'property is theft'. His solution was to give land to users. Before Proudhon and J.S. Mill, Thomas Paine (1737–1809) and Thomas Spence (1750–1814) had agitated for land reform. Paine, author of *Common Sense* (1776) and *Rights of Man* (1791), was influenced by Jean-Jaques Rousseau and believed that land is the common property of the human race. In *Agrarian Justice* (1797), Paine wrote: 'There could be no such thing as landed property originally. Man did not make the earth, and, though he had a natural right to occupy it, he had no right to locate as his property in perpetuity any part of it: neither did the Creator of the earth open a land-office, from whence the first title-deeds should issue' (Paine [1797] 2003: 374). Neither Abraham, Isaac, Jacob, nor Job, were owners of land, wrote Paine. Proprietors of cultivated land owed the community ground rent, that they should pay into a fund 'out of which there shall be paid to every person, when arrived at the age of twenty-one years, the sum of Fifteen Pounds sterling, as a compensation in part, for the loss of his or her natural inheritance, by the introduction of the system of landed property' (Paine [1797] 2003: 376). Thomas Spence disagreed with Paine, and wrote *The Rights of Infants; or the Imprescriptable RIGHT of MOTHERS to such a share of the Elements as is Sufficient to enable them to suckle and bring up their Young* (1797) in response to *Agrarian Justice*. Spence did not regard Paine's programme as just or satisfactory, because it only returned part of what was stolen to the victim. Spence thought that the compensation payments Paine suggested were 'poor, beggarly stipends, so contemptible and insulting' (Spence 1797: 46; cited in Marangos 2008: 319). Spence believed that landed interest was incompatible with happiness and independence. Like other radicals, he distrusted remote government and therefore did not propose the nationalisation of land; his solution was the parish system of property (Marangos 2008: 320). Parishes would own the land, make it available for use, lease it and collect the rent (Marangos 2008: 323).

Karl Marx was the most radical of land reformers and, together with Friedrich Engels in *The Communist Manifesto* (1848), suggested abolishing what they called bourgeois property. Marx analysed the land question from the point of view of production and concluded that landowners do not have a role in capitalism, yet there is a risk in the demolition of private ownership because private landownership has an ideological and legitimising function. In *Theories of Surplus Value*, he wrote:

The landowner, on the other hand, is quite superfluous in this mode of production [capitalism]. Its only requirement is that land should not be common property, that it should confront the working class as a condition of production, not belonging to it, and the purpose is completely fulfilled if it becomes state-property, i.e. if the state draws the rent. The landowner, such an important functionary in production in the ancient world and in the Middle Ages, is a useless superfetation in the industrial world. The radical bourgeoisie (with an eye moreover to the suppression of all other taxes) therefore goes forward theoretically to a refutation of the private ownership of the land, which in the form of state property, he would like turn into the common property of the bourgeois class, of capital. But in practice he lacks the courage, since an attack on one form of property – a form of private ownership of a condition of labour – might cast considerable doubts on the other form. Besides, the bourgeois has himself become an owner of land. (Marx [1863] 1968: 208)

From the point of view of capitalist production, argued Marx, the landowner has no function and therefore the capitalist class (commodity-producing industrialists) would be better off without land-lords and their claims for land rent. However, Marx continued, abolishing private landed property would be risky because it would question ownership in general. Therefore, a good compromise would be land becoming state property. More than the question of land, Marx was concerned with the question of labour, the disconnection of people from land and primitive accumulation that created conditions for capitalism.

The most famous of all land reformers is the American Henry George (1839–1897), who regarded land reform as the social reform capable of demolishing all the evils of societies, and managed to inspire a land reform movement still very much alive today. He did not propose the confiscation of land, but the taxing of land rent. George ([1879] 1920: VIII.II.12) wrote:

> I do not propose either to purchase or confiscate private property in land. The first would be unjust; the second needless. Let the individuals who now hold it still retain, if they want to, possession of what they are pleased to call their land. Let them continue to call it their land. Let them buy and sell, and bequeath and devise it. We may safely leave them the shell, if we take the kernel. It is not necessary to confiscate land; - only necessary to confiscate rent.

The tax on land rent was the only tax that was needed to cover public expenses, hence its name: single tax.

George drew his ideas from physiocrats, Smith, Ricardo and Mill, creating a populist synthesis. He used metaphors and appealed to common sense. To convince the reader of the injustice of private property in land, he wrote. (George [1879] 1920: VII.I.29):

> Has the first comer at a banquet the right to turn back all the chairs and claim that none of the other guests shall partake of the food provided, except as they make terms with him? Does the first man who presents a ticket at the door of a theatre, and passes in, acquire by his priority the right to shut the doors and have the performance go on for him alone?

Unlike Mill's platonic style, which did not stir the sensation Mill expected (Martin 1981: 33–34), George with his polemic style and simple political programme managed to create a controversy. A fierce single-tax debate followed after George published his doctrine and divided economists into two opposing camps. This division lasted for years, and blocked any reasonable discussion about land taxes. On the one side, there were those who were inspired by George's ideas. They founded schools, associations, journals and political parties, many of which still exist today, like the International Union for Land-Value Taxation and Free Trade, the Georgist school in New York and the *American Journal of Economics and Sociology*. On the other side were those who opposed the single tax or (if they regarded the tax on land values as a good idea) criticised the exaggerated political claims of the single taxers (Seligman 1915). Prejudice against George and Georgists still prevents reasonable discussion of the land value tax (LVT). The irony, as Mark Blaug (2000) noted, is that prominent economists like Paul Samuelson, Milton Friedman, James Tobin and Robert Solow regard a land tax as useful, or at least the 'least bad' tax. To emphasise his point, Blaug cites Arthur Schopenhauer, who said that an 'original idea is first ridiculed, then attacked and finally is simply taken for granted', concluding that 'the idea of LTV is not yet quite taken for granted – but it almost is' (Blaug 2000: 284).[2]

Henry George's book *Progress and Poverty* (1879) was a bestseller and, with its colourful language and rhetorical eloquence, a good read. George believed that the reason for all social problems is private landownership. Like Proudhon, George regarded private landownership as theft but, unlike Marx, he did not advocate the nationalisation of land. Nationalisation, claimed George, would arouse too much opposition. In order to avoid unnecessary political quarrels, George proposed a simple practical solution – taxing land, that is, confiscating the land rent. The effect would be the same as nationalising land. The dispute between Marx and George (Marx advocating the nationalisation of land and George taxing land rent) is one between an ideology and a practical programme. George recommended a practical solution: to tax rent and ignore the ideological battles over ownership; Marx, though, insisted on the nationalisation of land. In a letter written in 1881 (20 June) to Friedrich Adolph Sorge, Marx called George 'utterly backward' (Marx and Engels 1975: 322). The popularity of George made Engels, however, hesitate. In 1886 Henry George scored a big success in the New York municipal elections. In a letter to Sorge that year (29 November) Engels referred to this as 'the Henry George boom' (Marx and Engels 1975: 373) and in another letter to Florence Kelley-Wischnewetsky (December 28, 1886) wrote: 'It is far more important that the movement should spread, proceed harmoniously, take a root and embrace as much as possible the whole American proletariat than it should start and proceed, from the beginning, on theoretically perfectly correct lines' (Marx and Engels 1975).

George was an influential writer. Michael Silagi (1989) claims that he was a catalyst for British social reform. Thomas Paine, James and John Stuart Mill and several others had propagated land reform before George, but the sudden rise of the land reform movement from 1880 was due solely to George. Anthony Taylor (2004) suggested that Georgism was appealing and popular among British radicals at the end of the nineteenth century because it connected the American democratic ideal, admiration for American liberties, Jeffersonian ideas of small proprietors, lack of aristocracy, liberty rooted in John Locke, memories of 1688 (The Glorious Revolution) and the American Revolution, and political republicanism. When Henry George visited Britain in 1884 he was portrayed in newspapers as a David Crockett figure hardened in the wilderness and as a fighter against the slavery that the aristocratic government of Britain had supported in the US South (Taylor 2004: 53–55).

In Russia the great novelist Leo Tolstoy was a land reformer too, and was also influenced by George. Tolstoy was a landlord; he had inherited Yasnaya Polyana estate, including its serfs. The property and control over peasants' lives made Tolstoy remorseful, as he confessed in his novels and pamphlets. In *Resurrection* (1899), Prince Nekhlyodov teaches the doctrines of Henry George to his peasants and desires to relinquish his property. In an unfinished play, *The Light That Shines Through the Darkness*, Tolstoy depicts himself as Saryntson, a landowner feeling guilty about his property and the suffering it brings his peasants. Saryntson argues with his wife, who claims that the property is needed for the welfare of the family. As a compromise, Saryntson gives the property to his wife, yet remains tormented by the decision (Wenzer 1997). Following Henry George, Tolstoy came to believe that private ownership of land is unjust. The disconnection of people from land was the source of evil, and salvation is to be found in returning land to people, thought Tolstoy. Tolstoy also lived out his conviction, dressing like a peasant and promulgating a simple life made possible by the common use of land.

In China, the key land reformer was Sun Yat-Sen (1866–1928), a revolutionary who fought against the Qing Dynasty. He was the founder of the Republican Kuomintang (National People's Party) and president of the Republic of China. Influenced by the ideas of John Stuart Mill and Henry George, Sun Yat-sen had also observed land reforms implemented in a German colony in Kiaochow, China (where in 1898 Germany had leased land from China for 99 years). Here the Germans applied the doctrines demanded by the land rent movement of Adolf Damaschke and the German Land Reform League. A Memorandum Concerning Land and Tax Matters, published in 1898, became the basis for the Kiaochow Land and Tax Statue. This stipulated a land tax (6 per cent per annum of the land value) and an incremental tax to be levied in the event of any transfer of property (see Silagi 1984; Chen Cheng 1961; Woodruff 1980; Schiffrin 1956/57).

In 1912, after the establishment of the Republic of China and abolition of the last Dynasty, Sun Yat-sen set out his ideas for creating a good society. Land reform played an important role. The three principles for making a good society were those of Nationalism, Democracy and People's Livelihood. The first two principles (the national and political revolutions) were achieved with the establishment of the Republic of China; now in the new republic the time had come for the social revolution that was the third principle (Wei et al. 1994). At the core of the People's Livelihood principle was the equalisation of land rights; for Sun, this did not mean the nationalisation of land (mainly because the government did not have enough money to buy it all) but taxing the land according to land values. Sun proposed an interesting method to assess the value of land, namely allowing landowners to evaluate the tax (Sun 1924). If they valued their land too high they would pay excessive taxes, if too low they faced the risk that the government would buy the land at the value they assessed.

In the West, land reformers were left at the margins: Tolstoy continued to proclaim the panacea of Georgist ideas in his books, Finnish novelist Arvid Järnefelt preached on the moral duty of landowners and George, classified as an 'underworld economist' (Heilbroner 1992: 171), ridiculed academic economists. Despite George's common sense and appealing writings, the Georgist movement (that today more resembles a sect) has not succeeded in convincing the public and decision-makers as to the superiority of the land value tax. Warren Samuels (2003) suggests that this is because the idea of taxing land conflicts with 'the dominant ideology of property', that is the Lockean idea of property (see Chapter 2): people tend to regard the income that they derive from land as earned, thereby disregarding the social basis of land values and rent. Three methods have been used to overcome the obstacle of dominant ideology and implement land reform: revolution (nationalising land), modern land reform (gradual accumulation of a land bank) and neoliberal land reform (privatising land).

## Two Chinese Models of Land Reform

In China, land reforms adopted two different models. The People's Republic of China followed Marx and nationalised land. Tsiang Kai-sek took Sun's heritage with him to Taiwan and followed the practical path of Henry George. In fact, land tenure reform, writes Li Ling Hin (1999), has always played a vital part in Chinese politics:

> The Kuomingtang government lost the civil war in 1949 because they were seen as having a corrupt relationship with the big land-lords and causing a large number of landless farmers to suffer. They eventually took steps to alleviate the suffering, but it was too late. However, this experience did help them to set up a proper land reform system in Taiwan. The Communist Party won the civil war because of its promise to equalize property rights (Li 1999: 172–173).

In 1949, the Chinese Communist Party came to power and land reform was among its first actions. The People's Republic of China Land Reform Law was adopted in 1950 and applied to rural areas. The surplus land of rich farmers was confiscated and redistributed to poor farmers. Rural land was then collectivised and mutual aid teams, cooperatives, collectives and communes were established. The Urban and Urban Fringe Land Reform Law stipulated that urban land was to become state land and be managed by city governments. Li Ling Hin (1999: 14–16) identified three features of the nationalised urban land system that were valid until the mid 1980s. First, land was administratively allocated for different purposes, not by a market mechanism. Second, land was allocated to state authorities, armed forces, schools and state enterprises free of charge and free of rent and land-use fees. Third, land users were limited in their ability to sell, lease, mortgage, donate, exchange or perform any other act of land transfer. If users no longer needed land, it had to be returned to the relevant state department.

Taiwan, the Republic of China, followed a different path. After the KTM took power, land reform based on Sun Yat-sen's doctrine of equalisation of land rights was implemented in Taiwan (La Grange, Chang and Yip 2006: 58). In 1951 the Rent Reduction Act was passed, offering tenants the possibility of purchasing land, and in 1953 the Land-to-the-Tiller Act was adopted (Hsiung 1992). The government purchased the land of 106,000 landlords, and allowed 220,000 families to acquire their own land through the implementation of the 'sale of public lands' and the 'land to the tiller' programme (Chu 1996: 211). This land reform created what has become Taiwan's most characteristic economic feature – an economy dominated by small family-owned businesses. As Dobbs-Higginson (1993: 154) wrote: 'the dispossessed landlord no longer had an interest in local politicking; instead, they had incentives to enter business. Former landlords became small businessmen.'

Since the 1980s, the People's Republic of China has implemented another type of land reform, phased in gradually by the passing of a series of laws. In 1979, the Law of Sino-Foreign Joint Venture was enacted, stipulating that a land-use fee should be charged for joint ventures. In 1986, the State Land Administration was established, and a year later compensatory grants and a transfer system of land-use rights were implemented in Shenzhen. In 1988, the Constitution was amended to allow the transfer of land-use rights, and the state Council announced the Regulation on Land Use Tax Collection. In 1990 'The Provisional Regulation on the Granting and Transferring of the Land Use Rights over the State-Owned Land in Cities and Towns' and 'The Provisional Measures for the Administration of Foreign Investors to Develop and Operate Plots of Land' were enacted. Four years later, the 'Urban Real Estate Administration Law and Regulations' on urban real estate practices were passed. (See, for example, Qing 1995; Yeh and Wu 1996; Guo 2003; Haila 2007.)

The result of these laws is a new land-use regime, the main principles of which are enshrined in The Land Administrative Law of the People's Republic of China (adopted in 1986, amended in 1988 and revised in 1998). Land is still in socialist public ownership, meaning ownership by the people and collective ownership by the working people. There are two types of ownership: land in cities belongs to the state, while rural land is owned by collectives. What is notable in this modern Chinese land reform is the idea of separating ownership and use rights. Land is still owned by the state or collectively by villagers, but land-use rights (LURs) can be sold. State-owned land and land owned by rural collectives may be distributed to individuals for use. The facility to sell use rights opened the door for a feverish construction boom in Chinese cities during the 1990s.

These Chinese land reforms have led to suggestions that Marx's idea of primitive accumulation needs revision. Both in the Republic of China and the People's Republic of China the power of landowner class was broken but what make these land reforms unusual, argued Gillian Hart (2002: 201), is that they did not dispossess the peasant-workers from the land. Also, in post-Mao China, argued Giovanni Arrighi (2007: 361), collectively owned township and village enterprises absorbed rural surplus labour, making it possible for peasants to leave the land without leaving the village. These Chinese experiences, conclude Hart and Arrighi, call for a revision of the assumption of primitive accumulation as a concomitant of capitalist development. The Chinese reforms accumulated capital and reduced reproduction costs of labour, as housing was provided in the villages that remained viable. Singapore's land reform resembles this model. It reduced reproduction costs of labour and resettled people in public housing.

## Modern Land Reform

In Singapore, there was no need to stir up a revolution in order to reform tenure relations. The original inhabitants, the Orang Laut (see p. 26), had been dispersed and made no ownership claims. The colonial administration left behind a substantial land bank, and the powerful Land Acquisition Act enabled the government to gradually build on this to accumulate its huge land bank. Although the British colonial administration divided the area between ethnic groups (the 1822 Raffles town plan discussed in the next chapter), it did not create a racially discriminatory land tenure system but rather a single system for the city-state. This is different to what happened in some other colonies.

In Indonesia, Western colonialists created a dual system of land rights, which differentiated between Western individual property in the city and native land in the rural areas. In The Dutch East Indies, urban centres were governed by Dutch law, while areas inhabited by local people were governed by customary land rights (*adat*): non-natives were not allowed to own customary land (SarDesai 1994: 83; Evers and Korff 2000: 183; Wertheim 1958: 56). In Hong Kong, the British colonial government introduced a dual system. On Hong Kong Island the government became the owner of the land, as in Singapore, but the New Territories were treated differently. In 1898, the British leased the New Territories from China for 99 years and respected Chinese customary rights there. The land registration of 1904–1905 gave full ownership rights to sitting tenants (Watson 2011a), and British colonial officials 'granted special privileges to the descendants of original settlers encountered during the occupation of the New Territories, setting there *bendiren* (native peoples) apart from the *wailairen* (outcomers) who arrived in later decades. This dichotomy is still a hot button issue in Hong Kong politics' (Watson and Watson 2011b: 11). This legacy still has an influence: a New Territories villager who is the descendant of villagers living there before 1898 has a right to land, and the small house policy grants male indigenous villagers the right to build houses on village land. Through their influential committee, the Heung Ye Kuk, villagers have protested against government redevelopment plans.

In Singapore, the government became a significant landowner thanks to efficient land acquisition powers and the property bequeathed to it by the colonial administration. In 1956 the Land Titles Ordinance (the Torrens system)[3] brought into being a state-kept land register (which

**Table 4.1** Publicly owned (Crown or state) land in Singapore.

| Year | Per cent of publicly owned land |
| --- | --- |
| 1949 | 31.0 |
| 1960 | 44.0 |
| 1965 | 49.2 |
| 1975 | 66.0 |
| 1985 | 76.2 |
| 2002 | 90.0 |

Sources: Motha and Yuen 1999; SLA home page retrieved 2002.

substituted any necessity for deeds proving ownership), facilitating dealings in land, securing absolute certainty of title, and rendering those estates and interests registered completely indefeasible (Motha and Yuen 1999: 87). The Land Acquisition Act was passed in 1966. This made possible the compulsory acquisition of land 'needed for any public purpose, by any person, corporation or statutory board' and 'for any residential, commercial or industrial purposes'. What is unique in this land acquisition law is that expropriation is permitted for urban development, redevelopment projects and the building of new towns. Usually, expropriation powers are weaker, only allowing land acquisitions for purposes like the construction of railways, highways and military facilities. During the period from 1965 to 1988, over 1200 sites were expropriated and nearly 270,000 families were displaced (de Koninck 1992). Table 4.1 shows the gradual growth of publicly owned land.

Table 4.1 shows that when Singapore became independent in 1965, the government owned less than half of the land area. The government could have sold land to private owners, but instead decided to increase its land assets. This decision was to prove far-reaching. The deliberate nature of this policy is evident when compared to the situation in Malaysia (which had previously formed the Straits Settlement together with Singapore). In 1982, ownership of land in Malaysian towns was split as follows: individuals owned 55 per cent, companies 14 per cent, religious and other institutions 9 per cent and the government 22 per cent (Evers and Korff 2000: 179). Thus the large amount of government land in Singapore is not just a manifestation of its British colonial heritage, but the result of a proactive government policy.

One difficult question concerning land acquisition is that of compensation. John Stuart Mill (1848) believed that landowners had a right to compensation. George (1879) criticised Mill, and was adamant that to

**Figure 4.1**   Kampong housing, Buang Kok. Photo: Anne Haila.

give landowners compensation based on the market value of land would grant them a speculative gain, because the present market value contains the expectations of future value increases.

Singapore used two types of compensation: resettlement and monetary compensation (the old kampong housing still existed in 2014, see Figure 4.1 ). A central component of slum clearance programmes was the provision of alternative accommodation for displaced families (Ho 1993: 370). Minister for Law, Mr. E.W. Barker announced in the Legislative Assembly: 'Additional provision would be made in the Land Acquisition (Amendment No. 2) Bill to enable the Government to acquire land under private developers for rehousing of squatters who are Singapore citizens' (A land law ... 1965). Resettled households were offered affordable subsidised-rental flats on public housing estates. People were usually satisfied with their better quality new high-rise housing estate flats (Yeh 1995; Ho 1993). Some returned to their old neighbourhoods; this was explained by suggesting that they found it difficult to budget their expenses and wanted to save on food costs by rearing a few chickens in their old kampongs (Latif 2009: 79).

The new land acquisition law was controversial (S'pore Land Bill ... 1966) and especially the compensations were debated in the Parliament.

In the Legislative Assembly in 1964 Prime Minister Lee Kuan Yew enunciated two principles, 'namely, (i) no private land-owner should benefit from development at public expense and (ii) that the price paid on acquisition for public purposes should not be higher than what the land would have been worth had the Government not contemplated development generally in the area' (Singapore Government Press Statement 1964). In 1966 Minister for Law, Mr Barker, restated the general principles: the principle underlying the compensation provision 'is that no landowner should benefit at the public's expense, from any windfall gains resulting from enhancement of land values either through Acts of God or because of public expenditure in the neighbourhood' (Singapore Parliament Report 1966).

Monetary compensation was based on market value (Land Acquisition Act 1966). The Collector of Land Revenue evaluated the amount of compensation, and the Appeals Board resolves disputes between landowners and the Collector. The market value that was used in compulsory acquisitions was pegged to price levels set at specific dates in the years of 1986, 1992 and 1995 depending on the date of land acquired (Land Acquisition Act, revision 1995). This freezing of the price level used in compensation had the purpose and effect of preventing speculation, and gave the government control over any increase in land values. In 2007, the Land Acquisition Act was amended, and the use of a statutory date in determining compensation was abolished. While developers welcomed this (Channel News Asia, 13 February 2007), the amendment did not completely give way to market forces: the amended law orders that 'the market value of the acquired land shall be deemed not to exceed the price which a bona fide purchaser might reasonably be willing to pay', and that 'no account shall be taken of any potential value of the land for any other use more intensive than that permitted by or under the Planning Act as at the date of its acquisition'. During the more predictable and stable times prior to the Asian crisis in 1997 and global financial crisis in 2008, pegging compensation to a set price level had been possible; these reservations to the amended law continued to block land speculation, prevent absolute rent and keep any value increase through development under government control.

Amount of compensation based on market value is dependent upon property cycles. Singapore was in a fortunate position with regard to the reclamation[4] of new land. Lee Kuan Yew expressed this point well (cited in Latif 2009: 94–95):

Land reclamation started with the East Coast ... At that time, property prices were right down because people had no confidence in the future of Singapore. External investors had no confidence, and even our domestic investors were not certain of the future. So I could pass a law allowing all sea foreshores to be reclaimed without compensation. Otherwise, they would have demanded compensation for loss of seafront, and that would have been costly. At one stroke, we were able to reclaim the seafront. Later reclamation was extended to the West Coast also without any compensation for lost seafront. That enabled us to develop the whole coastline. If we tried to do it today we would have big problems. Private owners would get together and put up tremendous resistance.

In Singapore, land is simply either freehold or it is state land leased to users. Adverse possession (possession after continuous occupation) has been revoked in Singapore. There are no complicated and privileged categories of land tenure, as in feudal Europe with Crown, Church, manor and peasant lands all with different duties and privileges, or like in some Asian countries to this day: community land in Indonesia, indigenous lands in the New Territories in Hong Kong or privileged religious land in Thailand. In Singapore, even religious groups – regardless of whether they feel divine guidance with respect to a particular sacred place (Kong 2000) – have to play the market game and bid for land like all other land users. Cemeteries (Figure 4.2) can be redeveloped and the dead displaced, as depicted in the documentary film *Moving House* (2001) by Tan Pin Pin. The film tells the story of the Chew family, one of 55,000 Singapore families forced to relocate relatives' remains to a columbarium when their ancestors' graveyard was selected for urban development. In the film, the Chew family take a picnic to an ancestral grave and dig up the bones. The story is based on Tan's own family's experience: his family had to exhume his great-grandfather's grave in 1995.

Without radical Marxist or pragmatist Georgist land reforms, Singapore was endowed with conditions suitable for capitalist economic development: the government's land bank gradually accumulated, ownership was separated from use, and land became state property that was leased to users. Land became a factor of production, a driver for economic growth unhindered by social and political disputes over ownership. There was no rural landowners' class to hold back economic development. Government land serves the whole economy as well as public finance, creating the ideal conditions for public housing.

What is the origin of Singapore's far-sighted land acquisition policy? Henry George is not an authority referred to by Singapore's founding fathers and policymakers, although there are some similarities between Henry George's utopia and Singapore's land-use regime. Phang Sock-Yong (1995) remarked that 'the basic ideas of Henry George

**Figure 4.2** Old graveyard. Photo: Anne Haila.

have been implemented, in effect, in independent Singapore' and 'interestingly constitute the core of economic and social policy for Singapore'.

The ideas of Henry George might have influenced the founding fathers of Singapore through the ideas of the Fabians, who advocated land reform in the United Kingdom. In his memoirs *The Singapore Story*, Lee Kuan Yew tells of his studies in England during the 1940s when he heard one Fabian socialist speak.

> One person who made an impact on me in my first term at the LSE [the London School of Economics] was Harold Laski, a professor of political science, and a magnetic speaker. His Marxist socialist theories had a profound influence on many colonial students ... The two or three of Laski's lectures that I attended were my first introduction to the general theory of socialism, and I was immediately attracted to it. It struck me as manifestly fair that everybody in this world should be given an equal chance in life, that in a just and well-ordered society they should not be a great disparity of wealth between [a] person because of their position or status, or that of their parents. (Lee 2000: 49.)

Another old-guard leader who studied at the LSE and attended Laski's lectures was Goh Keng Swee, Singapore's first finance minister and the first defence minister, whom Lam and Tan (1999: 24) describe as 'the economic architect of Singapore'.

Fabian socialists were influenced by Henry George. Members of the Fabian Society like Edward R. Pease, Sidney Webb, H.G. Wells and George Bernard Shaw praised George's *Progress and Poverty* (Silagi 1989: 118–119), and George's influence is manifest in their programme: local authorities were to acquire land by using compulsory measures and taxing land values (separately from buildings) and then lease land as small-holdings and allotments (McBriar 1966).

Through the Fabians, Henry George may have influenced the thinking of the founding fathers of Singapore. There are, however, significant differences between George's ideas and Singapore's land regime. George opposed the idea of nationalisation of land, but in Singapore land is mainly state property, and became so without ideological battles or political movements. This made 'efficient use' of land possible. Pragmatic policy superseded ideological and political conflicts, and separating ownership and use allowed land to be used for economic growth and the welfare of citizens. This also affected conflicts concerning redevelopment. Instead of greedy landowners and land speculators (as in the West), in Singapore it is developers who lobby the government (discussed in Chapter 6).

## Land Value Tax

Henry George's ideas are kept alive by many Georgist schools, organisations, journals and activists. Among the Georgist organisations in the United States are the Fairhope Single Tax Corporation in Alabama, the Henry George Schools of Northern California, the Georgia League for LVT in Georgia, the Center for Economic Justice in Massachusetts, the Henry George Institute, the Henry George School of Social Science and Schalkenbach Foundation in New York, the Center for the Study of Economics and Incentive Tax League in Pennsylvania and Center for Public Dialogue in Washington. There are also Georgist organisations in Canada, the Dominican Republic, Great Britain, the Netherlands, Spain, South Africa, Korea and Australia. Georgist journals like *Land and Liberty* (published in London) and *The American Journal of Economics and Sociology*, founded in 1941, discuss issues addressed by George.

In their pamphlets, newsletters and leaflets, Georgists offer a synopsis of philosophers and economists, tracing a progression down the centuries.[5] They start with Moses (1400 BC), who said: 'the land shall not be sold forever; for land is mine'. Of the seventeenth-century philosophers, they mention Baruch Spinoza, who regarded the whole soil as public property, and John Locke who started from the premise that God gave land to the world in common for all mankind. From the eighteenth century, they draw upon the work of William Blackstone, who regarded the earth as the immediate gift of the Creator and therefore general property. Adam Smith is credited for his analysis of ground rent as revenue that the owner in many cases receives without effort, making it suitable for a specific form of tax. Tom Paine's belief that men did not make the earth is noted. Thomas Jefferson is credited for his belief that the earth is given as a common stock, upon which men can labour and live. J.S. Mill is honoured for the statement that 'landlords grow richer in their sleep without working, risking, economizing', and the declaration that any increase in the value of land should belong to the community. Abraham Lincoln appears for his ideas that God gave land to man for his home, sustenance and support, and it should never be in the possession of any man, corporation, society or unfriendly government. Herbert Spencer is included, as he believed that the world is God's bequest to mankind and that all men are heirs to it. From the contemporaries and supporters of George, Leo Tolstoy and Sun Yat-Sen receive a mention. Leo Tolstoy is esteemed because of his morality, declaring that solving the land question means the resolution of all social problems, and for comparing possession of land with possession of slaves (both are wrong).

Today, Georgists do not propagate the single tax, but advocate instead for a land value tax (LVT) or site value tax: a tax assessed on land values separately from the value of buildings and improvements. Georgists believe that taxing land value encourages the further improvement of property, leads to rehabilitation of slums and makes housing affordable. Several economists agree that the LVT has some merits; however, modern-day Georgists cannot ditch the idea that the LVT is a panacea, enabling an ecological and efficient use of land, discouraging speculation, increasing public funds, removing hunger, giving land to the landless, furthering liberty, democracy and equal opportunity, weakening the appeal of statist and communist solutions to social problems, and providing the means to achieve individual human rights and the pursuit of happiness.[6] In their newsletters, Georgists record their 'victories',[7] for example in Washington, Pennsylvania, which in 1985 became the state's sixth city to adopt a two-rate tax (taxing land at 6.05 per cent and buildings at 1.68 per cent).[8]

Academic Georgists have been less excitable, debating with economists about the neutrality and incidence of land tax – that is, whether land tax affects resource allocation and who bears the burden of the tax. Holland (1970) and Netzer (1966) believed that site value tax is 'neutral with regard to land owners' decisions since no possible response to the tax can improve the situation' (Netzer 1966: 205), whereas Skouras (1978) pointed out that the situation changes should the owner change the use of land in the future. In this case, land taxation is non-neutral, and therefore finding the optimal time for change of land use becomes an important question. As to the question of the incidence of land tax, Henry Gunnison Brown (1924: 375) summarised: 'it is held by most competent economists that, in general, a tax on land values cannot be shifted'. The disagreement concerns the question as to whether a tax on property can be divided into taxes upon site and upon improvements. Edgeworth (1925) denied the validity of this division and concluded that the tax would be borne entirely by the occupier, while Seligman (1910) distinguished a tax upon selling value from a tax upon house rent (Simon 1943: 398–399). Further, Martin Feldstein (1977) claimed that tax on pure land rents is at least partly shifted, and that the price of land may be increased by the imposition of a tax.

While academic Georgists retreated to mathematical language and argued for assumptions, devout Georgists keep on declaring the moral, social and political message of Henry George. John Kelly (1981) warned that the failure to act upon the land question is at the root of the threat of a new barbarism: the rioting in the slums, the looting and other crime across cities and rural areas, and rising levels of fear, paranoia and greed. Rev. Preston Bradley (1980), founder of the non-denominational People's Church, based his reading of George on biblical morality, believing in the application of ethics to economic life. Unlike these religious and moral Georgists, neoliberal land reformers base their arguments solely on economic efficiency.

### Neoliberal Land Reforms

In the 1990s, a new model for land reform emerged: privatise and commodify land, and let the market allocate land to users. The World Bank, a powerful institution advocating the new policy, saw government land reform as slow, bureaucratic and controversial. Mexico's land reform, for example, was contested for more than 50 years. The new solution, the World Bank suggested, was market-assisted land reform. 'Market-assisted land reform aims to facilitate the process of willing buyers striking deals with willing sellers, thus eliminating the usual delays and conferring immediate benefits on small holders' (Aiyar et al. 1995b: 2). What government can do is increase demand by giving grants to the poor, increase supply by selling its own holdings, and give subsidies to banks and pension schemes to convert potential sellers into actual sellers (Aiyar et al. 1995a: 3, 1995b: 3).

In *World Development Report, From Plan to Market* (1996), the World Bank recommended defining property rights and increasing private ownership. In *World Development Report, Reshaping Economic Geography* (2009: 203), the World Bank reiterated these ideas and stated: 'Indeed, formal titles are necessary for functioning land and property markets'. As evidence and good examples, the World Bank noted the enclosure movement in England in the sixteenth century, the transformation of communal land into private holdings in Denmark in the eighteenth century, and the United States Homestead Act of 1862, which gave individuals the right to 160 acres of unoccupied public land. 'Contemporary research confirms,' stated the World Bank (2009: 204), 'the role of well-enforced individual property rights.' As a bad example, the World Bank pointed to China, 'where land is collectively owned in rural areas and farmers do not enjoy clearly defined or fully protected land property rights. There, the conversion of land to industrial use generates social conflict' (2009: 204). Singapore and Hong Kong are mentioned as good examples, with property rights settled and no need to define property rights: Singapore has developed from a slum to a world city and Hong Kong, with its flexible planning and participation of the private sector, is a city where market forces lead the way and government follows.

In addition to citing Douglas North and the property rights theorists (see Chapters 2 and 3), titling, privatisation and commodification programmes are justified by referring to Hernando de Soto and his *The Mystery of Capital* (2000), a book praised by Margaret Thatcher, Ronald Coase and Milton Friedman. De Soto argued that the major stumbling block that keeps poor countries underdeveloped is their inability to produce capital. He thinks that the poor already possess the assets they need. The resources they have are their houses and land. Unfortunately, these resources come in defective forms, they are dead capital. The poor have land and houses, but not title to them. Their houses are built on land whose ownership rights are not adequately recorded. 'Because the rights to these possessions are not adequately documented, these assets cannot readily be turned into capital, cannot be traded outside of narrow local circles where people know and trust each other, cannot be used as collateral for a loan, and cannot be used as a share against an investment' (de Soto 2000: 6). Transforming dead capital into a live asset requires formal legal title and property registration, de Soto proclaims.

De Soto's suggestions are supported by some powerful political and funding institutions. The World Bank, The United Nations, The International Monetary Fund and think tanks such as the Institute for

Liberty and Democracy and the Cato Institute share an assumption that enclosing common property, defining property rights, privatising, titling property and allowing market mechanisms to allocate land must lead to economic growth. Experiments have been undertaken in Mexico, where *ejido* lands[9] have been enclosed, and in Peru, Egypt, Paraguay, Thailand and Vietnam. Furthermore, some academics have adopted the vocabulary and recommendations of the World Bank and de Soto. They see ambiguous property rights as problematic, especially in post-socialist cities, and suggest defining property rights and creating a market for land. In the case of China, the socialist administrative allocation of land is criticised for causing waste and inefficiency, public squatting (Tang 1989), work units taking more land than they need (because it is free) and problematic assessed value, which makes life difficult for partners in joint ventures (who use land as their share of the capital) and for Chinese companies (wanting to list on stock exchanges) (Li 1999: 22–23).

Critics of neoliberal land reforms – and de Soto's idea that property titling turns property into collateral, collateral into credit, and credit into economic growth – base their criticism on failed experiments of implemented titling programmes and argue that de Soto's neoliberal proposals have no proof. Timothy Mitchell (2007) claimed that titling renders land unaffordable, does not turn dead capital into live capital, fails to increase credit (because there is no housing credit market in less developed countries), leads to the concentration of property, makes it easier for large-scale owners and speculators to gain, and causes foreclosures and evictions. Mitchell and several others have shown that beyond the market there is not lawlessness but successful informal economies (Elyachar 2005), and beneficial moral and social obligations (Chatterjee 2004). It is also unclear whose rights should be formalised, because in several cases there exist multiple or overlapping rights to the same parcel of land. Daniel Bromley (2008) asked this question, and observed that banks have no interest in becoming owners of housing in slum neighbourhoods. Bromley also pointed out that formalising property rights erodes social relations.

## From Revolutions to Pragmatism

Land reformers have used religious, moral, economic, social and utilitarian arguments in defence of their programmes to challenge land tenure institutions; that is those legal, contractual and customary arrangements that give people access to land and regulate its use, defining various rights, obligations and duties. Neoliberal land reformers believe that secure private property rights lead to economic growth, whereas critics of neoliberal reform highlight the social consequences of land reform.

Although property rights theorists have managed to convince many as to the superiority of the economic efficiency argument, land reforms are not just economic reforms – they are also social reforms with social consequences requiring moral justification and political legitimation. Georgists are right in emphasising the moral aspect of land tenure relations, and neoliberal land reformers are wrong in ignoring peoples' discontent. Land reform sets social classes and their interests against each other, affecting different groups in different ways, mobilising people and inciting resistance. At the time of enclosure in England the land was fought over by the aristocracy and manors on the one hand, and peasants, the church and the Crown on the other. In the French Revolution of 1789, the bourgeoisie, peasants and workers challenged the privileges and landed properties of the Church and aristocracy. In the Mexican Revolution of 1910, the conflict was between the Church, landowners and foreign companies on the one side, and Indians and peasants on the other. The Mexican Constitution of 1917 promised to return *ejido* communal land to Indians and restricted foreigners' rights to own land. In South Korea, distribution of agricultural land formerly in Japanese hands to Korean tenants in 1948 was, Clyde Mitchell (1949: 144) argued, 'responsible for the repudiation of communism'. In the People's Republic of China, rural land was collectivised for the use of communes. In Taiwan, land reform gave land to tillers. In Egypt, the land reform and revolution of 1952 protected the rights of small-scale owners and tenants. Zimbabwe's fast-track land reform during the 2000s took land from wealthy colonial-descended white farmers and returned it to blacks (Matondi 2012). Today, land grabs by international corporations alienate land from indigenous users.

Compared to countries where politically contested land reform tore classes apart and left scars on society, in Singapore the government appropriated land gradually. Singapore was an immigrant city where no indigenous group claimed land rights. The Orang Laut of the Singapore River were dispersed and absorbed into the mainstream Malay population. Introducing land reform was easier than in places where past legacies hindered development: in Indonesia, the *adat* law affects grassroots organizations' romantic notions of community (White 2005; Irwan 2005), and in the New Territories in Hong Kong, villagers argue with the government and developers over urban development. In Singapore, there was no rural landowner class ('useless' in capitalism, as Marx said) whose power needed to be crushed. These conditions made implementation of land reform in Singapore easier than elsewhere.

Singapore followed the pragmatist model of Henry George in disregarding ideological battles of just ownership, but differed from the Georgist model in that the land became the property of the state, more following Marx's idea of making land state property. But such state land, although beneficial for urban development, caused a problem for Singapore's free market economy. How would the state create sufficient confidence among foreign companies and investors to reassure them that Singapore is a free market economy? The problem was solved by the Minister of National Development, who in 1970 stated that the government would not nationalise any commercial properties developed by corporate capital (Chua B H 1997: 133).

This solution, finding a balance between state landownership and the free market economy, is a uniquely Singaporean pragmatist solution (999-year leases still existed in 2015, Figure 4.3). It bypasses ideological debates about just property and focuses on consequences: economic growth, legitimacy of the government and (the greatest benefit for the people of Singapore) public housing. Also in the domain of land, pragmatism – regarded as Singapore's main policy and ideology (Chua 1995) – is the solution. In a 1995 interview with the international Chinese news weekly *Yazhou Zhoukan*, Senior Minister Lee Kuan Yew

**Figure 4.3**  Oceanfront Suite, 999-year lease. Photo: Anne Haila.

expressed this clearly. He said that Singapore succeeded not through following the textbook theories of Western liberals, but by being pragmatic
and learning through trial and error (Singapore's success ... 1996).
Pragmatism in Singapore recalls the classical Chinese idea of harmony –
balancing between scarce natural resources and fast economic growth.
Justification of property institutions applies a consequentialist argument
(good consequences being economic growth, public housing and stable
government); this is the only option in a small city-state without a hinterland. The next chapter analyses Singapore's pragmatic land development policies in practice, the role of the state and land institutions,
and shows how land reforms applied in agriculture and rural land are
remodelled in the urban context. Land reform implemented just once
in a rural setting is enough to give land to the tiller, whereas in a growing
city with scarce land resources there is a need to redevelop, and thus for
repeated land acquisitions.

## Notes

1 The two last sentences in the third edition of 1852 were: 'Public reasons exist
  for its being appropriated. But if those reasons lost their force, the thing
  would be unjust.'
2 Even the International Monetary Fund has warmed up to the land tax.
  When visiting Finland in June 2012, IMF's Lorenzo Figliuoli recommended
  Finland to increase its real estate tax.
3 The Torrens system (named after Sir Robert Torrens) was introduced in Australia in 1858.
4 The Foreshore Act passed in 1872 and revised in 1985 enables reclamations.
5 The following summary is from a leaflet (no date or author given) that I
  received at the 16th Conference of the International Union for Land Value
  Taxation and Free Trade, 4–11 August 1984, Cambridge, UK.
6 See, e.g., the pamphlet An Introduction to the Georgist Philosophy and
  Movement, by the Council of Georgist Organizations, New York 1984.
7 'Two New Real-World Victories!', headlined *Equal Rights* newsletter in Spring
  1986 referring to Scranton and Duquesne. January 1988 newsletter *Common
  Ground* headlined 'Three New Victories' referring to Harrisburg, Washington and Duquesne.
8 *Equal Rights* newsletter Fall 1984 and *Incentive Taxation* newsletter October
  1984.
9 *Ejido* lands are communally owned village lands in Mexico.

# 5

# Land Institutions and Housing

*The HDB was nothing if it was not political. (Asad-ul Iqbal Latif,* Lim Kin San. A Builder of Singapore)

Singapore's most remarkable story is the resolution of the housing question. The government authority responsible for providing public housing, the Housing Development Board (HDB), has succeeded in providing public housing for the majority of Singaporeans. In 2013, 81.6 per cent of the population lived in public housing. Also remarkable is the fact that residents in public housing are not tenants but own their flats, thus contradicting common understandings of owner occupancy. In 2013, the homeownership rate in Singapore was 90.1 per cent. This chapter explains how such a housing miracle was achieved. The key to the success of Singapore's housing policy is that it is not a stand-alone policy, but is linked to land, economic and social policies. This chapter, therefore (in contrast to most housing studies) analyses not only housing policies and housing institutions but also other state institutions and policies. I call these *land institutions*, and ask what kind of conditions state land ownership sets for housing policy.

The policies of Singapore's developmental state have been categorised as functionalist, in reference to Singapore's vulnerable geopolitical and economic position and to the PAP government's need for legitimacy. Instead of applying such functionalist arguments, or seeing the state either as liberal and fragmented or as a control apparatus, I analyse the state of Singapore as a web of institutions, balancing power among

*Urban Land Rent: Singapore as a Property State*, First Edition. Anne Haila.
© 2016 John Wiley & Sons, Ltd. Published 2016 by John Wiley & Sons, Ltd.

themselves and seeking to control scarce resources in the most efficient way. I do this by introducing a series of state land institutions which, once established, have formed a network of institutions regulating all aspects of development. Some have very similar responsibilities, but having such parallel institutions provides a system of checks and balances, avoiding too much power being concentrated in any one institution.

Singapore's land institutions aim at efficient use of scarce land resources; however, the 'efficiency' is understood differently than in the theories advanced by North and Thomas (discussed in Chapter 2): in Singapore the state is an important actor and the scarce land resource is used also for the public good. Neil Brenner (2004: 78) coined the term 'state space' (the space where state institutions regulate social relations and influence locational geographies at different scales), and differentiated between *state projects* (that change the state institutions themselves) and *state strategies* (that mobilise state institutions to undertake particular interventions). In the case of Singapore, the Singapore Land Authority (SLA) governs spatial relations, the Housing Development Board (HDB) regulates social relations, while the Economic Development Board (EDB) and the Jurong Town Corporation (JTC) have been responsible for making Singapore a favoured location among international companies. The land institutions in Singapore gradually developed from single-task offices into a web of institutions, almost as if a rational planner had been at the helm. These institutions generate unintended consequences, and the projects delivered change the state institutions themselves. The story of the development of Singapore's state institutions, strategies and projects is like a detective story, in which new institutions are introduced to solve emerging social problems.

Telling this story of evolving institutions in Singapore raises three important questions for urban studies. First, what is the difference and relationship between state and municipality? Second, how should state and local governments balance the use of their land for the public good on the one hand, and as a source of public revenue (fiscal rent) on the other? The third question relates to an urgent social issue of our neoliberal era: what is the value of public land? Singapore as a city-state, where state and municipal functions are interwoven, and government institutions, state projects and state strategies regulate at various scales (local, regional and international), offers a unique template.

### Land Institutions and the Second Round of Land Acquisitions

The land institutions responsible for development in Singapore are statutory boards, government-linked companies and government investment corporations. This chapter discusses statutory boards, whereas government-linked companies are discussed in Chapter 6 and government investment corporations in Chapter 7. Statutory boards are wholly owned public enterprises created to undertake specific functions. There are several statutory boards, ranging from the Board of Architects and Land Transportation Authority to the Health Promotion Board and the Casino Regulatory Authority. Here I discuss only those that are involved in urban development. They are the Economic Development Board, the Urban Redevelopment Board, the Singapore Land Authority and the Housing Development Board. In this chapter the focus is on housing; the public producer of industrial space, the Jurong Town Corporation, is analysed in Chapter 6.

Established in 1961, the Economic Development Board (EDB) provides business services for transnational companies locating in Singapore, and has played a key role in Singapore's economic development. It is praised by foreign companies for creating a good business climate. Using the vocabulary of North and Thomas ([1973] 1999: 97) discussed earlier (see Chapter 2), EDB reduces the transaction costs of searching, negotiating and enforcement. It helps companies to search for partners and advises in legal matters. Foreign companies locating in Singapore do not need to spend time and money negotiating with bureaucracies or the 'mafia' for protection. A World Bank study ('Doing Business') ranked Singapore the second-best place to do business, just below New Zealand and above the United States. In Singapore, it takes an entrepreneur just six working days to get a business going and the start-up costs are low (Teo 2005).

Another important statutory board is the Housing Development Board (HDB), Singapore's public housing authority, which is responsible for providing public housing (Figure 5.1). HDB is to thank for the fact that, unlike most global cities where soaring prices make housing too expensive for ordinary wage earners, in Singapore housing remains affordable. This has been beneficial for foreign companies locating in Singapore. They obtain access to a cheap labour force and can pay lower wages, because affordable housing makes reproduction costs of labour lower, just as Friedrich Engels anticipated (see p. 59). Jurong Town Corporation (JTC) is the public authority responsible for producing 'public' industrial space. Infrastructure provision, which is usually regarded a duty of the state, is in Singapore broadly interpreted so as to also include industrial estates. Thanks to JTC, foreign companies locating in Singapore can obtain suitable space without paying monopoly prices to speculative real estate developers. The third important statutory board responsible for the production of Singapore's landscape is the Urban Redevelopment Authority (URA), which takes care of town

**Figure 5.1** Early public housing, developed by SIT, Tiong Bahru. Photo: Anne Haila.

planning and conservation. The Public Works Department (PWD) was, until its corporatisation in 1999, responsible for infrastructure and the road network. Its duties were taken over by the Building and Construction Authority (BCA), responsible for building permits and the review of regulation (the Roads and Transportation Division of PWD was merged with the Land Transport Authority (LTA) in 1995), and CPG Corporation, an internationally active full-service professional development firm involved in everything from planning to design and management. The Singapore Tourism Board (STB) also participates in planning and urban development; it has, for example, drawn up plans to revitalise China-town and to develop islands lying off Sentosa (following the model of Italy's isle of Capri and Dubai's Palm Island). The National Heritage Board (NHB) was formed in 1993 after the merger of the National Archives, National Museum and Oral History department. It champions Singapore's heritage and promotes public awareness of it.

The statutory boards of HDB, URA and JTC are key actors in urban development. What is unique in this case is the fact that land-use planning, public housing, infrastructure and public works are coordinated by the Ministry of National Development. The physical development of

Singapore is its responsibility. On coming to office, the PAP government absorbed the City Council into central government (Lee S.A. 1976). Local and central authorities were merged, and city council functions were transferred to ministry level (Dale 1999: 77–97). The Town Council Act (1988) returned some power to the local level, and empowered local elected representatives and residents to manage and maintain common property (void decks,[1] corridors, open spaces, lifts, water tanks and public lighting). These tasks were previously carried out by the HDB. Town Councils are led by elected Members of Parliament, and they collect service and conservancy charges from the residents and commercial tenants in their jurisdiction.

The Housing Development Board was established in 1960. It replaced the Singapore Improvement Trust (SIT) that was founded in 1927 to provide public housing. In 1966, a section of the Building Department of the HDB was renamed the Urban Renewal Department (URD), and in 1974 the URD became the statutory board now known as the Urban Redevelopment Authority (URA) (Dale 1999: 80). The URA is Singapore's national planning authority. It deals with land sales[2] for residential, industrial and commercial development. Sites are usually offered on 99-year leases for commercial, hotel and private residential development, and 60-year leases for industrial sites. The usual sale method is through public tender or public auction.[3] Public ownership of land, and the practice of leasing it out, makes the implementation of plans in Singapore easier than in cities where land is privately owned.

Land is a scarce resource in this small city-state, and therefore an important policy aim in Singapore is to promote its best and most efficient use. The Singapore Land Authority (SLA) was founded in 2001, bringing together the Land Office, Land Registry, Survey Department and Systems Support Unit. Its task is to optimise the use of Singapore's land resources to 'ensure the best use of state lands and buildings'. It acts as an agent of the government, and is responsible for managing state land and buildings, land acquisitions, leases and sales. In 2011 SLA unveiled a new vision, *Limited Land. Unlimited Space,* embodying 'the notion that the scarcity of land in Singapore should not be a constraint. Rather it is an opportunity for greater innovation and creativity in land use' (SLA Annual Report 2010/2011). SLA sells land to statutory boards (HDB and JTC) and is responsible for ensuring that land sales by URA, HDB and JTC are conducted in an open and transparent manner through competitive public tender or auctions. The price of land sold by SLA is determined by the Chief Valuer. The government home page (retrieved 8 September 2002) lists the principles of using and pricing land: 'To ensure that the full cost of land resource is included in the provision of public service and not hidden in any government subsidy.

This will also motivate the public agencies to strive for more efficient use of land.' Land is leased to developers using the method of land auctions. A lease gives a right to use the land for a limited time period and under specified conditions. Auctions enable public and private developers to assemble land, make developers compete, affect the value of land and keep control of it in public hands.

Land leasing has a long history. Sir Thomas Stamford Raffles agreed a treaty with the local chieftain (discussed in Chapter 2); subsequent treaties ceded the land to the British, who began leasing it. After 1819, land was given (with verbal licenses) to settlers. In 1826, 999-year leases were issued, and then 99-year leases were introduced in 1838 (Motha and Yuen 1999: 17–18). The URA arranged the first sale of sites in 1967, offering 13 sites to private developers.

When land is leased out by the URA, it is subject to a set of conditions tailored to achieve the government's planning objectives. The URA applies the following terms and conditions: the development must be completed within a stipulated period; a new company must be formed to undertake the development; the new company must not be involved in any other business activity; sub-sale of the whole project to a single purchaser before completion is prohibited (URA 1995: 7). Such conditions are specifically designed to prevent speculation.

The early leases were free of rent, but after 1867 leases were subject to a rent charge known as quit rent (Motha and Yuen 1999: 18). Until the Second World War, a premium was charged, and in 1946 it was decided to stop the system of paying a premium and to charge 4.08 per cent of the full freehold value. The 4.08 per cent represented the sum necessary to generate the full freehold value over a period of 99 years at an interest rate of 4 per cent (Motha and Yuen 1999: 20). After 1948 lessees paid a premium (based on leasehold value) and rent.

At the end of the lease 'based on the common law principle both land and buildings would revert to the landlord' (SLA Press release 2008a), and 'in general, the Government's policy is to allow leases to expire without extension' (SLA Press release 2008a). The Ministry of Law's justification for this is that 'in land scarce Singapore, we need to recover land upon lease expiry to re-allocate it meet fast changing socio-economic needs' (SLA Press release 2008a). In the event of a new lease being granted, the lessee is required to pay a premium. Until 2008, the lessee paid both a land premium and a building premium, but in that year the building premium was waived 'so as to remove the disincentive for lessees to upkeep or upgrade their building' (SLA Press release 2008b). For short-term industrial and institutional leases the building premium had already been waived in 1997. 'The change was made on the recommendation of the Committee on Singapore's Competitiveness' (SLA

Press Release 2008a), and the aim of it was to 'encourage lessees to continue to invest on the upkeep and improvement of property' (SLA Press release 2008b). This is the Georgian two-rate tax, separating land and buildings in order to encourage improvement of land.

When a piece of land is allocated to the lessee, the lease document defines the conditions under which the government alienates the land, and how the land user can use the land. These conditions specify obligations the lessee must fulfil (for example, to develop it within a given period of time). In this sense, the leasehold system (that is also used in Hong Kong) is a civil contract between the government and an individual, as Lawrence Lai (1998) has emphasised. Such a contractual land development regime differs from private (land as a thing) and customary regimes, and recalls the early European concept of property as a right and relationship (the feudal land regime), reminding us that rent is a social relation. Lease contracts can also include social conditions, as in Hong Kong, where a clause in land leases requires operators of sport facilities, recreational spaces and private clubs to allow outside groups to use their amenities for recreational activities for a certain number of hours a week (Ng 2011).

Town planning as a regulatory regime complicates such a contractual method of urban development. Town planners determine the plot ratio, and this raises the questions of who owns development rights and how development rights are compensated. In some countries (like Finland), development rights belong to municipalities, while in some other countries, development rights belong to the land owner. In Singapore, development charge and differential premium allow the government to capture value increments resulting from increased development rights.

The development charge (DC) was introduced in 1965 and became an important levy in 1980 (Lim 1987). The Minister for National Development, Lim Kim San, defended it thus:

> With a view to securing to the state the increase in value of land brought about by community development and not through efforts of the landowner, the government has considered various measures including the acquisition of development rights in land, the acquisition of the freehold in land, and the freezing of land prices, but after very careful consideration, the government has decided that, as a practical and immediate measure, a development charge should be made on all written permissions for the development of land beyond the existing permitted use. The broad principle is that any written permission granted which allows development over what is normally permitted in the present Master Plan will attract a development charge. (Cited in Leung 1987: 136.)

The development charge is a tax on enhancement in land value resulting from approval of a higher-value development proposal (URA web page 3 July 2012). It is a Georgian land rent tax, aimed at capturing unearned increment. The justification given for the DC is that 'where a part of the enhancement in land value is taxed, [it] allows the State to have a share of the gains from the value enhancement arising from its grant of planning approval' (Ministry of National Development Press Release 18 July 2007). The development charge can also be used as a flexible policy instrument adapted to real estate cycles. In 1985, the recession year, the development charge was lowered from 70 per cent (of the appreciation in land value) to 50 per cent. In 2007, with a buoyant property market, the Development Charge returned to 70 per cent.

In 2000, the Differential Premium (DP) was introduced. State lands are leased at a price based on the use and intensity at the time of sale. If the subsequent use and intensity exceeds the use and intensity at the time of sale, payment of differential premium becomes applicable (SLA homepage 2 July 2012). Lessees of state leases may pay DP and be exempted from paying DC, or continue to pay DC (URA and SLA Circular 1 September 2011).

The Land Acquisition Act (1966) increased the government's land bank, making it the owner of 90 per cent of Singapore's land by 2002 (discussed in Chapter 4). Lease periods running for 99, 60 and 30 years restrict the government's ability to use land efficiently before the expiry of leases. In land-scarce and ever-growing Singapore, however, intensification and reuse of the land is a necessity. This has led to a second round of land acquisitions, this time not involving the resettlement of squatters but the resettlement of residents to higher-rise buildings. The case of the island state of Singapore (where population growth acts as a constant pressure to densify) demonstrates that one-off land reform is not enough in the context of cities – there is a need for repeated land acquisitions. Another round of land acquisitions began in Singapore in the 1990s. Land has been expropriated for extending subway lines, and high-rise buildings have been demolished to build even higher buildings. New legislation to facilitate intensification of land use has been introduced.

The Selective En Bloc Redevelopment Scheme (SERS) was introduced in 1995 to redevelop older HDB estates. Residents receive market-value compensation, are paid their relocating costs, and get a new replacement flat with a 99-year lease at a subsidised price. In 1999, the Land Titles (Strata) Act of 1967 (a stratum is defined as any part of land consisting of a space below, on or above the surface of the land and allowing several to own the property) was amended to permit collective sale of property should the majority of owners be in agreement (90 per cent if a development is less than 10 years old and 80 per cent if older). Prior to the amendment, all owners had to agree. Land can thus be sold to a developer to redevelop before the end of a lease. En bloc, or collective sales, legislation incites homeowners to sell a jointly owned building to a developer who wants to build a taller building on the site. One example is a 30-year old condominium in Mountbatten offered for collective sale in 2012. The previous condo had 118 units, while the marketing agent estimated that 392 units could be built (Tan Amanda 2012). Sim, Lum and Malone-Lee (2002) argued that en bloc sales avoid a tragedy of the anticommons (Heller 1998) (minority owners can prevent the efficient use of the property). The Strata Title Board hears applications relating to orders for collective sales and mediate in the event of disputes.

## National and Urban Development

Singapore is a young nation. Unlike many nation states that forged their national identities around memories of war, language and cultural symbols, Singapore built its national identity on programmes and campaigns. Between 1958 and 1984 there were 78 national campaigns, ranging from campaigns against long hair and condemning spitting in public, to encouraging courteous behaviour and the promotion of the Mandarin language (Quah 1987).

When Raffles landed in Singapore, the place was a tiny fishing village of sea gypsies, a wandering Malay tribe who preferred boats to houses and made their living as pearlers and pirates (Collis 2000: 134). Raffles drafted the first town plan and began a tradition of imagining Singapore's future, which remains important in urban strategies today. Raffles envisioned making this tiny village an entrepot between Canton and Calcutta, and he is remembered as the founding father of the city. Lee Kuan Yew (2011: 50) wrote: 'If Raffles had not come here in 1819 to establish a trading port, my grandfather would not have migrated to Singapore from Dapu county in Guangdong Province, Southeast China.' Lee (2011: 689) thanks Raffles for taking an island of 120 fishermen and turning 'it into an emporium on the sea route from India to China'.

The colonialists (the Portuguese with Goa and Macao, the Spanish with the Philippines, the British with Singapore and Hong Kong, the French with Indo China and the Dutch with their East Indies) brought with them a new urban order. European colonialists were obsessed with order and cleanliness. They classified and named everything they could in order to ease the anxiety of living in faraway lands (Low 1993). In the urban landscape, order was introduced through segregation and discriminatory zoning laws. Town planning in Singapore began with the

Jackson Plan (in 1822), which was based on Raffles' instructions and segregated the city into separate quarters for different racial and occupational groups. Europeans and Asians got their own neighbourhoods, traders from Amoy (Hokkiens) lived next to the European Town, and the Arab *kampong* was next to the Sultan's Palace (Yeoh 1996: 71). The new Town Plan also introduced a hierarchy of occupational zones: in allocating lands, first preference was given to merchants, second to artisans and third to farmers (Wong and Ooi 1989: 791; Eng 1994: 170). The legacy of colonial segregation remains evident today – tourists can visit Chinatown and Little India, hear stories of the Malay population formerly concentrated in Geylang and find expatriates doing their shopping in Holland Village.

The colonialists introduced segregation in Hong Kong too. Discriminatory zoning ordinances (the European District Reservation Ordinance 1888, the Hill District Reservation Ordinance 1904 and the Peak District Ordinance 1918) prohibited the building of Chinese tenements and any Chinese residents (except servants) on the Peak, the better neighbourhood reserved for Europeans (Lai 2001). Discriminatory ordinances were effectively implemented, and the result was segregation by race. 'The uppermost grounds, the Peak, were for affluent Europeans. The second level, the Mid-levels of Hong Kong Island, was occupied by Chinese and European residents who lived in luxury and ease. At the lowest level were the ordinary Chinese people, who lived in the rest of Hong Kong Island, the Kowloon peninsula, and the New Territories' (Lai 2001: 303). Today the housing price map of Hong Kong follows these colonial plans: houses on the Peak are still the most expensive.

In the beginning, town planners in Singapore had limited legal control over development. Slowly their power was increased. In 1887, the Municipality was empowered to prohibit building, and in 1927 the Singapore Improvement Trust (SIT) was established to implement urban renewal, the rehabilitation of buildings, land acquisitions for housing, public housing and development control (Dale 1999: 72). In 1958, the Master Plan to regulate land use and control urban development was introduced. In 1966, the Land Acquisition Act increased the implementation powers of the Master Plan by making possible acquisition of land for urban development and pegging compensation for acquired land, thus preventing speculation (see p. 75).

Singapore's planning authorities continued the colonialist tradition of bringing order, even to those chaotic elements of Asian cities that are romanticised and seen so archetypal: the labyrinthine back alleys and the hawkers. Shop houses (combining work and home) were typical in Singapore, built in rows and back to back. 'Back alleys' between shop houses were created only after urban renewal initiatives were introduced

**Figure 5.2**   Hawker food. Photo: Anne Haila.

in the early twentieth century (Ho and Lim 1992). 'Planned back alleys' (almost an oxymoron) were meant as public spaces, ensuring proper sanitation to remove waste and increasing light and ventilation, but were appropriated by the residents who stored their belongings there as visual markers of occupancy (Ho and Lim 1992).

The authorities also wanted to regulate hawkers, those mobile chefs typical of Southeast Asia who cook customers' meals on the street (Figure 5.2). In 1983, street hawkers and vendors in Chinatown were relocated into the Kreta Ayer Complex. According to members of the Singapore Heritage Society, this 'dislocated a lifestyle and ultimately drained the area of life and energy' (Kwok et al. 2000: 71). Hawkers are now concentrated in hawker centres and food courts located in shopping centres and HDB estates. The ordering of hawkers was not only spatial, but proprietary as well. In 1994 the government introduced the stall ownership scheme, enabling hawkers who had rented their stalls to buy them. The intention was to make hawkers entrepreneurs and asset owners, in common with 'the growing ranks of Singaporeans who own assets like HDB flats, HDB shops and Telecom shares', said Environment and Communication Minister Mah Bow Tan (Nathan 1994). Stall prices were determined by the Chief Valuer based on market prices, but the stallholders got their stalls at a discount. One case was chicken rice seller Foo Jung Cheng who took over his stall from his father (over 80 years old and too old to work). Mr Foo said, 'Owning our own stall will give us long-term security' (Nathan 1994). Another hawker, wanton noodle seller Madam Loke Yee Yaw, bought the stall she had been renting for more than a decade, only to sell it on. She had already found a buyer, and the resale would net her S$100,000 profit (Nathan 1994). The old Singapore with outdoors hawkers began to disappear.

In the 1960s, United Nations planning experts (E.E. Lorange, Otto Koeningsberger, Charles Abrams and Susume Kobe) were invited to Singapore to study its urban problems. Following the recommendations of these international advisors, Singapore initiated centralised planning, integrated development, public housing, urban renewal and industrial development (Dale 1999: 80). The government expropriated land for urban renewal, buying sites and amalgamating them. The government's extensive land acquisition powers made possible the thorough modernisation and comprehensive renewal of the built environment; public housing estates, industrial estates, skyscrapers and shopping malls replaced Chinese shop houses. New towns were developed to relocate populations from the city centre.

The basic principles of planning in Singapore manifested themselves in new towns and housing estates. New towns were planned to be self-sufficient in respect of basic services, and housing estates to have food courts. As the public housing authority, HDB has provided not only public housing but also shops. It allocates shops to tenants through competitive bidding, deciding the mix of business types to provide reasonably priced goods and services near to people's homes (Yeung and Yeh 1971: 74). The Home-Based Small Scale Business Scheme allows flat owners to conduct small-scale business from their homes. In 1992, HDB started to sell shops to sitting tenants at discounted rates.

Town planning in Singapore involves not only physical planning and provision of public housing, but the regulation of social relations. Singapore is known for regulations and rules. Even Singaporeans themselves joke about their society as being a 'fine' society. One can buy a T-shirt emblazoned with rules like no smoking, no littering and no durians. One strange rule introduced when I was living in Singapore was a fine for being naked in your own home. Unlike some rules in other Asian countries – for example Ne Win's currency reform in Burma that replaced 10-, 50- and 100-kyat notes with notes divisible by nine (Thant 2007: 316–317) – there is usually a valid reason for Singaporean rules. Paul Theroux, who taught at the University of Singapore in the 1970s, made fun of the fines for breeding mosquitoes in his *The Great Railway Bazaar* (1975). I too received a conditional imposition of a fine for breeding mosquitoes, but it seemed fair and rational (I was obliged to cut the grass in front of my house in order to prevent the spread of malaria and dengue fever).

Singapore's comprehensive regulatory regime showed its usefulness after the 2003 severe acute respiratory syndrome (SARS) outbreak. Singapore announced the drastic measure of closing all its public schools for nearly two weeks (Leung and Ooi 2003: 21). Singapore 'also invoked the Infectious Disease Act, under which all the people who have come into contact with infected victims have to be quarantined' (Leung and Ooi 2003). In Hong Kong too, the government used drastic measures, quarantining a whole residential block in the Amoy Gardens. Changi airport in Singapore (in common with Hong Kong airport) began checking the temperature of arrivals.

In Singapore new rules are adopted as new social problems are identified. One example is the social problem known as 'killer litter', which became a punishable offence. 'Killer litter' is a peculiarly Singaporean term for heavy objects thrown from high-rise buildings which can injure or kill a passer-by at ground level. *The Straits Times* (Leong 2000) reported that 'most people know about the family that got thrown out of their Housing Board flat in Dover Road in 1991, after one member was convicted twice of throwing killer litter'. Another case was 'a 43-year man who threw four motorcycle helmets, an oven toaster, a table fan, a wooden statue and a lamp from his sixth-floor flat' (Leong 2000). In 1986, an amendment in the Housing and Development Bill gave the Housing Board the power to repossess a flat should the owner, any member of his family or any authorised occupier above the age of 14 be convicted of a killer litter offence (Lim L 2000).

### Housing the Nation

The provision of public housing has been an important part of Singapore's nation-building story. When Singapore became independent, its slums and a severe housing shortage were among the most serious problems (Quah 1987: 78). The government initiated a public housing policy that has been a real success story. Upon opening the P.S.A. Blair Plain Housing Estate in 1968, Prime Minister Lee Kuan Yew said: 'Early in 1963, I thought the best way to give everyone, including our harbor workers, a stake was to give them a good home' (Prime Minister's Speeches ...). Singapore's public housing policy, moreover, is not just about providing housing, but entails much more: it is a social and economic strategy (Hill and Lian 1995: 113), a family policy encouraging the family as the basic unit of society (as Singapore's

**Table 5.1** Percentage of population in public housing in Singapore.

| Year | Percentage |
|------|-----------|
| 1960 | 9 |
| 1965 | 23 |
| 1970 | 35 |
| 1975 | 47 |
| 1980 | 67 |
| 1985 | 81 |
| 1990 | 87 |
| 1995 | 86 |
| 2000 | 86 |
| 2005 | 83 |
| 2009 | 82 |

Source: HDB Annual report 2008/2009.

'shared values' state) (Kong and Chan 2000) and the foundation of legitimacy and longevity underpinning the PAP's grip on the reins of power and governance (Chua 1995).

The provision of public housing in Singapore was a different choice from that made by Western countries, which after the Second World War selected another strategy: subsidising homeownership. In Singapore, the number of people living in public housing has increased gradually: in 1960, only 9 per cent of the population lived in public housing; by 1989, the figure was 87 per cent. Table 5.1 shows the gradual increase of population living in public housing until the year 1990, after which the proportion began declining. Providing public housing for over 80 per cent of the population means housing not only marginal groups or the working classes, but the middle classes as well.

The goals of Singapore's public housing policy have changed over the years and HDB has shown itself to be a dynamic organisation, adapting to new needs and trends. In the beginning, the task was to build homes quickly to solve the housing problem. Slum lands were expropriated, and those displaced were offered public housing flats as an alternative. Rental flats were in simple Corbusian-like slab blocks. Then the task was to improve quality, increase the proportion of the population eligible for public housing and (above all) allow people to purchase their own public housing flats. New planning ideas such as ecological living affected HDB policies, and in 2007 the HDB introduced a programme called Remaking Our Heartlands, with the eco-town of Punggol as its showcase.

HDB offers different types of housing, ranging from two-room flats to five-room flats. Studio apartments are designed for elderly residents and sold on 30-year leases. There are three-generation flats designed for multi-generation families. Executive condominiums (EC) are developed and sold by private developers. These are a hybrid between private and public housing. There are some restrictions concerning the sale of these flats, but restrictions expire after a certain number of years. They are meant for young graduates and professionals, who can afford more than a HDB flat but find private property to be out of their reach. Design, Built and Sell Scheme (DBSS) flats give greater choice to higher-income buyers. HDB provides loans, and private developers are involved in providing public housing and setting the price. DBSS flats were introduced in 2005 as part of a plan to increase the role of the private sector. HDB flats, especially the upper-scale flats, are not synonymous with bad-quality housing – in fact, quite the contrary. An example of luxurious quality housing flats are executive condominiums in Sembawang (advertised in *The Straits Times* (12 October 2013)) with an iconic sky park, 50-metre pool, club house, 200-metre sky park jogging track, spa beds and much more. The income ceiling was S$12,000[4] (per month), with a housing grant of up to S$30,000 available for first-time buyers. Private condominiums are mixed with HDB flats. HDB and URA have sold land adjacent to HDB estates to private developers. Private housing next to public housing makes it possible for HDB upgraders to stay in their own familiar neighbourhoods; for private housing residents, being in the vicinity of HDB estates guarantees access to good services.

From 1990, the proportion of Singapore's population living in public housing began to decline. Public housing seems to have been a temporary solution, and when the aim of housing the population was achieved, the focus shifted to increasing the quantity of private housing. This demonstrates the Keynesian rather than socialist character of Singapore's housing policy. As Keynes (1926: 47) wrote: 'The important thing for Government is not to do things which individuals are doing already, and to do them little better or little worse, but to do those things which at present are not done at all.' In the late 1990s, Head of Local Planning Section (URA) Seow Kah Ping expressed the new target for Singapore's public housing policy: 'to reduce the share of public housing to about 70 percent, with medium and low density housing moving up to 30 percent to meet the rising aspirations of people' (Seow 1998).

Compared to other countries, 87 per cent of Singapore's population living in public housing (in 1990) is a very high figure. Table 5.2 shows the proportion of households that are social housing tenants in European cities. The figures also show the great disparity among European countries. Amsterdam and Vienna are famous for their

**Table 5.2** Percentage of households
as social housing tenants.

| City | Percentage |
| --- | --- |
| Munich | 10 |
| Marseille | 16 |
| Helsinki | 17 |
| Copenhagen | 20 |
| Vienna | 40 |
| Amsterdam | 56 |

Source: Urban Audit the Yearbook 2000,
European Commission.

extensive public housing, whereas in many other European cities the
only option is to buy a flat.

In addition to the city-state's extensive public housing sector, an even
more surprising fact is that the majority of Singaporeans are homeowners. Before 1964, HDB flats were available as rentals. In 1964, the Home
Ownership Scheme was introduced, making the purchase of HDB flats
possible. In 2011, about 95 per cent of HDB residents owned the homes
they lived in (Mah 2011). The overall homeownership rate in 2012 was
90.1 percent (Statistics Singapore 2013). Compared to Western cities,
Singapore's owner occupancy rate is high. Table 5.3 shows homeownership in European cities (in 2000).

The reason for Singapore's high ownership rate is its compulsory pension savings system, the Central Provident Fund (CPF), which was inherited from the colonial government. The original purpose of CPF was

**Table 5.3** Proportion of households
owning their dwellings.

| City | Percentage |
| --- | --- |
| Amsterdam | 12 |
| Copenhagen | 16 |
| Vienna | 18 |
| Marseille | 44 |
| Helsinki | 47 |
| Singapore | 90 |

Source: The Urban Audit 2000. European
Commission.

that 'on retirement, individuals were paid benefits determined by total past contributions from themselves and their employers plus interest, rather than payments being made to retirees from the contributions of those still working' (Huff 1994: 334). People save for their retirement in their own individual accounts, instead of paying the pensions of those older than themselves. Although the term 'social policy' is relatively uncommon in public discourses in Singapore, CPF has been called 'social policy based on assets' (Sherraden et al. 1995), as distinct from Western welfare states' income transfer through social insurance and public aid. The term social policy is warranted because Singaporeans can use their CPF money to pay for their healthcare, insurances and education. The CPF system explains Singapore's high savings rate, which has also contributed to economic growth. The Home Ownership Scheme introduced in 1964, and augmented in 1968 (the Home Ownership Through CPF), allowed CPF members to use their CPF savings to purchase flats provided by HDB. In 1995, 87.2 per cent of buyers paid for their new HDB flats from their CPF savings (Report of the Cost Review Committee 1996).

Ownership of HDB flats means that owners can sell their flats in the resale market to eligible buyers of their own choice at a mutually agreed resale price. There are some requirements, for example the number of years an owner has lived in an HDB flat and racial quotas. With increasing house prices, Singaporeans have accumulated significant wealth through their public housing flats. Also, the families of deceased owners can (subject to satisfying certain eligibility criteria) choose to remain in their HDB flats.

Through public housing policy, the government has promoted the values regarded as important in Singapore (see the discussion on shared values in Chapter 1), namely family values. HDB eligibility criteria define a nucleus family, and offer extra benefits (for example, priority in the selection of a flat) to people moving to be close to their parents, young couples and families with children. In 2012, for example, the Multi-generation Priority Scheme gave priority allocation to parents and their married children submitting a joint application to purchase flats in the same project. Whereas the colonial government's solution to prevent racial conflict was segregation (see p. 95), HDB practises an anti-segregation policy. It defines ethnic quotas in HDB estates, thus preventing concentration of ethnic groups. An advertisement in *The Straits Times* (12 October 2013) offered public housing for sale in Clementi, but noted that: 'Ethnic group quota for Chinese has been filled' (meaning that Chinese buyers were ineligible in this case).

HDB flats provide not just shelter but a lifestyle. Within HDB new towns, there are swimming pools (with subsidised prices), mosques (for the Malay minority group), light industry (providing work-places) and schools. Modernists such as Le Corbusier, Otto Finck and Olle Enkvist dreamt about serviced houses (Hayden 1984). Services like cooked food provided on housing estates would liberate women from household work, pleasing early feminists such as Melusina Fay Peirce and Charlotte Perkins Gilman, along with socialists such as August Bebel. In Singapore, the HDB estates have food courts where hawkers cook cheap and delicious food, and further fulfil the serviced housing dream by providing a collective kitchen for social eating. Cheap prices – five dollars (three euros) for a portion of delicious fish soup – make it possible for families to dine out and meet friends. Diners from different ethnic groups and social classes eat together around the same table.

How does the HDB allocate flats?[5] At first, allocation was simply by a queue system. This functioned well until the Asian Financial Crisis in 1997, which caused people to withdraw from the queue and left the HDB with unsold flats. In 2002, HDB switched to the BTO (building flats to order) system whereby buyers ballot for the chance to select a flat and make a down payment; HDB proceeds with building when the majority of flats are reserved (Mah 2011: 31). This market model of public housing assembled solvent demand but could not satisfy the need for housing.

How are HDB flats priced? Originally, when there was no resale market, HDB adopted a zonal pricing system based on production costs. In the 1980s, HDB began allowing people to sell their HDB flats and noticed that people valued flats differently. This led HDB to start a market-based pricing system. New flats were 'priced based on what professional valuers assess similar flats would fetch in the open market, but discounted with a substantial subsidy' (Mah 2011: 47). The Minister of National Development, Mah Bow Tan, asserted that this system ensures fairness across generations: 'Owning HDB flats gives Singaporeans an asset that grows in value along with the country's progress' (Mah 2011: 47).

How is affordability ensured with market-based pricing? This is one of the challenges of HDB and with the rapid increase in housing prices the question of affordability became a hot political issue in the 2011 elections. The situation was especially difficult for first-time buyers, and for them new flats were subsidised. How many subsidies are needed to make housing affordable? First, we must distinguish between different kinds of subsidies. Between 2007 and 2010, the average loss on the sale and development of HDB flats was about S$600 million a year (Mah 2011: 73). The government subsidises HDB flats through price discounts for new flats and through offering grants (for first-time buyers and low-income households). HDB also offers housing loans at concessionary interest rates. For needy Singaporeans, HDB provides rental flats (in 2013 the income ceiling was S$1500 a month). Second, if these subsidies are deducted, does the provision of public housing need subsidies? Singaporean economists Amina Tyabji and Lin Kuo Ching (1989: 29) pointed out the difficulty in calculating subsidies: 'Had the government set up a Ministry of Housing in 1960 rather than the HDB, this Ministry would have received annually a budgetary allocation like any other Ministry, without the necessity of loans and subventions. This would have made it easier to calculate costs and subsidies as can be done for example for education or health.' They compared rents in HDB and private market flats (in 1998 the difference between these for a two-room flat was S$166 per month) and calculated the subsidy in the case of selling a three-room HDB flat (in 1985) to be S$33,785. This includes S$33,085 land cost. Third, how the land costs are calculated is not a simple question. In 2004 I interviewed Tony Tan, the senior advisor of Surbana Consultants, and asked him whether public housing is subsidised; he answered that it is slightly subsidised because of the subsidised land. The land 'subsidy', however, depends on how costs are calculated, and whether revenue from any alternative use is calculated as a cost. From the point of view of society the whole rent is surplus (as Joan Robinson wrote, discussed in Chapter 3), and public ownership of land prevents price-increasing land speculation (absolute rent).

   Through land acquisitions, the government resolved the land question and created conditions for resolving the housing question without tearing Singapore's classes apart, and through resolving the housing question it created the propertied class that became a stabilising force in Singapore. Singapore's public housing programme is undoubtedly a success.[6] Still, it remains largely neglected by housing analysts. Chua Beng Huat (1997: xiii) suggested that the reason for this neglect is the perception of the PAP as an authoritarian regime. Singapore's impressive results in its public housing programme are thought to be achievable only through repressive measures, and hence do not provide a useful lesson for more democratic societies. However, the reason for the success of Singapore's public housing programme is land policy and public ownership of land; and this is the significant lesson it can offer. As Chua (1997, 134) concluded, Singapore's different strategy towards land acquisition 'demonstrates that in an advanced capitalist society it is possible (i) to eliminate private small landlords without jeopardizing the economy or the legitimacy of the state, and (ii) to provide public housing without threatening the dominant position of capital, or, more generally, to provide for a fairly high standard of collective consumption goods without undermining capitalism.'

## Housing Welfare

The homeownership rate of a country depends on its culture and level of urbanisation. Owner occupancy rates are higher in rural than in urban areas. In Asian countries, where urbanisation is low, the homeownership rate is high; for example 78 per cent in Pakistan, 85 per cent in India, 89 per cent in the Philippines and 90 per cent in Bangladesh (Saunders 1990: 18). Homeownership and public housing rates also depend on a state's political regime. Socialist countries tended to invest less in housing because housing investment was regarded as non-productive. Ivan Szelenyi introduced the concept of under-urbanisation to describe the effects of such under-investment in housing. Socialist policy favoured heavy investment in urban industry. Consequently, there was insufficient investment in urban housing, and the result was overcrowding and the emergence of a new working class – peasants who left full-time employment in agriculture and took up industrial employment in the cities, but remained in the villages and commuted to their work (Konrad and Szelenyi 1977). Singapore's housing policy, drawing inspiration from the socialist ideas of the Fabians and social democratic Sweden,[7] differed from this Soviet model. Although the PAP government emphasised economic growth, it understood the importance of workforce availability, and thus the importance of accommodating the urban working class. The housing question was resolved by building public housing, and thus lowering the wage companies needed to pay for their labour force.

In providing public housing and reducing the social reproduction costs of labour, the PAP government was implementing an agenda similar to those of welfare states. Welfare states provide employment benefits, healthcare and education. Although they differ across the Nordic countries, continental Europe and Britain (Esping-Andersen 1990; Kosonen 1995), what they all share is that housing is not included in universally provided welfare services but is provided only for marginal groups. Asian countries have been regarded as welfare state laggards. East Asian countries, however, are not without safety nets. Extended families and clan associations provide some of the duties that welfare states perform. Goodman and Peng (1996) describe social welfare in Japan, Korea and Taiwan as a combination of Confucian and Buddhist tradition. 'While the Confucian rhetoric extolled the virtues of filial piety, diligence, and conflict avoidance, the Buddhist teachings further reinforced these values with the notions of karma – the idea of benefit and obligation – and of private charity and acceptance of the status quo' (Goodman and Peng 1996: 199).

Is Singapore's welfare policy a mix of Western welfare state policy and an East Asian welfare model reliant on family, clan and voluntary charity? To answer this question, I compare Singapore's safety net to that of a developed welfare state. Finland has an extensive welfare state. All citizens are entitled to unemployment benefits, public assistance for food and clothing, childcare, free education (up to and including university level), health services and pensions. Low-income citizens, the unemployed and students receive housing allowances provided by municipalities. Municipalities also provide shelters and homes for the homeless. Despite these provisions there is no security of housing. This became evident during the recession that Finland experienced in the early 1990s. With increasing unemployment and interest rates, households ended up paying mortgages on homes that they had lost. Compared to this scenario, Singapore's housing policy may be seen as a social protection policy by virtue of having assured security of housing.

Singapore's public housing policy, however, cannot be regarded as a welfare state policy. First, in Singapore, welfarism (together with individualism and liberalism) is among those Western values contrasted against 'superior' Asian values of collectivism, discipline, family and ethnic kin (as discussed in the first chapter). On 14 January 1996 the cover story of *The Straits Times* headlined with: 'Will Britain become a nation of coolies?' The former colonial master's welfare system was compared to Singapore's anti-welfare ideology: 'Unlike the "tiger" economies, Britons live in a dependency culture.' Britons 'demand the state increase their pensions, house them, feed them, medicate them and support them ad infinitum'. In Singapore 'old people must not only be supported, if necessary, by their families, but now have a right to sue their children if they fail in this "filial duty".' Britons 'pay income tax [and] have no idea what happens to the money once it disappears into the Treasury's maw: The politicians can spend it any way they like.' 'When a Singaporean contributes to the CPF, he knows that money is his and he receives the equivalent of bank statements to let him know how his fund is doing. Moreover, the Singaporean knows he is saving for his own future welfare and pension needs, not the current needs of the spendthrift or lazy people next door (Will Britain become ... 1996).'

Second, Singapore's public housing is not welfare state policy, because housing is not a social right in Singapore. 'Housing in Singapore is not provided as a right and cannot be regarded as a legal entitlement of citizenship. The acquisition of a public housing flat is a business transaction between client and tender, since the HDB operates as a corporation which is financially and administratively independent of government' (Hill and Lian 1995: 129). The government is committed to the universal provision of public housing, but public housing 'is defined in terms of private property rights and has never been a matter of welfare provision' (Hill and Lian 1995: 129). Public housing is a

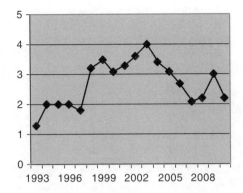

**Figure 5.3** Unemployment rate in Singapore.
Source: MAS Annual Reports (several years).

business transaction and the public housing sector operates like an enterprise. Public housing is a universal good available to everyone who earns it. It is public housing, not 'social housing' as in Western cities, where municipal housing is provided only for marginal groups.

There is a Keynesian element to Singapore's investment in housing. Keynes suggested that the ultimate cure for unemployment is to spend 'on public housing, better roads and improvements to the electricity grid' (Wapshott 2011: 33). Singapore's government has invested in all these, and the unemployment rate remains low compared to Europe and the United States. Figure 5.3 shows the unemployment rate in Singapore, which peaked at 4 per cent in 2003.

### Private, Expatriate and Migrant Housing

In addition to public housing, there is private housing that includes non-landed condominiums and landed houses and bungalows (Figure 5.4). To satisfy the increasing demand of a growing affluent middle class, the government allowed Singaporeans to use CPF to buy private housing, and began selling 99-year leases to private developers for the construction of private high-rise condominiums. As Chua (2000: 53) commented, this created 'a new category of private housing with similar tenure category as public housing, different from conventional lease-hold private ownership'.

In the private housing market, demand is increased by foreigners who can buy an apartment within a building and restricted residential property (landed property, detached, semi-detached or terrace houses)

**Figure 5.4**  Reflections, Keppel Bay, luxurious condominiums, Daniel Libeskind. Photo: Anne Haila.

after approval. Rents in the private market are high, and are paid by transnational companies. When I lived in Singapore, my university-subsidised housing cost me one-tenth of what Finnish businessmen paid to live in private housing (they, of course, had their rent paid via generous housing allowances from Finnish companies like Nokia, Kone and Wärtsilä). In the 1990s, Finnish companies were still sending families to Singapore, even though these postings with high housing allowances and schooling costs were expensive. The wives of Finnish businessmen, who in Finland had worked as teachers and doctors, spent their days by the pool and learnt brush painting, discussing 'the maid problem' and their fear that their husbands would take a local wife. Times were changing, however, and companies reconsidered their policies. One large transnational Finnish company I interviewed had four types of contract. Family contracts covered schooling expenses for children, single contracts offered more trips back to Finland, girl-friend contracts gave benefits to a local girlfriend and local contracts came without extra benefits. Older expatriates refused to accept local contracts, seeing them as eroding expatriate benefits, whereas younger generation expatriates were ready to accept local contracts and were tempted to stay in Asia after expiry of their contracts. The changes down the expatriate generations meant changes in expatriate housing demand: less family housing and more studio flats.

Singapore's government has helped house the expatriate workforce. After the 1997 Asian crisis, in order to attract more foreign professionals the Jurong Town Corporation (JTC, statutory board discussed in Chapter 6) launched a public housing scheme for Housing Foreign Talents (SHIFT), offering eligible foreigners – highly skilled workers, professionals and graduate students who had worked in Singapore for less than two years and did not own property in Singapore – HDB flats at monthly rentals up to 40 per cent lower than market rents, without stipulating an income ceiling. JTC's scheme followed the Prime Minister's National Day rally speech that announced government moves to provide more affordable housing for foreign professionals in order to persuade them to stay in Singapore (Tan C 1997).

In addition to highly educated and well-paid expatriate professionals with their generous housing allowances, there are low-paid labourers who need housing too. Accommodation is invariably a problem for low-income groups in global cities, as Saskia Sassen (1991) observed. How do low-paid migrants who are ineligible for public housing find accommodation in Singapore's expensive private housing market? One example of foreign workers' housing in Singapore is the People' Park Complex in Chinatown. Ang Yiying (2009) reported that apartments here were partitioned to create extra rooms for rental to foreign workers. The complex's units were typically occupied by rather more people than an average family: bunk beds were common, some units accommodated as many as 30 people, shoe racks with 15 to 30 pairs of shoes were a telltale sign outside apartments, vast expanses of laundry were strung out on window grilles, racks in hallways and staircase landings, kitchens were turned into bedrooms, and notices on doors reminded occupants to keep quiet or to shut the door. The URA investigated whether such conversions of apartments into workers' quarters had been authorised.

### Challenges

No matter how good Singapore's housing system is (Figure 5.5), it generates conflicts and inequalities. What housing conflicts and inequalities exist in Singapore? I examine four aspects. First, how is Singapore's scarce land area allocated between private and public housing? Second, how does the lowest income group live? Third, are there inequalities connected to race? Fourth, what kinds of conflicts have there been?

Based on calculations by Addae-Dapaah (1999), in 1991 – when about 82 per cent of Singapore's population lived in high-density housing (plot

**Figure 5.5**   The Pinnacle@Duxton, HDB housing is not synonymous for bad quality housing. Photo: Anne Haila.

ratio greater than 2.1) – 6.1 per cent of the total population occupied 40 per cent of residential land and lived in low-density housing (plot ratio less than 1.4). It can be concluded that Singapore's scarce land is unequally distributed, and the Singaporean landed property dream is out of reach for the majority of people. There are also spatial inequalities. Although Singapore is a small island, transportation is pretty good, there are neighbourhoods that are more expensive than others just around the corner. As *The Easy Guide to Investing in Singapore Real Estate* by James Chua (2013: 92) points out: 'Just like how men will naturally gravitate towards pretty women, savvy property investors … have gravitated towards certain areas or districts in the city.' Among such areas are Orchard, Cairnhill, River Valley, Bukit Timah, Holland Road and Tanglin.

To find out how low-income groups live, we can use the estimates of homeless people and those living in HDB rental flats. Belinda Yuen (2007) estimated that about 170–300 people in Singapore are living on the streets in any given year.[8] In addition to these there are those who live in HDB rental flats. In 2011, about 95 per cent of HDB residents owned the flats they lived in (Mah 2011). This leaves 5 per cent

**Table 5.4** Homeownership rate among
resident households in Singapore.

|          | 1980 | 2005 |
|----------|------|------|
| Chinese  | 61.9 | 92.9 |
| Malay    | 49.7 | 93.2 |
| Indians  | 42.2 | 83.1 |

Source: Adapted from MCCY 2013.

living in HDB rental property. Phang (2001: 447) regards the public rental sector as representing the 'social' housing sector in Singapore. For the lowest income group, HDB provides heavily subsidised rental flats. Among the criteria for obtaining a HDB rental flat is that the applicant's income is below S$1500 per month and the applicant be part of a proper nucleus family. Rental flats are smaller than four rooms, and more than 90 per cent are one- or two-room flats. The proportion of HDB residents in rental flats has decreased from 15.5 per cent in 1987 to 3.7 per cent in 2013 (HDB Sample Household Survey 2013: 15).

The decreasing percentage of rental flats implies that the homeownership rate has increased. Homeownership has increased even more markedly for those ethnic groups that used to be predominantly renters. Malay households are still less likely to be owners of private homes than Chinese or Indians: in 2005, 16.3 per cent of Chinese households lived in private housing, whereas for Malays and Indians the figures were 2.3 per cent and 12.4 per cent respectively (MCCY 2013). Table 5.4 shows homeownership rates among residential households.

Making people from Malay and Indian minority groups into homeowners supplements HDB's ethnic quota anti-segregation policy and boosts other institutions (responsible for promoting shared values, integrated schools, English as the first language, and the CMIO system) aimed at promoting integrated multi-ethnic communities and preventing racial riots. As recently as 1964 and 1969, there were riots in Singapore, with the Malays 'moved out of Chinese-majority areas and the Chinese fled from the Malay quarters' (Chua M H 1996).[9]

En bloc sales legislation was amended in order to facilitate intensification of land use. Giving up the requirement that all owners have to agree provoked conflicts, and the issue was debated in the parliament. The critics of the new majority rules appealed to the emotional value of their home and community. The defenders of en bloc sales argued that collective sales of strata titles ensured optimal use of land, prevented buildings from falling into disrepair and prevented the 'tyranny' of the minority over the majority (Wu 2007: 89). The en bloc debate also raised the issue of the extent of the property. Wu Tang Hang (2007) suggested that the rights of strata title owners are comparably fragile, making homeowners susceptible to displacement by a majority of neighbours. The Minister of Law, Professor Jayakumar, argued that strata title holders possess their property as tenants-in-common with their neighbours, saying that 'in the case of strata titles, to put in layman's terms, [the strata title holder] does not own an identifiable part of the land as being his but he owns it in common with other subsidiary proprietors' (cited in Wu 2007: 89).

Collective sales split residents between those supporting the sale and those opposing it. One controversial case was Gillman Heights, where a minority of owners did not want to move and tried to overturn the collective sale of their estate (to CapitaLand, Hotel Properties and two private funds). The Strata Title Board had approved the sale at a price that was 40–55 per cent above the figure residents would have received if they had sold their flats individually. The residents who opposed the sale said that price had never been the problem. They claimed that there was no other place like Gillman Heights in Singapore (Teo J 2008c). The Land Titles Strata Act allows a person to object to an en bloc sale if he suffers a financial loss, whereas emotional attachment is not taken into account (Wu 2007: 90). Minority owners compared a collective sale to compulsory acquisition.

Another case was the Clementi Park development, where residents mobilised to save their neighbourhood and resist en bloc sale. On their movement's website (read 8 April 2012), they characterised en-blocers as owners who had left the development, did not live in it, or who wanted to cash in or have a second home. They called themselves 'stayers', wanting to preserve the quality of life enjoyed here over the previous 10 or 20 years. Stayers regarded their condos as irreplaceable and did not want to live in 'shoe boxes'.

The residents who opposed the sale of Gillman Heights said that price was not the problem. Housing prices, however, are one of the main frictions in Singapore, and rising prices have generated inequality between generations. Those residents who received public housing in compensation for their slum dwellings benefitted from the price increase when they sold their property and were able to accumulate wealth. After the rise of housing prices (especially after flows of 'hot money' into Singapore after the subprime and euro crises), housing became a problem for first-time homebuyers. They faced unaffordable housing prices. The housing question for the younger generation was one important issue in the election of 2011 and again during the 2013 Punggol by-election. As a result, special measures were introduced to help first-time buyers.

## The Value of Public Land and Fiscalisation of Rent

Urban economists and property rights scholars assume that the market mechanism is a better method of allocating land than administrative allocation by the state. Planners, as Hayek thought, can never know the best and most efficient use of land. Critics of the market model argue that the state has several roles in making the market work, and claim that the whole idea of *laissez faire*, the free market or an invisible hand is a myth (Medema 2009; Martinez 2009). The state protects and enforces property rights, and constructs the legal environment for the market. In urban development, governments do even more. They appropriate land and deliver urban renewal. The developmental state of Singapore owns land and leases it to developers in public auctions, appropriates land for private developers, makes private developers compete, provides public housing and industrial space, intervenes in the real estate market and promotes 'good values'. How can such multiple tasks of the state be analysed? The first important distinction to be made is between intervention in the economy versus the real estate market. They are different things, although often confused. A perfect illustration is that transnational companies find good business environments in Singapore and Hong Kong because there is little business regulation; in urban development, however, there is plenty.

To distinguish between intervention in the economy and the real estate market is important, because the axioms that are true for the productive sector do not apply to the real estate market: in urban development the issue is not just about efficiency but also a matter of justice, externalities, exclusion and environmental preservation. The property rights doctrine's trust in the market as the mechanism to allocate land uses can be criticised in several ways. First, the market mechanism excludes those without means, who cannot move to gated communities and buy club goods even if they wanted to. The second problem is the assumption that rights are equal. Rose (1994: 280) has remarked that the metaphor of the bundle of rights suggests that the component entitlements in that bundle are all more or less alike. This homogenisation of rights in the bundle is problematic as to land use and urban development. Development rights are a very different type of rights from, for example, a right to sell. The former can be regarded as the collective property of citizens and not alienable. Further, in cities there are shared, collective and common rights, overlapping and changing rights. Third, land use and urban development bring positive and negative external effects. Chapter 2 discussed criticism of North's idea that well-defined property rights lead to efficiency and pointed out a fallacy of generalisation in property rights scholars' reasoning. If individuals take better care of what they own, it does not follow from this that, in cities where individual action produces externalities, the result is 'efficient' and good. Whether a factory has the right to pollute or residents the right to clean air are not equal choices; the task of town planners is to protect residents (particularly those without negotiating power) and promote social welfare. Fourth, assuming that negotiations solve land-use conflicts ignores practical problems and power in participation (noted, for example, by planning theorists like Patsy Healey, John Forester and Judith Innes). Fifth, efficiency is not the only goal of land-use decisions. Critics of the utilitarian view of planning, like Timothy Beatley (1994), advocate ethical planning and have introduced alternative goals to efficiency and utility maximisation. These objectives are to prevent harm, protect certain land-use rights, promote and distribute justice, preserve the environment and other forms of life, protect the interests of future generations, and consider impacts beyond the borders of a particular city. These factors are all important in cities and they are beyond measurable utility.

The second distinction we should make is that between the state and the city. Often when scholars debate public intervention, they talk about the state without distinguishing between state and municipality. In the 1970s and 1980s, when landownership and government intervention in the land market were still popular research topics, scholars tended to study market intervention and town planning using the language of neoclassical economics (excusing intervention in the case of market failure) and without delineating the difference between state and city (see e.g. Balchin and Kieve 1977; Hallett 1979; Dunkerley 1983; Barlow 1993). Since the rise of neoliberal ideas of privatisation and deregulation, interest in landownership and intervention has disappeared (Werczberger and Burukhov 1999). These are important issues and should be analysed again.

One question is: does it matter whether the intervening body is the state or the city? Singapore is the state and the city. The state and municipality functions have been difficult to separate since the Rendel Commission 'recommended streamlining local government functions into one island-wide city and Island Council' (Turnbull 1982: 268). In 1959 'the PAP absorbed the city council into the central government' (Turnbull 1982: 276), and local government functions were either absorbed into government ministries or assigned to the Public Utilities Board established in 1963 (Lee S A 1976). Local and central authorities were merged, and city council functions were transferred to the Ministry of National Development. The ensuing institutions provide the services that in European cities are supplied by municipalities. HDB developed public housing, JTC developed industrial estates and URA was responsible for town planning. The key actors in urban development are coordinated by the Ministry of National Development.[10]

The story of HDB explains why municipal housing offices often fail to provide enough affordable housing: they have too little power. The predecessor of HDB, the Singapore Improvement Trust (SIT), founded in 1927, had the task of providing low-cost housing. Despite an alarming housing shortage, it directed its energies 'to working on back lanes and ordinary planning duties' (Latif 2009: 53). It was regarded as a failure because 'it was less a housing authority than a municipal body', remarked Latif (2009: 57), who also noted that the new organisation, the HDB, 'would have to be a proper building authority' (Latif 2009: 58). The HDB was provided with land, funds, legal powers and the support of the state.

Given the autonomy and power of statutory boards such as HDB and JTC that operate like enterprises, what prevents them from misusing the power and become corrupt? What is the relationship between town planning and the action- and development-oriented programmes of HDB and JTC? Ole Johan Dale (1999: 85), who worked for several years in the URA, commented on the centralisation of planning under the URA with the Ministry as final decision-maker. He noted that it reduced competition between different ideas, but made the planning process and coordination easier. In this, Singapore differs from the urban development system in Hong Kong, where planning and development powers are fragmented into various semi-autonomous departments (like town planning, housing and land) without a single agency or strategic planning unit to coordinate matters or take care of the 'public interest'. The result is that there is bureaucratic discretion, micro-powers at the individual level and elastic conditions for land speculation in Hong Kong (Curthbert 1991).

In Singapore, there are two ministries involved in land development. Land-use planning, public housing, development control, land development and conservation and urban redevelopment all fall within the remit of the Ministry of National Development. Land policy and selling and leasing land, however, are within the remit of the Ministry of Law and the SLA (Singapore Land Authority). When I asked a Singaporean civil servant why the SLA (managing Singapore's land resources) answers to the Ministry of Law but the URA (Urban Redevelopment Authority, in charge of town planning) answers to the Ministry of National Development, he replied that the reason is to 'prevent too much power being concentrated in any one office'.

Singapore's national-level coordination of local urban development raises the question of the division of labour between state and municipality. The legal status of the city, comments Gerald Frug (1984), has been a puzzle for liberal theorists. Cities seem to be between the state and the individual, and fail to fit neatly into liberal theory. The European medieval town was 'a group of people seeking protection against outsiders for the interests of the group as a whole' (Frug 1984: 243). For Max Weber 'city air made men free', and city residents comprised a class of economically independent petty burghers together with others who were legally free (Weber 1966: 93). From these origins, European cities developed as collective actors (Le Gales 2002) contributing to the common good of their citizens. In their roles as collectors of taxes and providers of public services to their citizens, European municipalities have come into conflict with nation states. A characteristic of European history, argued Patrick Le Gales (2002), has been the continuous battle between cities and states. In Finland, for example, that fight today concerns the duties (public services) the state demands that municipalities must provide, and the taxes it collects from municipalities for redistribution. As to the managing of land resources, there are differences among the European countries. In James Barlow and Simon Duncan's (1994) comparison between Britain's liberal approach to land and housing, France's corporatist approach and Sweden's social democratic approach, the Swedish system (with its state regulation and municipal land banking) stands out as the most successful. The Swedish system bears a resemblance to Singapore's model.

The growth machine theory (Molotch 1976; Logan and Molotch 1987), although important and influential, has blurred the difference between the state and the 'local state', and cast doubt on local governments: cities are arenas of selfish interest-seeking, lobbying and coalitions. The growth machine theory is correct in arguing that local actors can pursue self-interest. This explains why, for example, officials are reluctant to use expropriation powers even when they have such powers. This leads to the dilemma of land acquisitions: municipal decisions-makers are too close to local interests, while the state is too far removed from local issues to be interested. This dilemma has been solved in Singapore: the developmental state of Singapore, independent of social classes and special private economic interests, has appropriated land for the purposes of municipal uses and services – the most important of which was public housing.

Land is an important resource both for the state and the city. Does it make a difference whether the land is owned by the state or the municipality? Marx proposed the nationalisation of land; in Mao's China, land became state property; Thomas Spence distrusted remote government and suggested that parishes should own the land, collect rent and provide services with rent revenues; and the Fabians recommended that municipalities should appropriate and lease land (see Chapter 4). European cities were endowed with municipal land used for the common good to provide public services (Häussermann and Haila 2005) and the most centrally located municipal land used as a market square and the site for key buildings (like the principal church and the city hall) was not for sale (Martinotti 2005). In Finland, such halcyon days of land used for the public good seem to be over. After the recession of the 1990s, the state concentrated its real estate assets within state real estate corporations, which began managing these assets as corporate private property with the goal of maximising rent revenue. This led to conflicts with tenants (such as universities) accustomed to using public land for the public good. A decade later, the City of Helsinki adopted a similar policy. It concentrated its real estate within the Premises Centre, and began collecting market rents from schools, libraries, day-care centres and public-housing tenants. This led to protests and an urban social movement; residents, shop-keepers and users of public services demanded that rent increases be cancelled. These developments in Finland raise the question: what is the value of public land? This question puzzles citizens and the corporatised state and municipal real estate departments not only in Finland but in all countries and cities thinking about what to do with their real estate.

Singapore offers an answer. When the JTC (the producer of 'public' industrial space, discussed in the next chapter) measures the productivity of industrial land, it takes into account not only the monetary value of the use of that land, but also productive use (that is the type of use). When the SLA sells land to statutory boards like the HDB, the Chief Valuer determines the price and ensures that 'the full cost of land resource' is included in the public service provision and 'not hidden in any government subsidy' (SLA principles of using land, see p. 90). And yet, public housing accommodating the majority of people and the provision of industrial space have been possible. The private housing market is kept separate from public housing, and an important reason why public housing prices are affordable is the absence of land speculation. Whether the provision of affordable housing without subsidies is possible depends on how the price of public land is calculated; there is no 'natural price' or 'equilibrium price'. If the revenue from an alternative use is counted as a cost, then the price is higher than in a case where use determines the price. This is a conclusion we can draw from the history of rent debates and the contribution of Joan Robinson who differentiated the various points of views (discussed in Chapter 3). From the point of view of society, land is provided free and the whole rent is surplus. From the point of view of a particular industry, transfer payments are a part of supply price. From the point of view of an individual, the whole rent is a cost of production. The variety of points of view also complicates the use of monetary compensation in land acquisitions. Whose costs are included in compensation, let alone any value inherent in social relations? HDB's solution to resettle people on public housing estates with shops and services was an unusual policy trying to take into account social value. The solution also affected peoples' social relations. As the 2007/2008 HDB Annual report stated: 'as HDB transformed the physical landscape, it also played a pivotal role in our social development'.

To return to the question: what is the value of public land? There is no 'natural value' for public land. Rather, the value depends on the role the city and the state assume as landowners, their point of view and whether they count alternative costs. If they decide to make money through their real estate and maximise rent revenue – becoming players in the real estate market – they replace schools, libraries and day-care centres with offices, restaurants and hotels that can bid more rent for the land. If they value social consequences and the public good in their land allocation decisions, they calculate the use value of their land.

The use of state land for the public good is restricted in both Singapore and Hong Kong, because their governments derive a considerable amount of revenue from land leases. The Hong Kong Government gets between 20 and 40 per cent of its revenue from land leases (Wu C 1989; Schiffer 1991; Henderson 1991). In Singapore, the government receives land-related revenue from land sales, property tax (on buildings, land and development sites based on annual value), stamp duty, road use (Electronic Road pricing) and government-linked development companies. I call land and real estate-related revenue *fiscal rent*. Some estimates of fiscal rent in the case of Singapore are as follows. In 1995, land sales were the largest source of government revenue (Low 1998: 180). Dale (1999: 44) estimated that the real estate sector comprised up to 30 per cent of the GDP in Singapore. In 2008, the total receipts of the Singapore Government were S\$64,306 million, of which revenue from sales of land were S\$7675 million, motor vehicle taxes S\$1834 million and property tax S\$2856 million (Singapore Budget 2010). The pros and cons of the revenues from sales of land are the same as those of the real estate tax: owners cannot escape the tax, but the amount of it depends on cycles. Revenues from land sales have varied from S\$1870 million in 2003 to S\$13,000 million in 2007 (Singapore Budgets 2005, 2009). On the other hand, property and real estate taxes can be used as an instrument to affect cycles. For example between 1986 and 1995, land under development was exempted from property tax to help developers during the economic downturn. The question of real estate cycles is discussed in Chapter 8.

The next chapter looks at those other actors additional to HDB active in urban development. These are development companies that develop for profit. Their activities bring further complications to the determination of land and housing prices that can include monopoly and absolute rents, and can be influenced by the speculative activities of developers.

## Notes

1 Void decks are the ground levels under apartment blocks.
2 Although they are called 'sales' they are actually leases.
3 URA web pages, 18 July 2001.
4 In 2013 one euro was S$1.75. The exchange rate of the Singaporean dollar per euro between 1999 and 2013 was 1.68 in 1999 and 2.24 in 2004.
5 Eligibility criteria have changed over the years. They concern citizenship, family status, income, age and previous property history. They differ for new HDB flats and resale HDB flats. Two points are important: the criteria have over the years been applicable to up to 87 per cent of the population and have been connected to other policy aims, for example, promoting family values.
6 In 2010, the HDB was awarded the UN Habitat Scroll of Honour Award (the world's most prestigious human settlements award, inaugurated by the United Nations Settlements Programme).
7 Lim Kim San, before he worked at the Housing Development Board, visited Vallingby in Sweden, where he discovered that the municipality was the biggest owner of land (which made it easy to build for the public) (Latif 2009: 95).
8 This is low for a city of 4.6 million inhabitants (in 2007). The number of homeless people in Finland (with a population of 5.4 million) in 2009 was 8150, and in Helsinki (with a population of 576,632) it was 3465 (ARA 2010).
9 Singapore's policies and institutions aimed at racial and ethnic harmony have been widely discussed; see Benjamin 1976; Chiew 1985; Siddique 1990.
10 Town councils were introduced in 1988 in order to increase democracy and devolve estate management duties from the HDB. Community Development Councils within districts assist the needy, promote bonding among residents and connect the community.

# 6

# Property Tycoons and Speculation

Property development companies are complex organisations that differ from companies producing commodities like cars and mobile phones. One important difference concerns land. While commodity-producing companies need land for their location, for development companies land is a factor of production to be developed. To acquire land, development firms must spend time negotiating land deals, and to secure building permission they must negotiate with planning authorities. Such transaction costs increase the costs for developers. Many actors are involved in the development process: landowners, developers, planners, building permission authorities, real estate brokers, construction companies, and their staff, construction workers, bankers and final users. Given such a variety of actors, it is no surprise that a popular approach to studying the construction and development industry has been to analyse actors and their behaviour. In addition to the questions of acquiring land and building permission, a further important question for development companies is whether they seek their profit from development, trading or speculating with the asset value of land. This raises a question that has been debated for long time: the difference between building rent and ground rent. Adam Smith distinguished building rent from ground rent and defined building rent as the profit of the capital expended in building the house and ground rent the part over and above reasonable profit.

This chapter investigates developers and their profits, the difference between land and building rent. It begins by discussing rent-seeking and

*Urban Land Rent: Singapore as a Property State*, First Edition. Anne Haila.
© 2016 John Wiley & Sons, Ltd. Published 2016 by John Wiley & Sons, Ltd.

lobbying, the main sins that developers stand accused of. Various kinds of developers and development companies, along with their types of business, are distinguished: conglomerates with their real estate departments in Japan; tycoons in New York and Hong Kong; pension funds and insurance companies in Europe. These are introduced in order to demonstrate a distinctive feature of Singapore: the presence of the state in the development market. In addition to statutory boards such as the Housing Development Board (HDB) and Jurong Town Corporation (JTC), the provider of industrial land, government-linked companies such as CapitaLand develop properties in Singapore.

### Rent-seeking

The concept of the developmental state (discussed in Chapter 1) was introduced to explain the disconcerting puzzle of the rising Asian economies. Another attempt to solve the conundrum involves the notions of 'rent-seeking' and 'cronies'. The question to be resolved was whether there are true entrepreneurs in Asia. In economic theory, entrepreneurs are the main actors of the production process. They seek and earn profit because of their risk-taking and productive activity. Asian entrepreneurs did not seem to fit the model of capitalist entrepreneurs, and it became common to call them not entrepreneurs, but rent-seekers, cronies and speculators. It was claimed that state patronage provided opportunities for rent-seeking and thus prevented the rise of a productive entrepreneurial class (i.e. 'real capitalists'). That is why, it was suggested, one does not find 'real' entrepreneurs in Asia, just cronies and corrupt businessmen. Chapter 3 defined rent-seeking as the use of resources to acquire, through political pressure, special privileges whereby the injury to others is greater than the gain to those obtaining rents (Tullock 2005). The World Bank, which adheres to the concept of property rights theory in its reports, defines rent-seeking as 'manipulation of the law or of government authority in order to generate or appropriate an economic rent' (World Development Report 1996: viii). Economic rent – defined as earnings from productive factors in excess of the minimum payment needed to keep that factor in its present use – can arise through the acquisition of a resource whose ownership is ambiguous, or through a change in government policy that creates artificial scarcity (World Development Report 1996).

In the economic development literature, the term rent-seeking has been applied widely across all societies in which the state intervenes in the market and distorts incentives, wastes resources, creates monopoly privileges and slows down economic growth. The concept has been applied, for example, to the Cameroon economy (De Lorme et al. 1986) as well as to military expenditure (Looney 1989). Tullock (2005) uses the term rent-seeking extensively. He used it to analyse Imperial China's examination system, the potlatches of the Pacific Northwest, and the purchase of government jobs under the *ancient régime* in France. In all these cases, individuals invested resources in seeking rents (future revenue) which are not transferable to other uses and therefore have a negative social impact. They are waste.

The concept of 'rent-seeking' has been applied to Asian economies in particular. In fact, the concept has its origins in Asia. Gordon Tullock (2005) notes that three early contributors to the rent-seeking literature – J.M. Buchanan (1980), Anne Krueger (1974) and Tullock himself – 'have all spent a good deal of time in the Far East, where there coexist a number of immensely successful cultures capable of generating high-quality art, literature, etc. Yet, many of these civilizations, despite their cultural successes are economically backward' (Tullock 2005: 27). The puzzle was that the *émigré* Chinese of Southeast Asia and the United States, as well as the *émigré* Indians of Africa, were extremely successful; 'only in their homelands do they fail to perform well' (Tullock 2005). Rent-seeking, according to Tullock, 'offers a powerful general explanation of this apparent paradox' (Tullock 2005). The benefits that flow to rent-seekers, cronies and speculators have prevented Asian economies from increasing their productivity.

In debating the recent rise of Asian economies, the concept of 'rent-seeking' has been used to show the close relationship between the state and entrepreneurs and explain the less entrepreneurial mindset of Asian entrepreneurs. In his study of Malaysia, Peter Searle (1999) applied the concept of rent-seeking to cases where businessmen seek special commercial favours (such as licenses, contracts, concessions and the privatisation of state assets) from relevant authorities. Politicians became businessmen through relationships with their party (UNMO)[1] and government machines, which helped them to acquire land, resources, contracts and loans, Searle claimed. The dependence of businessmen on shifting political relationships prompted a preference for investments likely to turn a quick profit (property and speculation on the stock market) (Searle 1999). In Indonesia, 'the business activities of the Suharto family are legendary' (Long 1997). In China, businessmen have relied on *guanxi* reciprocal relationships, granting favours and business opportunities to their relatives (Yeung and Olds 2000).

K.S. Jomo (2000) has criticised the entire rent-seeking literature for a simplistic juxtaposition of state and market. The hidden agenda of the rent-seeking discourse, claimed Jomo, was to accept and legitimate the neoliberal ideology and structural reforms of the World Bank and the International Monetary Fund. Government intervention was crucial in the case of Asia's newly industrialising countries, and the problem was not rent-seeking but whether values are enhanced or diminished because of government intervention. As Jomo emphasised, rent-seeking and government intervention can have socially desirable outcomes. Rents are not only connected to state intervention, but also to what Jomo, following Khan (1996), calls a 'regime of claims'. In Southeast Asia, because of weaker industrial policy than that applied in Japan and other first-tier industrial countries, the bourgeoisie 'have been much more "lumpen" in nature, with much more wealth derived from financial and other non-industrial investments as well as political power and influence' (Jomo 2000: 27).

The concept of rent in the rent-seeking literature is the generalised concept of rent, that is economic rent that can be created by using any factor of production (not just land). Businessmen can derive additional profit through manipulation of the law and monopoly privileges. I use the concept of rent in relation to land, and in Chapter 3 suggested using the concept of political rent-seeking and manipulated rent for such manipulative activity. In this chapter I am interested in whether Singaporean developers put pressure on the government and try to gain from monopoly privileges. Do they claim a share in the distribution of the produce through their ownership, as John Stuart Mill assumed landowners did? Or do they compete and develop their productivity? Have foreign and government development companies made Singaporean developers compete and develop their entrepreneurial spirit, or have they sought quick profits in speculation, like those Malaysian businessmen mentioned by Searle (1999)? To address these issues, I ask three questions in this chapter. First, who are the rich in Asia and what is the source of their wealth? Second, what sort of companies are Singaporean development companies? Third, what kinds of business do Singaporean development companies do?

## Property is a Hot Topic in Singapore

International comparisons show that the rich in Asia are property owners and real estate developers. The *Forbes* 1996 list of the world's highest net-worth individuals showed that the rich in Asia – Li Ka-shing (Hong Kong), Yoshiaki Tsutsumi (Japan) and Tan Yu (the Philippines) – all derived their wealth from real estate. Western tycoons on this list – Bill Gates (USA), Warren Buffett (USA) and Paul Sacher (Swiss) – accumulated their fortunes from other types of businesses. The *Forbes* list ten years later in 2006 included a new group of rich individuals, the

Chinese, with several among them also involved in the property business. The second richest was Xu Rongmao (real estate), and the third
richest was Larry Rong Zhijian (real estate and banking).

The 2009 *Forbes* list showed that, of the twenty richest Singapore-
ans, nine were involved in the property business: Ng Teng Fong (Far
East Organization), the Khoo family (Goodwood Group of Hotels), the
Kwee brothers (Pontiac Land), Zhong Sheng Jian (a China-born but
Singapore-based businessman; Yanlord's Land), Kwek Leng Beng (City
Development), Ong Beng Seng and his wife (Hotel Properties), Peter Fu
Chong Cheng (Trading and property group Kuo International), Chau
Thian Poh (Ho Bee Investment) and Kwek Leng Kee (Hong Leong
Group). In Hong Kong too, many of the richest are real estate devel-
opers or otherwise involved in the property business. Property is 'the
main factor in growing prosperity of two-thirds of names on Forbes top
50' (Sito 2013). Li Ka-shing chairs Cheung Kong Holdings and Hutchi-
son Whampoa. Lee Shau-kee chairs Henderson Land Development, and
Thomas and Raymond Kwok control Sun Hung Kai Properties.

Have these wealthy developers in Singapore and Hong Kong amassed
their fortunes by seeking rents, manipulating the law and lobbying government authorities, as the rent-seeking literature leads us to believe?
To answer this question I look at one episode in Singapore in 1997.

After moving to Singapore in the 1990s, a strange phrase caught my
attention in the pages of *The Straits Times*. This was 'property lobby'. I had
no idea what a developers' lobby could be. I had heard about lobbies in
Washington DC, and in Finland peasants from Lapland (called the 'fur
hat delegation') descended on Helsinki to protest outside the Parliament House demanding changes in the government's agricultural policy. Trying to find out what the odd expression 'property lobby' meant
led me to understand a crucial feature of the real estate market in
Singapore: the role of the government. The term makes sense in a system in which the government has land assets and is willing to practise an
active real estate policy – not that many governments have and do. The
following story illustrates how the property lobby works in Singapore.

In July 1997, one year after the introduction of the anti-speculation
measures by the government, and in the midst of the Asian economic
crisis, the Real Estate Developers' Association of Singapore (Redas)
appealed to the government to ease off its land sales. A letter signed
by the president of Redas, Heng Chiang Meng, was sent to the Minister
of National Development, Lim Hng Kaing. Redas was concerned about
the fall in property prices and warned that the property market could
collapse. 'Heng said that the market has "nowhere to go but decline"
because of "a sick local property, a lousy regional outlook, a local economy which hardly looks like it's going to recover vigorously soon (and)

most importantly, the prospects of a huge [land] supply"' (Singapore Redas ... 1997).

The letter was reported in the media and aroused a public outcry. Local newspapers received angry letters from readers who criticised developers for urging the government to curb land sales and for not accepting that prices in a market can fall just as they can go up (Oon and Hadhi 1997).

Four months later, in November, Heng Chiang Meng reiterated his appeal to the government to do something to improve market confidence. He suggested that the market was not booming like it was in 1996, when the government had introduced its anti-speculation programme. The Asian crisis had affected the property market. He proposed that the government should slow down future land sales. 'Today, market sentiment is so poor, mainly because of what is happening in the region, economic uncertainty and the huge oversupply of land' (Lee J 1997). Soon after 'Deputy Prime Minister Lee Hsien Loong announced a series of measures to cut back [land] supply and stimulate transactions by suspending stamp duty payable by those who sell after holding their purchase for less than three years' (Tan S S 1997). The question that can be asked is whether the lobbying of Redas influenced the government decision.

In December, Mr Heng Chiang Meng resigned from his position as executive director of the Far East Organization (one of the large development companies in Singapore) and president of Redas. It was disclosed in the newspapers that Prime Minister Goh Chok Tong had sent a letter to Mr Heng. In his letter the Prime Minister wrote that 'the Government's decisions must be based strictly on the merits of the issues. It cannot yield to lobbying pressure' (Goh 1997). The Prime Minister expressed concern that when Mr Heng spoke publicly on the state of the property market and the need for government intervention, it was not always clear if he was speaking as an MP (Member of Parliament) or in his capacity as a senior property company executive. 'This has confused the public,' the Prime Minister said. He made a distinction between an MP's role in public office (necessitating the upholding of the high standards which Singaporeans expect of their MPs) and any private positions held: 'Excessive lobbying by interest groups is counterproductive. It is likely to cause the public to misunderstand the rationale for the Government's actions. Ministers who are easily swayed by the vested interest pleadings of their colleagues in Parliament are not fit to be in Government' (Goh 1997). In his reply, Mr Heng said he hoped that by quitting his positions in both Redas and Far East it would be clear that he was committed to upholding the standards required of him (Heng 1997).

Home Affairs Minister Wong Kan Seng commented on Mr Heng's resignation: 'Had property not been a hot issue, then there's no reason why Mr. Heng shouldn't be president of Redas. Because it is a subject of interest to so many people, that's why people feel that there is some possible confusion' (Change to avoid ... 1997). At a press conference, Deputy Prime Minister Lee was asked whether he was succumbing to pressure from developers. He made clear the government's position. 'We have to do the right thing, not for the developers but for Singapore. And Singapore includes homeowners as well as home-buyers. And home-owners greatly outnumber the home-buyers although they do not write so many letters.' (Ang L 1997).

After Heng's resignation, Redas elected a new president at an emergency meeting. The new president Daniel Teo clarified the position of Redas. He announced that in future Redas would be less vocal. 'We will have dialogues with the government when necessary but we would not like to be seen as a pressure group,' Mr Teo said (Ang W M 1997). Teo also said that Redas would try to improve the public image of developers. 'We need better understanding and a better image for developers by having dialogues with the public, forums, seminars and more chit-chat sessions with the media.'

Subsequently, Prime Minister Goh Chok Tong removed Member of Parliament Leong Horn Kee from his position as chairman of the government Parliamentary Committee for National Development, not on account of any misconduct but because of Mr. Leong's dual positions as a Parliamentary Committee chairman and as an employee of developer Orchade Parade Holdings (Oon 1997). Unlike Mr Heng, who resigned from the private sector to serve the public sector, Mr Leong remained in the service of the private sector. However, Mr Leong's removal from his public sector position created a new problem in this city-state striving for excellency – developers serving the public sector are experts, and their specialist knowledge can benefit the government. These issues were discussed after Mr. Leong's move (Fernandez and Tan 1997).

The events of 1997 demonstrate four features of the real estate market in Singapore. First, the developmental state has relative autonomy from specific economic interests. The interests of developers, property owners, homeowners, homebuyers and Singapore as a whole are different, and the government has to strike a balance between them. Second, interests are identified and negotiated through public debate. Contrary to characterisations of Singapore as lacking transparency, having 'no politics' (Clammer 1985: 161), and suffering depoliticisation of public participation (George 2000: 45), I was surprised at the openness and articulation of the property debate. Compared to Finnish newspapers, *The Straits Times'* reporting on land and property issues is more open, radical and politicised. Finnish newspapers will report incidents of fraud committed by construction companies and planning authorities intimidating inhabitants with their plans, but there is no open political debate concerning the effects of government laws and programmes upon various interests groups. What explains this open (compared to Finland) public debate on land questions? One plausible explanation is Singapore's land reform (discussed in Chapter 4) that, without tearing the classes apart, settled the majority of people in public housing flats. The third feature this episode demonstrates about Singapore is that the term property lobby makes sense when the government owns the land to auction, and is willing to regulate supply and demand for land. In addition to fiscal and zoning measures, the Singaporean government has its land sales programme to balance supply and demand. The government has actively used land auctions to regulate the property market, an intervention that reacts to property cycles, and a policy that I have called real estate policy (Haila 1999). Fourth, in Singapore the property lobby is the developers' urban property lobby. This differs from Finland, for example, where landowners defending their interests are invariably rural landowners, or from the suburbs of California, with homeowners defending their property values (Davis 1990). Developers in urban Singapore lobby the government collectively to change government policies and influence market conditions.

### Rumours in Hong Kong

As in Singapore, the government in Hong Kong leases land through land auctions to private developers, and there are rumours that developers have formed a cartel to put pressure on the government. On 31 May 1994, Singapore's *The Straits Times* reported on a land auction in Hong Kong with the headline 'HK developers deny cartel plot to force down property prices'. *The Straits Times* cited Hong Kong's newspaper *Sunday Morning Post* and wrote: 'developers here have rejected suggestion that they had operated a cartel to force down property prices as a warning to the government not to introduce tough market-cooling measures' (HK developers … 1994). What had happened was that 12 companies had banded together to buy two sites well below market value at a government land auction. Big developers were defending this act. Mr Li Ka-shing said developers had not teamed up to push down the bidding price, but were 'only sharing the risk under the present circumstances' (HK developers … 1994). New World Development's Mr Cheng said: 'We have never meant to act in concert against the government but the site was so big that everybody has become more cautious' (HK developers ... 1994). Sino Land chief Mr Robert Ng said prices were lower because of uncertainty about measures the government would be introducing imminently to bring down sky-rocketing residential prices. A developer who had helped organise the deal said that the idea was mooted only minutes before the auction, when several of those concerned met in the City Hall coffee shop. It was 'totally unrehearsed'. Hong Kong's public authorities saw things rather differently. Deputy Secretary of Planning, Environment and Lands, Canice Mak Chungfong, said: 'what we saw was obviously something quite different from a normal auction ... they (the developers) walked around the auction hall and caused minor chaos' (HK developers ... 1994). Mr Mak said that his department would look into whether the auction had allowed fair competition.

Four years later, in May 1998, less than a year after the onset of the Asian financial crisis, Li Ka-shing's Cheung Kong offered for sale a project at a price lower than expected. Other developers followed and cut their prices. The ensuing price war was described as the 'most intense price war since 1982' (Ku and Yeung 1998). *South China Morning Post* reported that the Chief Executive of Hong Kong, Tung Chee-hwa, had met developers. 'Mr. Tung said he did not want to see a collapse in prices, and pledged the Government would be flexible about land supply. But he was under increasing pressure to drop his target of building 85,000 homes a year' (Ku and Yeung 1998). A spokesman for Mr Tung confirmed that 'the Government absolutely does not want to see a great fall in property prices. The stability of the property sector is very important to Hong Kong's overall stability and to the stability of our banking sector' (Ku and Yeung 1998). A Planning, Environment and Lands Bureau spokesman rejected calls for the government to halt its land sales plan, adding that 'hasty changes to long-term housing strategy would give the false impression targets could be changed because some people make some noise (Ku and Yeung 1998)'. He said that the government was monitoring the price war, and that officials were aware of recent reports that developers were still enjoying a profit margin of 37 per cent despite the price cuts.

The government arranged a land auction in May as planned. The prices offered were lower than expected. Developers denied that there had been plans to boycott the land auction as a mean of pressing the government to revise its land-supply policy. Some developers admitted that, although there were no boycott plans, they had delivered a clear message to the government through various channels to temporarily stop holding land auctions (Sito 1998). Later, on 23 June 1998, the *South China Morning Post* reported that the government had decided to suspend land sales until the following April (Ko and Li 1998). This suspension was welcomed by developers. The Real Estate Developers Association said it would 'not only help stabilize the property and stock markets but also boost the people's confidence in the economy' (Ko and Li 1998). Henderson Land Development's chairman said that 'suspending land sales would be "an effective way of restoring confidence"' (Ko and Li 1998).

Newspapers in Singapore commented on the events in Hong Kong. *The Business Times* (Quak 1998) reported on developers' plans to repatriate their offshore finances and commented:

> Funny how all of a sudden, companies like Cheung Kong and Henderson Land have become so forthcoming about their offshore finances by revealing the amount of money (and even the date in the case of Henderson) that they plan to move back into local deposits ... Notably, the repatriation talk by the tycoons also followed the government's announcement that it would suspend all land sales until March next year. Inevitably, several analysts have begun to ask if there had been some kind of deal struck between the tycoons and the government since they immediately revealed plans to bring funds back after the land sales suspension was announced.

In the same edition of *The Business Times*:

> 'wonders what assurance, if any, the Tung government has given to the tycoons in order to convince them to bring their deposits onshore. If the corporates have been keeping their money offshore when local deposits rates were shooting through the roof in more turbulent times, why would they want to bring them back now to earn lower and more stable interest rates? What makes them think it is safer to park them in local deposits now unless they are assured of the survival of the Hong Kong dollar peg or compensation of some sorts? Are we missing something here?' (Quak 1998)

*The Economist* (Tung constrained ... 1998) also commented on the episode. It referred to Tung's promise to solve a chronic housing shortage by building 85,000 new apartments a year and developers' willingness to cooperate in the days when property prices had been rising.

> 'Since then, home prices have fallen by 35 %. As a result, the property cartel, in effect, went on strike by refusing to bid at government land auctions, and by suspending some development. Worse, Hong Kong's banks almost stopped offering credit. The government faced the prospect of collapsing revenues and an imploding

economy. Mr. Tung has been forced to retreat from his home building targets, for now. Home-buyers have been offered tax breaks on
their mortgages, developers are again bidding at auction and the
banks are lending.'

Such episodes illustrate the Hong Kong government's difficult position.
On the one hand, developers can act in concert to foil government
plans. On the other hand, the government is dependent on revenues
from land sales. On average the government receives a third of its revenue from the sale of land leases, but revenue also varies depending on
cycles in the property market.

These stories introduce Singaporean and Hong Kong property
tycoons as lobbying businessmen. They lobby the government to affect
government land sales and government's real estate and land policy,
but they do not lobby the government in order to obtain monopoly
privileges as the theories of rent-seeking and 'cronies' suggest. Their
business environment is created by government regulation and land
sales. However, despite government landownership and regulation, both
Singapore and Hong Kong development companies have become large
and successful, making fortunes for their owners. In order to identify
the distinctive qualities and business environment characteristics pertaining to Singaporean and Hong Kong developers I now briefly portray
the development companies of Japan, the United States and Europe.

### Conglomerates, Dynasties and Pension Funds

Japan is known for its large conglomerates like Mitsubishi, Mitsui and
Nomura, which all have their own real estate departments. Some of
these companies are old (Mitsubishi was founded in 1890 and Mitsui
in 1673). In addition to their development activities, Japanese companies also act as town planners. In the 1950s, for example, Mitsubishi
drew up the Marunouchi Master Remodeling Plan for central Tokyo,
and in the 1980s it initiated the Marunouchi Intelligent City Plan
(Mitsubishi Corporate Profile 1992). Japanese companies also do business abroad. Mitsubishi hit the headlines when it bought a 51 per cent
interest in the Rockefeller Group (the owner of New York's Rockefeller
Center). Mitsui began its overseas operations in Singapore in 1972, and
it has since bought landmark buildings in the United States, such as the
Exxon Building in New York and the AT&T Tower in Los Angeles. The
Japanese Shuwa Corporation was founded by Shigeru Kobayashi who,
after working with his father making furniture, started his own shipping
business. When it subsequently went into bankruptcy, he discovered that

the company's land had become very valuable in Tokyo's booming post-war redevelopment market. So Kobayashi entered the real estate business, and in 1986 he bought the Arco Plaza complex in Los Angeles and the ABC building in Manhattan. Since then, wrote Karl Schoenberger (1989), 'Kobayashi has been the conspicuous symbol of Japan's massive investment in the United States'. Kobayashi gave $1 million to the Ronald Reagan Presidential Library, and made a substantial donation to the Los Angeles Museum of Contemporary Art.

In New York, property developers are celebrities with widely recognised names and faces, like Donald Trump, John Jacob Astor and Bill Zeckendorf. 'Visions of Donald Trump making big stake deals often come to mind when people think about real estate developers' (Pisani and Pisani 1989: ix). Wayne Barrett's biography of Donald Trump, *Trump, The Deals and the Downfall* (1992) portrays him as a manifestation of the spirit of greed driving the speculative real estate business. The personal qualities of developers are emphasised in their biographies. 'Successful developers/entrepreneurs are often identified by their personal profile, which can be summarized as follows: self-reliance, leadership, propensity toward risk, opportunity seeking, action and goal oriented' (Pisani and Pisani 1989: vii). In the American context, developers are real estate entrepreneurs who explore and search markets in order to differentiate themselves from their competitors. They analyse demographic and lifestyle trends in order to guess the future demand for housing. Books chronicling the history of New York have been written largely as a history of real estate dynasties, like Tom Shachtman's (1991) *Skyscraper Dreams - The Great Real Estate Dynasties of New York*. Ideas, imagination, courage, personal skill, risk taking, visions, ego, ambition and cunning are seen as the driving forces behind urban development. As Harry Helmsley, who (together with Larry Wien) bought the Empire State Building in 1961, stated: 'Every morning you look out the window and the building is staring you in the face. So, you'd say, "well, I gotta buy it"' (Shachtman 1991: 219). It is the imagination of the developer that has forged the New York landscape (Wyckoff 1988). Land speculation is another important theme in the US real estate literature. 'America from its inception was a speculation', began Sakolski (1932) in his land bubble story (cited in Wyckoff 1988: 7). Land speculators on the frontier preceded the settlers, chose locations, purchased and surveyed the land and sought to channel immigration there (Gates 1942; Wyckoff 1988).

In the United States, real estate entrepreneurs and other real estate professionals are organised, and have founded organisations like National Association of Real Estate Boards (NAREB) to promote the interests of their sector. The US real estate industry is known for its dynamism and innovation. An example is that of the private company, Sears, that attempted to sell houses just like it sold watches and jewelry – by mail (Stevenson and Jand 1986). Another type of innovation concerns real estate finance. In the late 1960s, JMP Realty in Chicago introduced a new idea for financing real estate, the syndication of real estate packages. 'Instead of turning to banks for between 80% to 100% of the capital needed for a particular real estate project, the developer in a syndication sells off pieces of his equity to a multitude of small and medium-sized investors. He is thus able largely bypass the banks, put up very little of his own money, and by packaging subsequent similar deals build a large portfolio of real estate that he controls and may either sell or continue to manage' (International Directory of Company Histories 1991: 702).

In Europe, the building boom after the Second World War saw the emergence of development and construction companies. In the United Kingdom, property companies had their origins in the urban estates of Victorian industrialists, public property companies such as the City of London Real Property Company and large landowners (Marriott 1967; Fraser 1984; Smyth 1985). Later, shares in successful property companies came to be publicly traded. The first postwar boom ended in the mid 1960s, and the number of property companies declined. A big change in the United Kingdom, and indeed elsewhere in Europe, followed when pension funds and insurance companies began investing in real estate. McIntosh and Sykes (1985: xv) wrote that: 'over the last two decades there has been a revolution in the ownership of property within almost all towns and cities in the United Kingdom. Many office buildings, shops, shopping centres, warehouses, industrial units and even agricultural holdings are now owned by insurance companies, pension funds and property unit trusts.' Ownership by pension funds and insurance companies completely changed the real estate market. Because pension funds and insurance companies are required to make safe investments, the role of *yield* and value of real estate compared to use value became more important than before. This shift in investment sources also forged a link between financial markets and property markets (discussed in Chapter 8).

In Finland, individual landowners enjoy rights to develop out in the countryside, while in urban areas development rights belong to municipalities that have 'a monopoly of zoning'. Because the right to develop belongs to society, companies construct rather than develop, and the pejorative term 'developata' is used for those cases in which a company buys land, subdivides and develops it. In practice, Finnish cities have found themselves contracting with construction firms who own the land.

Cities' construction markets came to be controlled by a few companies that had established a monopoly position through their land possessions. Until the recession of the early 1990s, Helsinki was dominated by four construction companies, who excluded others from the market and were thus able to sell at monopoly prices. The source of their power was the land bank they had accumulated. In 1985, the four largest development companies combined had a 63 per cent share of housing construction, and owned 75 per cent of the land suitable for housing construction (Junka 1988). These companies did not compete with each other over prices or quality, as land ownership enabled them to acquire market share and avoid competition. Their land banks gave them power in negotiating with planning authorities (who in principle enjoyed the planning monopoly). Because the land owned by these companies was on the urban fringe, the result of this public–private partnership form of development was urban sprawl. In the recession of the early 1990s, with decreasing property values and increasing interest rates, these land banks turned into toxic assets and private construction firms went into bankruptcy. The recession caused the state to corporatise its real estate assets, establishing state real estate companies to manage and develop them. Established under the auspices of the Ministry of Finance, these state real estate companies adopted keenly entrepreneurial policies; they sought to maximise rent.

In Hong Kong, companies producing commodities invest in real estate as a sideline. Development and real estate investment is combined with all sorts of other types of businesses, like plastic flowers, garments, biscuits and shipbuilding. A large number of companies in Hong Kong are, at least partially, property and development companies. In 1998, 103 of the 639 firms listed in the Hoenig Guide to the Companies of Hong Kong (1998) were property companies. Hong Kong is also known for its property tycoons and, as in New York, they are public personalities. Alice Poon (2005: 13) noted that many property development companies are controlled by Hong Kong families: the Lis of the Cheung Kong/Hutchison group, the Kwoks of the Sun Hung Kai Properties, the Lees of the Henderson group, the Chengs of the New World Development group. The best known is Li Ka-shing, who is often in the limelight. In 1986, *South China Morning Post* (28 May) reported: 'Five minutes after the scheduled time for the opening of bidding the territory's most powerful property mogul, Mr Li Ka-shing, entered the room, to be met with gasps of recognition from the crowd. With an impeccable sense of theatrical timing, and to the accompaniment of television are lights and camera flashes, Mr. Li took his seat. The game was on.' (Cited in Walker and Flanagan 1991: 39–40.) Hong Kong development companies are global players. Cheung Kong has projects in Singapore, the UK and China. New World Development has hotel business in China, Southeast Asia, the United States and Canada (Barings 1991). Hongkong Land operates in China and Southeast Asia.

Japanese conglomerates, New York's celebrity real estate entrepreneurs, anonymous insurance and pension funds in Europe and well-known property tycoons in Hong Kong – all represent a stark contrast to the private and government-linked development companies that between them share Singapore's development market.

### Private and Government-linked Companies in Singapore

Singapore's development industry is a mixture of private and state enterprises. Some companies started as trading and shipping companies, like Keppel Land with its origins in the nineteenth-century Straits Steamship Company. Another development company, City Development (CDL), has its roots in Fuzou, China, from where Kwek Hong Png arrived in Singapore during the 1920s. Kwek derived his wealth from trading commodities, and his Hong Leong trading company flourished during the rubber boom caused by the Korean War in the 1950s (Searle 1999: 214). In 1965, the company split into Singaporean and Malaysian branches. Among its projects in Singapore are Republic Plaza, designed by Kisho Kurokawa, and the Palais Renaissance shopping mall. The largest private developer in Singapore is the Far East Organization. Its Hong Kong-based sister company, Sino Group, is among the largest developers in Hong Kong. Among Far East's projects in Singapore are Far East Shopping Centre (built in 1974) and Lucky Plaza (built in 1978). The company develops residential, commercial and industrial properties.

In addition to private companies, statutory boards (the Housing Development Board and Jurong Town Corporation), corporatised statutory boards and government-linked companies also develop land. Government-linked companies (GLC) are companies in which the government has an equity holding; they are linked to the government holding companies like Temasek Holdings. Government-linked companies are not like SOEs in China or state enterprises that have a social purpose. They are run as private companies on a competitive and commercial basis and are, as the International Monetary Fund (Ramirez and Tan 2003: 1) stated, 'ostensibly without government privileges'. Government-linked companies may also be listed on the Singapore Exchange. In the 1980s, there were about 600 GLCs (Peebles and Wilson 1996: 32).

Since the 1980s, the government has carried out a privatisation programme, selling shares in government-linked companies and corporatised statutory boards and government departments. In 1987, for example, DBS Land's government shareholding was reduced from 44.7 per cent to 21 per cent (Low 1990: 172). According to Linda Low (1990: 154), privatisation did not mean a transfer of control, only a transfer of ownership. In 2003, HDB's Building and Development Division was corporatised and renamed Surbana Corporation in 2005. When I interviewed Senior Advisor Tan Keng Joo Tony in 2004, he explained the importance of picking the correct moment to give up a public sector business and let the private sector do the job. In 2004 HDB Corp was acquired by Temasek Holdings and in 2011 CapitaLand acquired a 40 per cent stake in Surbana. Port of Singapore Authority (formed as a statutory board in 1964) was corporatised in 1997 and renamed PSA Corporation Limited. In the list of the world's 100 largest infrastructure TNCs (ranked by foreign assets in 2006), PSA International was ranked at 41st.

DBS Land was one government-linked development company in Singapore. Its parent company was DBS Bank (Singapore's development bank). DBS Land developed shopping malls (Plaza Singapura) and serviced residences (not just in Singapore, but also abroad, in Ho Chi Minh City, Jakarta, Manila and Shanghai). Another company, Pidemco, was a property investment subsidiary of Singapore Technologies. It developed residential, commercial and industrial properties in Singapore and overseas (for example in China and Myanmar) (Who's Who in Real Estate Redas Directory 1997). In 2000, DBS Land merged with Pidemco. The new company, CapitaLand, became the largest property company in Singapore and Southeast Asia, one of the 10 biggest developers in Asia, and Asia Pacific's largest serviced-apartment operator (Tan C 2000) (Figure 6.1). The merger disconnected DBS Bank's activities from the volatile property market (the relationship between the financial and real estate sectors is absolutely crucial, and is discussed in Chapter 8). I interviewed CapitaLand's Vice President (Research, CapitaLand) Boaz Boon in 2002 and asked him about the privileges of being a government-linked company. He stated that CapitaLand benefits from the good reputation of the government. He also told me that government-linked companies are quicker to adopt new technologies than family-run private companies. This interesting comment contradicts the assumption that small companies are more flexible in adapting to new markets than state-run companies. Small family-run companies can be traditional and conservative too.

Today, CapitaLand is a giant listed real estate company, comprising subsidiaries such as CapitaMalls Asia (shopping mall owner, developer

**Figure 6.1**   Interlace, CapitaLand Residential, architects: OMA and Ole Scheeren. Photo: Anne Haila.

and manager), CapitaMall Trust (Singapore's first real estate investment trust), Ascott Residence Trust and CapitaRetail China Trust (Singapore's first 'pure-play' China retail REIT). CapitaLand develops, invests, owns and manages homes, offices, malls, service residences and mixed developments. It operates in Singapore, China and Australia. It works in partnership with world-famous architects, submitting bids, for example, for the Marina Bay IR (integrated resort) (with Kohn Pedersen Fox as architect) and for Sentosa IR (with Frank Gehry as architect).

CapitaMalls is Asia's leading mall developer, owner and manager. It has developed a business model combining real estate investment, shopping mall development and retail (Figure 6.2). The increase in shopping and shopping malls is, of course, a universal trend; specific to Singapore, however, has been the development of a real estate business concept out of this trend. While in many cities shopping malls are still new and few, Singapore has already witnessed several shopping mall generations come and go, with new shopping malls being developed frequently to grab the attention of shoppers (who, in Singapore's shopping mall landscape, soon become professional shoppers). There are older shopping malls like Lucky Plaza (popular among Philippine maids) and new malls like, Vivo, Ion and 313@Somerset. Real estate professionals specialised

**Figure 6.2** ION shopping mall, Orchard Road, a joint venture between CapitaLand and Sun Hung Kai Properties (Hong Kong). Photo: Anne Haila.

in shopping malls talk about Singapore's professional and serious shoppers and try to find out their preferences in order to create the right ambiance for shopping.

### Industrial Landscape and the Jurong Town Corporation

Jurong Town Corporation (JTC), a statutory board developer providing industrial space and science parks, deserves a detailed discussion. Although there are several studies of public housing in Singapore and economic geographers have analysed Singapore's science parks, the character of JTC as a government provider of 'public' industrial space has been neglected. Even landscape studies ignore the highly visible feature of Singapore's environment – its industrial landscape. Before introducing JTC, I make a brief comparison between industrial policy in Hong Kong and Singapore.

Industrial policy has an important role in developmental states (Jomo 2000: 32). National industrial policies comprise macro- and micro-programmes, plus incentives such as subsidies, taxes, import quotas, tariffs, monetary policy and so on. In both Hong Kong and Singapore,

the government as landowner is an important actor in industrial policy and subject to lobbying by industrialists. In Hong Kong in the 1950s,
the nascent manufacturing sector lobbied the government to increase
industrial land supply. The government responded and planned a land
auction for industrial sites. Industrialists demanded a semi-closed land
auction, arguing that an open auction would make them compete and
pay overly high prices (Chiu 1992). Nonetheless, the government took
no heed of the industrialists' protestations or their threats to boycott
the auction, and arranged the first public auction in 1956 (Chiu 1992:
399–401). Stephen Chiu (1992: 403) suggested that one reason why the
state acted against industrialists' interests was because it had a more inti-
mate relationship with the financial–commercial bourgeoisie than with
industrialists.

Contrary to Hong Kong's weak industrial policy, Singapore's industrial policy has been notably interventionist. The government has developed science parks, invested in information and telecommunication
technologies, and provided industrial land. At the height of the IT
(information technology) boom, Singapore publicised the ICT21 Master Plan (Information and Communication Master Plan), with the goals
of making Singapore the world's leading IT city and its ICT (information, communication and technology) industries Singapore's key growth
sector. In his inaugural speech, the new Minister for Communication
and Information Technologies, Mr Yeo Cheow Tong, said: 'Our vision
is to transform Singapore into a dynamic and vibrant global ICT capital with a thriving and prosperous Net economy by the year 2010' (Tee
1999: 1).

Such visions and plans were not unusual, especially during the IT
boom days. What is unique to Singapore is that the government provides industrial space. The authority responsible for this is the Jurong
Town Corporation (JTC), a government development agency. Founded
in 1968, JTC is a statutory board (like HDB) with the power to acquire
properties and lease them. Its duties are to develop and manage industrial estates, and to provide facilities to enhance the operation of industries. It builds not just factories and industrial space, but also housing,
public gardens and sports facilities. The extension of the JTC's tasks
led to the foundation of new companies in 2001. Ascendas was established by merging JTC International (which took care of the JTC's overseas businesses) with Arcasia Land (which developed the JTC's science
parks). Ascendas develops business space for the information, communication and biomedical sciences sector, as well as constructing industrial,
science and business parks and their infrastructure.

Singapore's affordable housing is a much-vaunted attribute, but its
affordable industrial space is less well-known. The industrial space

provided by the JTC, Singapore's largest landlord, has helped make Singapore an excellent location for transnational corporations. Industrial space provided by the JTC is priced not in order to maximise rent, but by taking Singapore's competitiveness into account, and the JTC's industrial parks provide sophisticated facilities at ordinary factory prices (Yeow 1998). In its real estate policy the JTC has to pay attention to property cycles and, for example in 1997, the JTC froze factory land rents for one year to maintain Singapore's competitiveness as a manufacturing hub (Hadhi 1997). The JTC has developed a method of measuring land productivity (using the output as the measure of productivity) to ensure that every inch of Singapore's scarce industrial land is put to optimal use. Measuring land productivity in Singapore is as important as measuring labour productivity elsewhere. There are two key concepts in this process: *intensive use* of land and *productive use* of land (comparable to differential rent). A 1998 calculation showed that the most productive use of land was pharmaceutical space, followed by electronics, printing and publishing, apparel, and instrumentation equipment. The three least productive were petroleum, basic metals and wood product industries (JTC sets out to make ...1999).

The Jurong Town Corporation, in providing industrial space and calculating the most productive use of land, may be seen as acting like *property capital*. This term was introduced by Francois Lamarche (1976: 91), and refers to a form of capital that is separate from industrial, commercial and interest-bearing capital, and specialises in tailoring space in order to increase the efficiency of commercial, financial and administrative activities. In Singapore, the public provision of industrial space benefits not only private industries, but also contributes to the economy and generates revenue for the government from the use and sale of industrial land (fiscal rent). The more expensive the land, the more revenue the government gets. High prices, however, are not good for the lessees, and the government has to strike a balance between high revenues and affordable industrial space.

### Private and Government Companies Sharing the Market

Given that the development and real estate market is shared by private and government companies in Singapore (Table 6.1 lists ten large Singaporean development companies), and that land is leased in government land auctions, two important questions arise. First, how does the government treat private companies? Second, what is the relationship between government and private developers?

**Table 6.1** Singaporean development companies.

| Company incorporated/ listed | Industry | Projects | Subsidiary/affiliation | Revenue 2013 S$ million |
|---|---|---|---|---|
| CapitaLand public 2000 government link | Real estate Hospitality Residential Shopping malls | Sky Habitat Interlace The Star Vista ION Raffles | CapitaMalls Ascott 40% of Surbana | 3980 |
| Ascendas private government link | Master planning Developing Managing Industrial, business, science parks Office and retail space | Singapore Science Park | a-reit (ascendas reit) a-itrust (ascendas india trust) a-htrust (Ascendas hospitality trust) | 322 |
| Koh Brothers public 1994 | Construction Building Materials Real Estate Leisure & Hospitality | Punggol waterway Marina Barrage Choa Chu Kang HDB Housing Changi | | 371 |

| | | | | |
|---|---|---|---|---|
| Far East Organization Private Sino Group 1971 | Private residential Retail Office Hospitality Industrial | Lucky Plaza Far East Plaza Fullerton | Far East Orchard Far East Hospitality Trust Yeo Hiap Seng Sino Group (Hong Kong) Ng family | 3900 |
| Keppel Land public | Residential commercial | Marina Bay Financial Centre, Tower3 One Raffles Quay Reflections | Keppel Group | 1460 |
| City Developments 1963 public | Office Industrial Retail Residential Hotel development | Republic Plaza Sentosa Cove The Sail@Marina Bay | Millennium & Copthorne Hotels plc (M&C) City e-Solutions Limited (CES) Hong Leong & Kwek | 3162 |
| Wheelock Properties (Singapore) public 1981 | Luxury residences Retail | Scotts Square Wheelock Place | Wheelock and Company Limited | 117 |
| UOL Group public 1963 | Residential Commercial hospitality | Pan Pacific Singapore Park Royal Hotel Velocity@Novena Square | Pan Pacific Hotels Group Limited (PPHG) | 1059 |

(continued)

**Table 6.1** (*Continued*)

| Company incorporated/ listed | Industry | Projects | Subsidiary/affiliation | Revenue 2013 S$ million |
|---|---|---|---|---|
| Wing Tai Holdings public 1989 | Property development hospitality Lifestyle retail Hospitality management | The Tembusu Draycott 8 Belle Vue Residences | Wing Tai Asia Cheng Family | 1332 |
| Singapore Land public 1963 | Retail Residential | Singapore Land Tower Gateway SGX Centre | Parent UIC (United Industrial Corporation) | 610 (UIC) |

Sources: CapitaLand (www.capitaland.com)
Ascendas (www.ascendas.com)
Koh Brothers Group (www.kohbrothers.com)
Far East Organization (www.fareast.com.sg)
Keppel Land Limited (www.keppelland.com)
City Developments (www.cd.com.sg)
Wheelock Properties (www.wheelockproerties.com.sg)
UOL Group (www.uolgroup.com.sg)
Wing Tai Holdings (www.wingtaiasia.com.sg)
Singapore Land (www.singland.com.sg)

First, the government and private developers cooperate. The government expropriates land on behalf of private developers: it buys land, amalgamates sites and leases land to private developers for development. This cooperation between government and private companies is often perceived as a major benefit of the Singapore model. In its planning principles, URA states that it recognises the potential value of a development and works together with developers to realise it. For example, the project of conserving the landmark Fullerton building was given to private developers Far East and Sino Land (Figure 6.3). The private building industry also benefits 'from lower costs brought about by standardization, from the availability of building materials, and from a growing skilled labour force' (Latif 2009: 93) thanks to the HDB's building programme.

Second, private developers (like CDL and Far East) and government developers (the HDB, the JTC and CapitaLand) compete against each other. A frequently asked question is whether the government discriminates against private developers: do land auctions favour government developers and do government-linked companies receive monopoly privileges and favours?

**Figure 6.3** Fullerton, Conservation project, private developers Far East and Sino Land. Photo: Anne Haila.

From the private sector's point of view, the public sector might look like 'unequal public sector competition' (ARC Report 1977). In Singapore's case, where over 80 per cent of the population lives in public HDB housing, private sector complaints about unfair competition are understandable. In the housing development sector, the public developer (HDB) has dominated, and the private sector share of residential building has decreased from 67.1 per cent (in 1965) to 13.6 per cent (in 1976) (ARC Report 1977). The pre-eminent role of the public sector makes Singapore's housing market unique, but the housing question is itself unique too. As Singaporean real estate scholars Ho Chi Wing and Sim Loo Lee (1992: 5) commented: 'The issue in Singapore is not one of meeting the housing needs of people, but rather one of who can afford private housing. With about 10 per cent of the total units each year to be provided by the private sector, the private housing market in Singapore is highly sensitive to demand and government regulations.' This unusual scenario of a solved housing problem has made private housing into a marker of distinction, and owning landed property the Singaporean housing dream (discussed in Chapter 2). In an environment where more than 80 per cent of the population lives in public housing, living in private sector housing has become a way of distancing oneself from the masses. Singaporean sociologist Chua Beng Huat (1999: 218) wrote:

As the overwhelming majority of the population resides in public housing, it provides the background for break away from the masses to be readily noticed. Housing becomes the marker for differences in comparative consumption capabilities. For many in the emerging middle class, to be away from the public housing estate is more important than an economically unsound decision to purchase a substantially smaller flat in a 99-year lease condominium built by a private developer in a location poorly serviced by public transportation and other daily necessities.

In the office market, private companies have a greater presence than in the housing market. In the early 1980s, 78 per cent of all office space completions in Singapore's central area were developed by the private sector (Ho and Sim 1992: 53). The public sector (the Jurong Town Corporation, the Housing and Development Board, the National Productivity Board, and the Port of Singapore Authority) has developed projects beyond the central area, with suburban office developments in Jurong, Bukit Merah and Alexandra Road (Ho and Sim 1992: 56). Private developers have thus been at the receiving end of location differential rent.

The question of whether government land auctions treat private and government bidders equally has provoked concern in Singapore as well as in Hong Kong. There are rumours that the government favours big developers. Alice Poon (2005: 15) suggested that 'it is no secret that government policies have most of the time favoured large developers'. Chua (1997) argues that the Land Acquisition Act (1966), which empowered the Singapore government to acquire land on behalf of private developers, made it possible to amalgamate small lots for large private development projects, thus favouring large developers at the expense of small developers.

The government offers sites at auction to private and public developers alike, who compete against each other for the land offered. The explicitly stated policy of the URA has been to lease sites to the highest bidder. In order to find out whether government land auctions are fair (treating private and government bidders equally), I have employed two methods: looking at all tenders over a specific time period, and looking in more detail at individual auctions. Based on these studies, I conclude that: government land auctions are fair; the highest bidder gets the site; government companies are not favoured; and foreign companies are not discriminated against.

I examined tenders relating to 35 sites between the years 1997 and 2002,[2] finding proposals from both government-linked and private companies, and discovered that tenders were awarded to both private and government-linked companies. In addition, tenders were always won by the highest bidder. It is interesting to note that tenders and tendered prices are readily available public information.

The two individual auctions I scrutinised in more detail showed that private developers closely follow government auctions, and that the government does not discriminate against foreign developers.

The first case was an October 1998 auction in which the URA offered sites to bidders. Among those successful was government-owned Arcasia-Land. The prices of the leased sites were 60 per cent below previous peak levels. This upset developers who had earlier leased sites at higher prices. 'Hardest hit are Far East Organization, Boustead, Pidemco Land, MCL Land and individual investor Cheng Heng Tiu and partners who bought comparable sites in Tuas and Ubi in 1996 and early 1997 for between $2\frac{1}{2}$ and three times the prices of the recent tender' (Oon 1998). The reason for these lower prices, however, was not that the successful party was a government bidder, but the Asian financial crisis that had decreased the price level.

The second case is that of Suntec City (Figure 6.4) in the heart of Singapore's business district, comprising the International Convention and Exhibition Centre, offices and entertainment centre. At the

**Figure 6.4**  Suntec City. Photo: Anne Haila.

time of completion it was among the most spectacular constructions in
Singapore. It was developed by a Hong Kong group that had entered
and won the bidding competition. The Urban Redevelopment Authority
had selected the plot of land for tender in December 1995. The tender
for the project was announced in 1996; at that time it was Singapore's
largest private development project. There were three bids. The highest bid of S$200.9 million was from Suntec City Development, with I.M.
Pei as architect and backed by tycoons including Li Ka-shing, Cheng
Yu-tung and Lee Shau-kee. The second bid of S$175 million was from a
group comprising Kuok (Singapore), Shangri-La Hotel and UOL Investment Holding, using Japanese architect Nikken Sekkei and Singaporean
architects. The third bid of S$120.9 million was from Sino International
Real Estate Agency, part of Far East, belonging to Singapore's property
tycoon Mr Ng Teng Fong, with John Portman as architect (Wee 1988).
The winning bidder was Suntec, a foreign firm.

### Transnational Property Companies

One of the paradoxes in Singapore and Hong Kong is that the development companies of these city-states – where land is scarce and in
public landownership – are global players. A list of the world's 100 largest

companies in 1993 (*World Investment Report* 1995) showed that all these 100 companies were based in developed countries. Their fields of industry were oil, electronics and automobiles. There were no property or development companies among the largest 100 TNCs in the world. A list of the world's top 100 non-financial TNCs (ranked by foreign assets) in 2006 also featured no real estate companies (*World Investment Report 2008*). Looking at a 1993 list of the 100 largest companies in the developing world, several are involved in development and property, like Hutchison Whampoa (2nd largest, Hong Kong), New World Development (13th largest, Hong Kong), CITIC Pacific (19th largest, Hong Kong), Keppel Corporation (14th largest, Singapore) and CDL Hotels International (41st largest, Hong Kong). Singapore and Hong Kong are well represented among these transnational property and development companies. A 2006 list of the top non-financial TNCs from developing countries (ranked by foreign assets) (*World Investment Report* 2008) has Hutchison Whampoa in first place (its industry activity is classified as diversified). New World Development was 22nd and City Developments 58th. CapitaLand (with its industry activity classified simply as real estate) was ranked 17th.

The real estate literature informs us that development companies tend to be local companies. Legal and planning systems, difficulties associated with buying land, and restrictions on foreign ownership, make entry into new markets difficult and act as barriers to foreign companies. Development companies from Singapore and Hong Kong, however, are not only local but also global players. Singapore's Keppel Land has undertaken projects in Manila, Hanoi, Ho Chi Minh City, Mandalay, Suzhou, Shanghai, Jakarta, Bintan, Yogyakarta and Manadao (Keppel Land Annual Report 1994). Singaporean DBS Land has had projects in Beijing, Shanghai, Suzhou, Jakarta, Johor, Selangor, Penang, Bangkok and Ho Chi Minh City (DBS Annual Report 1994). Hong Kong company Sun Hung Kai had offices in Thailand, the Philippines, Singapore, London and New York in 1998 (Hoenig Guide to the Companies of Hong Kong 1998). CapitaLand conducts business in China, Australia, Japan, the Philippines, India, Malaysia, Thailand, Vietnam, the Middle East, Africa, Europe, Russia and Kazakhstan. CapitaMall Asia develops, owns and manages 99 shopping malls in 51 cities.

With its commitment to regionalisation programmes, the Singaporean government has encouraged and assisted Singaporean companies to expand overseas. In the late 1980s, the Economic Development Board (EDB) began to facilitate outward foreign direct investment (FDI). A program entitled Regionalisation 2000 (introduced in 1992) encouraged Singaporean firms to do business abroad. EDB offered assistance analysing foreign market potential, matching projects, providing support for loans, and abolishing some taxes on overseas earnings (*World Investment Report 1995*: 34, 335). One example of a government-supported project is the sub-regional economic zone on the Indonesian island of Batam. Batamindo Industrial Park is jointly owned by Indonesia's Salim Group, Singapore Technologies Industrial Corporation (STIC) and Jurong Environmental Engineering (JEE) (Grundy-Warr et al. 1999). Another example of such a project, this time in China, is Raffles Square in Shanghai. It was led by DBS Land, with partners including OPH Realty, Singavest Investments (a Government of Singapore Incorporation Subsidiary) and Hong Lim Investment (a Temasek Holdings subsidiary) (Teh 1998).

The government of Singapore has exported its public housing concept. In the Suzhou Industrial Park (jointly developed by Singapore and Chinese authorities), Shanghai developer Yang Junde built housing modelled on Singapore's HDB flats, subsidised by the Chinese government and financed using a provident fund scheme modelled on Singapore's CPF (Chua L H 1997). Surbana Corporation (the corporatised entity of HDB) exports HDB's housing and development knowledge. Surbana's business includes township development, building and infrastructure consulting and fund management. Its vision has been to become a premium global buildings and infrastructure provider, shaping townships and cities worldwide. Having gained experience in developing new towns in Singapore, Surbana outgrew the city's market and looked abroad. It has undertaken projects in 90 cities across 26 countries: middle-class housing and townships in China, luxurious hotels in the Middle East, and other projects in India and Vietnam. Surbana offers master planning and urban design, builds infrastructure, and develops residential, commercial and industrial areas. Among its trophy buildings projects are Al Raha Beach Hotel and the Grand Corniche Hotel, both in Abu Dhabi.[3] In 2008, the Surbana Urban Planning Group, together with Singapore Cooperation Enterprise (formed by the Ministry of Trade and Industry and the Ministry of Foreign Affairs to export Singapore's expertise), won a contract to develop a detailed master plan for the Republic of Rwanda's Kigali City (Singapore Cooperation Enterprise News Release 15 September 2008).

### Capricious Landlords and Mean Developers: Absolute Rent

Compared to companies that produce commodities, companies that produce the built environment are complex entities. Their fields of business vary. Property and development companies develop properties, invest in properties and own, trade and manage properties. Their most important factor of production is land, and fluctuations in land values affect their operations and viability. Development companies differ among different cultures. New York is known for developers like Donald Trump and Larry Silverstein. In the United Kingdom, institutional investors are pre-eminent. Japan is home to conglomerates like Mitsubishi, Mitsui and Nomura that have their own real estate departments. In Finland, the state's real estate companies seek to maximise rent returns. In Hong Kong, companies invest in property as a sideline, and a distinct feature of Singapore is its government-linked development companies. An important reason explaining such cultural differences is the landownership and planning system, and particularly who owns development rights.

Landed property can turn an industrialist into a developer, as in the case of Japan's Shigeru Kobayashi. After the bankruptcy of his shipping business, he discovered that the company's land had become very valuable in Tokyo's postwar redevelopment market. Companies have been bought and sold solely to acquire their land. How developers obtain land is an important issue for development companies. Buying and leasing land can involve long and complicated negotiation. Chapter 2 discussed the treaty Raffles agreed with the local chieftain of Johor to cede Singapore to the East India Company. The following cession treaties from United States history further illustrate the complexity of land acquisitions.

In Ohio, the 1789 Treaty of Fort Harmar allowed the Wyandot, Delaware, Ottawa, Chippewa, Potawatomi and Sauk Indians to hunt on the territory they ceded, but limited their commercial dealings. The Great Chickasaw Cession negotiated by Andrew Jackson in 1818 promised $300,000 to the Chickasaw nation for relinquishing all lands north of Mississippi. Jackson stipulated that the treaty minutes be kept secret, to avoid disclosing the substantial cash payments and other favours granted to Chickasaw negotiators. In 1835, 20 Cherokees signed the treaty of the New Echota that transferred all tribal lands east of the Mississippi River in exchange for $5 million (all members of the Cherokee Nation would move to Indian Territory by 1837). In New Mexico in 1853, the treaty of Fort Atkinson allowed the US to develop roads, depots and military posts on tribal land. In 1855, Chief Lame Bull and other Native leaders agreed to maintain peace with the government and to allow the construction of roads, telegraph lines and military posts. The treaty of Little Arkansas River in 1865 provided allotments of land to the survivors of the Sand Creek Massacre, but prohibited Indians from leaving their reservation without the written consent of a government agent.[4]

These treaties show that what had been negotiated was not just a land deal, but a bundle of rights – hunting rights, the right to develop roads, telegraph lines and military posts – and obligations restricting commercial trade or passage from the territory. The medium of exchange was sometimes money, sometimes an agreement to maintain peace. Modern real estate deals are no less complicated than the early treaties in the US or Singapore, and take substantial time to negotiate. An example is the sale of the Empire State Building in New York in 1961, as recounted by Shachtman (1991: 219–221). Larry Wien, partner of Harry Helmsley, a major real estate owner, concocted a complicated sale-and-leaseback scheme. An investment syndicate would buy the building from the Crowns of Chicago (who owned the building) for $65 million and the land from Prudential (which owned the land) for $17 million. $46 million would be loaned by Prudential. Then the syndicate would sell everything to Prudential for $29 million. Prudential would then lease the building back to Helmsley and Wien for four successive terms of 21 years at an annual charge of $3.2 million. That would give Prudential a 7% return on its income (previously it was obtaining 6%). Closing the deal at Prudential's corporate headquarters in Newark involved 150 people. The signing of documents took more than two hours. One lease alone (among many) was 400 pages long.

Purchasing land demands time and money: transaction costs (negotiating the price of land and the bundle of rights and obligations) can be high. Additionally, the landowner (the seller in the land deal) is not necessarily a rational economic partner. Land is not just a commodity but can also give name and fame, and an owner may be sentimentally attached to his land (discussed in Chapter 2). Researchers on landowners and their behaviour have, therefore, taken non-rational behaviour into account, differentiating between various types of landowners. Traditional landowners (the Church, aristocracy, gentry, the Crown estates), industrial entrepreneurs (industrialists, manufacturers, farmers, retailers) and financial institutions (banks, property companies, investment funds) (Massey and Catalano 1978) all have different motives and modes of behaviour. Landowners may be emotionally attached to their property and demand a price that differs substantially from the buyer's price. Furthermore, landowners are not necessarily motivated by monetary revenue from land at all; their behaviour can be affected by subjective motives (Denman 1957), they can make decisions by feel or stomach (Feagin 1987), follow a herd instinct (Fainstein 1994), share common beliefs (or *Vermeinungsmonopol*, as used by von Nell-Breuning 1965) or believe that prices can only keep rising (Akerlof and Shiller 2009).

Capricious landlords are unpredictable business partners, and through their monopoly position they can restrict the supply of land, wait for land prices to go up and capture the increased price (absolute rent). Urban development is awash with stories of landlords hindering development. One of the most famous 'withholder' cases of recent years was in Chongqing, China, where the Wu family refused to move from their home, whereas all their neighbours accepted compensation for redevelopment and left, thus vacating the land. The developers dug around the family's house, leaving it on a small site surrounded by a deep pit. In China such houses are called 'nail houses', because they are nailed to the ground by their owners' stubbornness.

Compared to complicated cession treatises, arcane real estate deals like the Empire State Building sale, and negotiations with stubborn landlords emotionally attached to their land, Singapore's land auctions and leases are simple and transparent. Development companies obtain land at government land auctions, there is no need to hoard land, lease contracts define the terms of development and the state coordinates the uses and users. Government appropriates land on behalf of developers and amalgamates small sites. Thus, the state significantly lowers the transaction costs for the developer. It is in the private property market system where transaction costs are highest. This highlights the illogical reasoning of property rights theory: advocating the market system and criticising state intervention on the one hand, and demanding minimisation of transaction costs on the other. Through the state's landownership and land auctions, the government of Singapore creates the conditions for companies to develop and compete to obtain profit, not absolute rent.[5] Such conditions still turn out to be profitable for development companies.

In addition to land, development companies need labour.[6] The construction industry is a labour-intensive industry and some of its problems are due to this. The use of informal, low paid, immigrant and non-unionised labour is one reason for the poor reputation of the construction industry. In the European Union, freedom of movement of labour means that the Polish plumber (and in Finland the Estonian construction worker), working as informal and low-paid labour, has become a well-known phenomenon. Singapore (where development companies exclusively develop, using contractors for building) is not without problems relating to subcontracting low-paid labour. The construction industry, a labour-intensive sector demanding technical skills and a low-paid labour force, is effectively a collection of sub-industries. The Directory of Registered Contractors (2001), issued by the Building and Construction Authority (BCA) that regulates Singapore's building and construction industry) listed about 10,000 registered firms. Although there were some foreign contracting firms (from Japan and Korea), the majority of firms were local. Only a few were public companies and some were family firms. Over 70 per cent of site workers were foreigners. In the nineteenth century, Indian convicts were used as free labour (Beamish and Ferguson 1989: 11). Today, pick-up trucks transporting Sri Lankan

construction workers are a familiar sight in Singapore, and the Tamil language widely heard in Little India every Sunday, when migrant labourers
meet up with each other.

The use of informal labour is one reason for developers' poor reputation. Michael Ball (1988: 1) begins his book *Rebuilding Construction*
by stating that 'of all industries in Britain, construction has one of
the worst public images'. Developers are represented as immoral (like
Leona Helmsley, the fabulously rich New York real estate developer and
hotel operator nicknamed 'the Queen of Mean' (Harrington 2007)), or
likened to the Devil at a Halloween party, as Hong Kong's Li Ka-shing was
by Thomas Lau Kwok-fai (Wan 2010). Developers and related organisations are well aware of their industry's murky reputation and have established ethical rules, like NAREB's (National Association of Real Estate
Boards) Realtor's Code of Ethics in the United States (Weiss 1987: 24).
In addition to the use of informal labour, another reason for the development industry's poor reputation is land speculation. At the Urban
Land Institute's Fall 2000 meeting in Chicago, one topic debated was
speculation. Some participants claimed that the US real estate sector
had become more 'disciplined', by which they meant that there were
fewer speculative projects and less speculative money than previously.
Sceptics at the meeting challenged these assumptions about a suppos-
edly 'healthier' business, suggesting that all the speculative money had
simply moved into Internet companies. Soon after, the dotcom bubble
burst and speculative money flowed back into real estate. Defining speculation, however, is not a simple issue.

## Land Without Speculation

In neoclassical economic theory, speculation is not a problem.
Economists look at speculation from the point of view of market equilibrium and even regard speculation as good. Milton Friedman (1953:
175) wrote: 'People who argue that speculation is generally destabilizing seldom realize that this is largely equivalent to saying that speculators lose money, since speculation can be destabilizing in general only
if speculators on the average sell when the currency is low in price and
buy when it is high.' Writing about land markets, Walters (1974) suggested that speculators who buy when the price is low and sell when the
price is high are doing a 'socially useful' job of reducing swings in price
levels and strengthening the element of stability. Real estate economists
Jaffe and Sirmans (1986: 25) think that 'it is difficult if not impossible
to distinguish between investors and speculators'.

From the point of view of urban development and the built environment, land speculation presents a problem. Modernist architects

and the garden city movement criticised land speculation for its harmful effects. In 1928, the CIAM (Congres Internationaux d'Architecture Moderne) declared that the chaotic division of land resulting from speculation must be outlawed. In Ebenezer Howard's garden city ideal, land was to be bought by the community before planning and development began. Land was then to be leased to residents and businesses, and the revenue used for the public good. Unfortunately, this progressive anti-speculation legacy of the early modernists and garden city builders was forgotten; their message was understood to relate to physical form, rather than the social and economic aspects of urban development. Peter Ambrose (1986: 262) commented on this amnesia and ascribed the shortcomings of planning to the concern with built form instead of production process.

Continuing the progressive legacy of modern architects and garden city builders is to analyse the harmful effects of land speculation and policy measures to prevent land speculation. Land speculators in withholding use of land delay development. This raises the question of the optimal timing of development debated by land economists. Richard Ely (1920) claimed that land speculation is a socially valuable activity, because it keeps land undeveloped until it is the most efficient time to develop it. Nicolaus Tideman (2004) denied this, and referred to US cities with one- and-two-storey buildings within a block of skyscrapers: obviously the optimal time of development had not been identified by their owners. Tideman further argued that when the future value of land is uncertain, the person bidding the most for it makes the greatest upward error in estimating its value and believes that its value will rise. Therefore, he is disinclined to invest in it now and so keeps land out of production. Referring to Henry George's theory of land speculation and the modern theory of the winner's curse[7] (Milgrom and Weber 1982), Tideman concluded that shifting the burden of taxation from production and exchange to land rent decreases the selling price of land and speculation (see Chapter 4).

Another harmful effect of land speculation is that it inflates prices. Why are housing prices high? Economists would say because of too little supply. Town planners are often blamed for increasing housing prices, because they zone far too little residential land and create a shortage of supply leading to high land prices. There is a fallacy in this reasoning. As Graham Hallett (1979: 248) remarks: 'House prices determine land prices, not *vice versa*.' This was demonstrated by Ricardo in his rent theory. Rent is a residual and is paid after the costs of other factors of production are paid; prices are not high because a rent is paid, but a rent is paid because prices are high. 'Corn is not high because a rent is paid, but a rent is paid because corn is high', as Ricardo wrote (Ricardo [1817] 1974: 38). If a builder buys an expensive piece of land, the land price is his cost and he will factor it into the price of housing. In this case too, house prices are not high because rent is paid, but rents are high because a builder pays a high price for land.

The question then becomes: who is selling the land to the builder? Empirical studies show that speculators often step in, buy raw land, subdivide it, sell sites to builders and make a quick profit. Those who benefit from pre-construction value increases are not the original landowners or developers, but middlemen who buy land cheaply from the original owner and sell it on at a higher price to developers. In their Boston study, Edel, Sclar and Luria (1984) observed that ownership of land often changed just before subdivision. Professional landlords owning ten or more units of housing were selling land to developers. In other words, those who receive land rent and benefit from value increases are not the original landowners or the community or developers, but professional speculators. 'Much of the area had passed into the hands of outside landowners before becoming ripe for revitalization', commented Edel, Sclar and Luria in the case of Boston (Edel et al. 1984: 86). This, then, raises the question of how land rent is divided.

One old debate concerns the difference between building rent and land rent. Adam Smith ([1776] 1904: V.2.68) long ago distinguished building rent from ground rent. The building rent in Smith's theory was the profit of the capital expended in building the house, and 'whatever part of the whole rent of a house is over and above what is sufficient for affording this reasonable profit naturally goes to the ground rent'. More recently, Michael Ball (1985a: 518) argued that 'for most existing buildings, with the exception of those on leaseholds (where ground rents and fines on improvements or changes of use have to be paid to the landowner) ... rent is paid for the use of the building so it is a payment to a building owner not a landowner'. Therefore, Ball claimed, 'many urban structures pay no land rent at all' (Ball 1985a). Eric Clark (1987: 266) criticised Ball for confusing building rent with land rent, arguing that the differentiation between building rent and land rent is important because it stresses – citing Marx in Capital 3 – that 'it is ground rent and not the houses themselves that forms the real objective of speculative building' (Marx [1894] 1981: 909).

Developers earn both profit and rent because, as Michael Ball (1988: 35) identified, developers have a dual role as producers and merchants. As producers, they seek profit and invest in and improve the land. As merchants, developers have an interest in the exchange value of their property, and are tempted to speculate with the asset value of land. Speculation can bring them absolute rent, but hoarding a large land bank may cause them harm.

Why have development companies in Singapore and Hong Kong succeeded in making fortunes for their owners and becoming global players? Is it because of political rent-seeking and lobbying to obtain monopoly privileges and manipulated rent? Or have difficulties in political rent-seeking obliged them to look abroad and made them more productive? What explains their survival in cities where the land is in state ownership, and where there is no fringe or rural raw land to hoard? There are four reasons.

First, if land rent is captured by the government, developers have less incentive to speculate with land values. When I interviewed the Vice President of CapitaLand Research and asked him about the company's profits, he told me that 'they get building rent and the government gets land rent'. The reluctance of development companies in the West to build social housing (on public land) refers to the same point: land speculation is where they get their fattest profits. In Singapore, the URA restricts the sale of buildings before completion and thus prevents speculation on uncompleted properties.

Second, although land banks guarantee future opportunities for development companies, they can also be a burden. Land banks tie up developers' capital, and are vulnerable to cycles and fluctuations in asset prices. Land can become a liability rather than an asset for a developer if the market situation or interest rates change. Keeping land vacant while awaiting development is costly, and developers cover these costs by factoring them into the prices they charge when they come to sell the houses they have built. Developers' assets can also sink into negative equity when interest rates rise and property prices go down. In Helsinki during the 1990s recession, the land banks built up by Finnish construction companies reduced in value and became a burden rather than an asset: Finland's construction companies became easy acquisition targets for Swedish companies. Development companies in Singapore obtaining their land at auction for immediate construction are spared having to own vacant land, have none of the costs incurred by keeping land vacant, and are less affected by cycles and fluctuations in property prices.

Third, a land regime with public landownership and fair land auctions makes developers compete and seek their profit from the construction business, not from land rent. When 'Mr HDB', Lim Kin San, took office he discovered that its predecessor, SIT, used only four contractors. In his biographical notes (cited in Latif 2009: 68), he states: 'The businessman will tell you that if only four chaps have got the power to tender, they will very soon form a ring and see that the prices go high. We broke that and said "nothing doing". We will allow everyone who thinks that he can build for us to tender.' In Singapore, the state (following the liberal traditions of the former colonial masters) does not interfere by means of subsidies in the private market. 'If a project is not viable, then the developer should not expect support from public funds but find other solutions' (Dale 1999: xi). Less competitive companies fall by the wayside, and the government that captures land rent makes developers compete by creating a disincentive to speculate on land values. Government land auctions also test market sentiments (and sometimes they fail because developers do not bid). For a government, this solves the Hayekian problem of how planners know what to plan.

The fourth reason concerns available information and the transparency of real estate markets. Buyers and sellers may wish to keep prices and contracts secret, as exemplified by US President Jackson with the confidential minutes of the Great Chickasaw Cession, or industrialists in 1950s Hong Kong who demanded a semi-closed land auction for industrial sites (arguing that an open auction would make them compete and pay overly high prices). The modern global real estate industry is concerned about the transparency of real estate markets, and factors this in when calculating 'country risk'. Singapore's real estate market is regarded by real estate investors as low-risk compared to Thailand, the Philippines and Indonesia, which are perceived as high-risk due to lack of transparency (Adis 2009a: 40). A transparent real estate market weakens the monopoly of landowners, preventing them from charging absolute and monopoly rent.

In this globalised world, the ability to invest using financial instruments and across borders affects investment in land. Land speculation is not simply about buying low and selling high or predicting future profits. Both John Maynard Keynes – who, in *The General Theory of Employment, Interest and Money* (1935), distinguished between speculators forecasting the psychology of the market, and enterprises forecasting the prospective yield of assets – and Hyman Minsky (1986: 347) – who distinguished between speculators making money through appreciation in the value of their assets, and enterprises making money from yield – focused attention on asset values and yields affected by the interest rate. Interest and money, in addition to the interdependence of markets, affect land prices, opportunities to speculate and development companies' profitability. The two following chapters examine these issues.

## Notes

1   UNMO (United Malays National Organization), established in 1946, is the most important political party in Malaysia (Leifer 1995: 242).
2   Source: URA web pages.
3   Surbana home page 7 May 2010.

4   The information on these treaties was gathered at the National Museum of the American Indian, Washington DC, 24 November 2009.
5   In the debate concerning land rent in socialism (i.e. the state as an owner of land), it was argued that in the Soviet Union differential rent existed whereas absolute rent did not (Smirnow and Winogradow 1973).
6   One debate during the 1970s concerned absolute rent and the assumed backwards nature of the construction industry. Following Marx, it was argued that because of lack of competition, the production technologies in the construction industry were less developed compared to the average across all industries and therefore the construction industry produces more surplus (because of using more labour) that is captured as absolute rent (Frank and Joares 1973).
7   The winner's curse is the danger that the winner of a bidding competition will lose money because he has underestimated his costs.

# 7

# Diversification of a Real Estate Portfolio
## The World is Singapore's Hinterland

*Singapore has got to re-position itself in this world.* (Minister Mentor Lee
Kuan Yew in Parliament in 2005)[1]

Globalisation was one of the hottest topics in social sciences at the turn
of the millennium. Economists studied foreign investment, sociologists
analysed the transnational class, communications scholars focused on
the Internet, and cultural studies investigated the homogenisation
of cultures. Immanuel Wallerstein's world system theory, Roland
Robertson's analysis of the globalisation of ideas and Manuel Castells'
three-volume study *The Information Age* are just a few examples of
globalisation studies. In urban studies, John Friedmann and Goetz
Wolff (Friedmann and Wolff 1982) called for research on world cities
and launched a boom in global city studies. Much of the global city
research was descriptive and sought to produce rankings of cities in
the global hierarchy. The concept of the global city introduced by
Sassen (1991) was broad – chaotic even, to use Andrew Sayer's concept
(Sayer 1992: 138) – lumping together unrelated features. Global cities
have been understood as strategic places, control centres, nodes in
networks and having a function in the world economy. Critics of
global city research have accused global city scholars of legitimising
and advocating economic globalisation (Smith 2001), and in so doing
eclipsing ordinary cities (Robinson 2002, 2006).

*Urban Land Rent: Singapore as a Property State*, First Edition. Anne Haila.
© 2016 John Wiley & Sons, Ltd. Published 2016 by John Wiley & Sons, Ltd.

Globalisation was studied either by focusing on places (global cities, offshore financial centres and economic zones, see Sassen 1994) or on networks (markets and technologies connecting places). I combine these approaches, and analyse Singapore together with the investment flows into it and from it. I look at Singapore as a hub expanding its boundaries across the world and attracting investment from abroad. The world is Singapore's hinterland and extensive margin. Another topic I add to the globalisation studies mix is real estate, which has been largely neglected by global city scholars.

Before the economic rise of the smaller Asian tigers (Singapore, Hong Kong, Korea and Taiwan), the surge in Japanese economic power during the 1980s created anxiety in the Western world. An important reason for this concern was Japan's real estate investments. The Japanese invested in real estate markets abroad because of low interest rates in Japan, Japanese banks' willingness to grant low-cost loans, the appreciation of the yen, and the scarcity and high price of land in Japan. In the late-1980s Los Angeles, for example, the Japanese owned 16 out of the 31 foreign-owned buildings in the downtown area. One Japanese real estate company I interviewed in 1993 estimated that the Japanese owned 20 per cent of the office space in downtown Los Angeles (and 40 per cent of the first-class office space). Japanese investment created tensions, far more so than earlier investments by the British, Dutch and Canadians. Douglas Frantz and Catherine Collins (1989) entitled their book on the subject *Selling Out: How we are letting Japan buy our land, our industries, our financial institutions and our future*. Newspapers published stories on the dangers of Japanese investment. Headlines like 'Great Japanese Land Rush' (Frantz 1989) and 'Could Japanese Realty Holdings Hurt U.S.?' (Collins 1989) prompted fears that Japanese ownership was creating dependence upon Tokyo and 'a loss of sovereignty'. This anxiety aroused by the Japanese points not only to sentiments attached to landownership but also racial discrimination in the real estate market.

Some countries restrict foreign ownership of land. In Indonesia, Malaysia and Thailand, foreigners cannot buy land. In Singapore, the government has since 1973 imposed restrictions on foreign ownership of private residential property in Singapore and sought to strike a balance between giving Singaporeans a stake in the country by being able to buy and own residential properties at affordable prices, while attracting foreign talent and giving foreigners a chance to purchase properties for their occupation. The government attracts foreign investment into Singapore, as well as encouraging overseas investment among Singaporean firms and indeed investing abroad itself. Striking a balance between the benefits of an open real estate market and the potentially harmful effects of foreign investment inflows is a difficult task. While on the one hand an open real estate market brings investment and maintains Singapore's credibility as a financial centre, on the other hand asset inflation provoked by foreign investment necessitates regulation. The next chapter analyses regulation, whereas this chapter looks at overseas investments by Singaporean companies and individuals, and the Singaporean government's overseas investment corporations. I ask the following questions. What has the government done in order to facilitate global real estate flows? Who invests in Singaporean properties? Who are the Singaporeans investing in properties abroad? To answer these, I investigate the rules and institutions of Singapore's real estate market, and discuss property investors' motives.

The global reach of Singapore numbering just five million people is astonishing. Among its distinctive features are its sovereign wealth funds (SWFs) that invest in real estate globally and real estate investment trusts (REITs) owned by shareholders around the world. Singapore's government investment corporation owns real estate in Paris, London and even in the small Finnish city of Espoo, and its REITs own shopping malls in China and industrial parks in India. SWFs and REITs are new kind of real estate investors interested in the yield rather than trophy buildings. Whereas in the 1990s businesses such as banks would probably own their premises and corporations their headquarter premises, since the 2000s buildings are owned by REITs and display the logo of the proprietor REIT on their facades, the same logo in each global city.

### Safe Haven for Global Real Estate Flows

The government in Singapore has facilitated the flow of real estate investments into and out of Singapore. It has drawn up strategic programmes to define Singapore's position in the global marketplace, refashioned Singapore's built environment into an attractive environment for the transnational business elite, and passed laws making Singapore a reliable investment environment and its real estate more liquid.

The visioning of Singapore's future began with Sir Thomas Stamford Raffles. Since the 1960s, the pace at which new visions have been introduced has increased. There have been strategies to develop Singapore as a financial city, the Renaissance City, Tropical City of Excellence, an information city, and the Global City for Arts, to mention just a few. Derek da Cunha (2010: 7) commented on this constant redrawing of new visions: 'The most curious thing about these aspirational objectives is that every time Singapore has "remade" itself, it has assumed a new identity without actually discarding its previous identities.'

The objective to become a global city was established back in the early 1970s, before urban scholars began talking about global cities. Singapore's foreign minister, S. Rajaratnam, suggested developing Singapore as a global city. Referring to Arnold Toynbee's book *Cities on the Move* (in which Toynbee wrote about a new type of city, Ecumenopolis), Rajaratnam commented in 1972 on the tragedy of separation between Singapore and Malaysia, and envisioned the future of Singapore:

> times are changing and there will be less and less demand for the traditional type of entrepot services Singapore has rendered for well over a century. Its role as the trading city of Southeast Asia, the market place of the region, will become less and less important. This is because it is transforming itself into a new kind of city – the Global City ... If we view Singapore's future not as a regional city but as a Global City then the smallness of Singapore, the absence of a hinterland, or raw materials and a large domestic market are not fatal or insurmountable handicaps ... because for a Global City the world is its hinterland. (Rajaratnam 1972, in Kwa 2007: 229–232)

Before Rajaratnam, Singapore's first Finance Minister Goh Keng Swee had suggested that cities are not the creations of their hinterland, but quite the opposite; they create their hinterlands (Kwa 2007: 171), and paradoxically the lack of a hinterland turned out to be an advantage. With no need to subsidise underdeveloped regions and redistribute surplus produced at the centre, the government has been able to concentrate its efforts on developing the stimulus of urban agglomeration, called sometimes 'Jane Jacobs externalities' (Jacobs 1969; Henderson 1994; Soja 2010). Further, as a city-state with closely guarded borders, Singapore has been able to control its in-migration. As Chua Beng Huat (Chua 1996: 208) noted: 'the severing of the rural hinterland of Peninsular Malaya from the island nation of Singapore turned out to be a blessing in disguise. It meant the elimination of all the problems attached to rural-urban migration, faced by cities in developing nations.'

Some of these strategic visions have been implemented as urban renewal projects. The government invested more than S$4.5 billion developing Marina Bay, hoping it would become a magnet for global investors seeking premium office space in a prime location (Figure 7.1). URA town planners Ching Tuan Yee and Benjamin Ng compared this flagship project to Canary Wharf in London and Pudong in Shanghai (Ching and Ng 2008). Right in the city centre, Marina Bay is a mixed-use project comprising housing, offices, shops, hotels, recreational facilities and public space. It was advertised as a tropical living environment sited among lush greenery, a bustling global business hub and indeed

**Figure 7.1**   Marina Bay Sands, architect Moshe Safdie, developer Las Vegas Sands, three skyscrapers topped by a ship-form construction. Photo: Anne Haila.

a lifestyle, with a kaleidoscope of entertainment and leisure choices. Its 70-storey Sail@Marina Bay residential tower is 245 metres high. A casino, two theatres, two floating crystal pavilions, its ArtScience Museum, distinctive designed gardens and mist sprayed into the air to cool the tropical temperatures make a futuristic environment.

Strategic programmes have consolidated efforts to make Singapore a world-renowned destination and urban development projects have made Singapore a pleasant living environment for expatriates, but the main factor making Singapore attractive for real estate investment has been rule of law in its real estate market. Commercial and public housing developments are kept separate and the government has passed legislation to make real estate a liquid investment object and its real estate market open, transparent and safe for foreign investors and developers. There are no laws like the Bumiputera[2] laws in neighbouring Malaysia, which discriminate against some investor groups and favour others. Unlike many other countries, there are hardly any restrictions on foreign investment (Khublall 1988). Foreigners can purchase land and landed properties with government approval, and apartments in buildings without any need for approval.

Although the land is owned by the government and the majority of the population live in public housing, commercial properties are in private ownership and the ideological climate of investment is liberal. As Chua Beng Huat (1997: 133) commented, the assurance given by the 'Minister of National Development in 1970 that the government would not nationalize any of the commercial properties developed by corporate capital ... was necessary to attract foreign capital into a city-state whose political and economic viability was then very much doubted by all concerned, and not least by the government itself.' That was important for a city-state that 'identified foreign investment as the engine of its economic growth' (Chua 1997). Singapore has used its stable government and political climate to attract investment and foreign companies. As Lee Kuan Yew (2011: 62) recalls: 'China was in the mad throes of Mao's Cultural Revolution. Most investors thought Taiwan and Hong Kong too close to China and headed for Singapore. We welcomed everyone, but when we found a big investor with potential for growth, we went out of our way to help it get started.'

Like Singapore, Hong Kong has benefitted from its legally secure and liberal business environment, attracting investment especially from China. Since the inauguration of the Open Door policy, Chinese money has flown from China into Hong Kong. Barry Naughton (1999) coined the phrase 'property rights arbitrage' to describe the benefits that Hong Kong (with its secure and transparent system of property rights) enjoys compared to China (with its vague and uncertain property rights regime). 'PRC residents come to Hong Kong in a steady stream, looking for opportunities to transform assets over which they have uncertain claim into secure and liquid assets' (Naughton 1999: 86).

Singapore benefits from its secure and transparent property rights regime that has made it a safe haven for global real estate investment. Singapore combines a predictable legal environment with very few restrictions. A real estate investor with experience in Australian and European markets described the Singaporean property market to me by saying that its system is 'just simple'. There are no complicated obligations inherited from the feudal past; no privileged religious land. The two sets of laws that have made real estate investments in Singapore easy and simple are the Land Titles (Strata) Act and the REITs regulations. Introduced in 1967, the Land Titles (Strata) Act has made it possible to own parts of real estate, giving owners a share in land and making it easier for purchasers to secure loans from financial institutions (Motha and Yuen 1999: 95–100). Real estate investment trusts have made real estate more liquid, and also made it possible for small investors to invest in real estate.

**Real Estate Investment Trusts**

A real estate investment trust is a company that owns and manages real estate (offices, retail, industrial, hospitality, healthcare and residential property) and pays dividends to its shareholders. In Singapore, REITs are regulated by the Monetary Authority of Singapore (MAS), which is Singapore's central bank. MAS requires that REITs pay out 90 per cent of their profits as dividends and restricts gearing (the ratio of debt to total property value). MAS requires that REITs have their properties valued every year by a professional valuer. The REIT investors also get tax benefits compared to direct investors in property, who pay property tax and tax on rental income. The dividends from REITs are tax-exempt, and REITs do not pay any corporate tax (Jayaraman 2012: 19). In addition to dividends, REIT investors may also gain from the appreciation of the underlying asset. Table 7.1 lists some of Singapore's REITs.

The first REIT to be listed in Singapore was CapitaMall Trust in 2002. Soon afterwards, Hong Kong's biggest developer, Li Ka-shing's Cheung Kong, planned its first property trust – not in Hong Kong, however, but in Singapore (Cheung Kong's ..., 2003). The reasons for favouring Singapore were the different methods of calculating the allowed borrowings (based on net asset value in Hong Kong, total asset value in Singapore), the percentage of dividends distributable (100 per cent in Hong Kong, 90 per cent in Singapore) and requirements in Hong Kong that REITs should be local and exclude hotels and theme parks (whereas Singaporean trusts can hold overseas properties) (Cheung Kong's ..., 2003). The REITs managed by ARA Asset Management (an affiliate of Cheung Kong) and listed in Singapore are Fortune REIT, Suntec REIT and Cache Logistics Trust. In addition, the world's first Islamic REIT (which is also the world's largest Shari'ah-compliant REIT) was listed on the Singapore Exchange (SGX) in 2010 (MAS Annual Report 2010/2011). By 2010, Singapore's Real Estate Investment Trust sector had become the largest REIT market in Asia, excluding Japan (MAS Annual Report 2010/2011: 33). In an Annual Report (2007/2008: 36), MAS remarked that Singapore is 'the premier real estate financial centre in Asia'. In 2013, there were 25 REITs listed on the Singapore Stock Exchange.

REITs have provided good investment returns at a time of low interest rates. The yields offered by REITs vary, and depend on the type of REIT. Jayaraman (2012) identifies three REIT cycles in the short history of REITs in Singapore: the bull phase (2002–2007), the panic sell-down (2008–2009) and the stabilisation period (from mid 2009). A comparison from the bull phase (in 2004) shows that Singapore's REITs

**Table 7.1** Selection of Singaporean REITs.

| REIT | Listed | Properties | Total asset S\$ million 2013 | Group |
|---|---|---|---|---|
| CapitaCommercial Trust | 2004 | Office | 7218 | CapitaLand |
| CapitaMall Trust | 2002 | Retail | 10,017 | CapitaLand |
| CapitaRetail China | 2006 | Shopping malls in China | 2184 | CapitaLand |
| Ascott Residence Trust | 2006 | Serviced residences | 3582 | CapitaLand |
| Keppel REIT | 2006 | Office | 6775 | Keppel Land |
| Mapletree Industrial Trust | 2010 | Industrial | 2968 | Mapletree Investments |
| Mapletree Logistics Trust | 2005 | Singapore, Japan, Hong Kong, Malaysia, Vietnam | 4237 | Mapletree Investments |
| Mapletree Commercial Trust | 2011 | PSA Building, VivoCity | 3886 | Mapletree Investments |
| Mapletree Greater China Commercial Trust | 2013 | Commercial Hong Kong, China | 4873 | Mapletree Investments |
| Ascendas Real Estate Investment Trust | 2002 | Industrial | 6959 | Ascendas |
| Ascendas India Trust | 2007 | Bangalore, Chennai, Hyderabad | 1065 | Ascendas |

Sources: CapitaCommercial Trust (www.cct.com.sg)
CapitaMall Trust (www.cmt.sg)
CapitaRetail China Trust (www.crct.com.sg)
Ascott Residence Trust (www.ascottreit.com.sg)
Keppel REIT (www.keppelreit.com.)
Mapletree Industrial Trust (www.mapletreeindustrialtrust.com)
Mapletree Logistics Trust (www.mapletreelogisticstrust.com)
Mapletree Commercial Trust (www.mapletreecommercialtrust.com)
Mapletree Greater China (www.mapletreegreaterchinacommercialtrust.com)
Ascendas Real Estate Investment Trust (www.a-reit.com)
Ascendas India Trust (www.a-itrust.com)

produced 16.08 per cent yield, compared to yields on UK REITs at 0.24 per cent and those on US REITs at 5.54 per cent (Brounen and de Koning 2012). In addition to their impressive performance against a backdrop of low interest rates, Singaporean REITs have also benefitted from strong sponsors,[3] such as CapitaLand. Within specialist sub-sectors of the market, REITs focused on healthcare have done well due to an ageing population, industrial REITs have prospered on account of low vacancy rates and hospitality REITs have thrived thanks to high tourist numbers.

The REITs listed in Table 7.1 have links to the government. Capita-Commercial Trust, CapitaMall Trust and CapitaChina Trust are trusts within the CapitaLand Group (see Chapter 6). Mapletree Industrial Trust, Mapletree Logistics Trust and Mapletree Commercial Trust are trusts within Mapletree Investment, tracing its origins to the Port Authority of Singapore (corporatised as PSA and non-port properties, transferred to Temasek) and JTC, which divested its properties into Mapletree. Mapletree is the real estate unit of Temasek Holdings. Ascendas Real Estate Investment Trust and Ascendas India Trust have their origins in JTC and Arcasia (see Chapter 6). In addition to these trusts, there are also REITs like Frasers Centrepoint Trust (retail), Lippo MallsIndonesia Retail and CDL Hospitality Trust listed on the Singapore Exchange.

The real estate investment trusts listed in Singapore include offices, shopping malls and business parks within their portfolios. In Singapore, where 90 per cent of residents are homeowners, the only residential REIT is Saizen REIT, offering investors the opportunity to invest in residential properties in Japan. Ascendas REIT and Mapletree REIT originally acquired property from JTC and PSA, the former providing affordable industrial space and the latter taking care of ports. What happens to affordability when industrial space[4] is managed by REITs that use short 30- to 60-year leases? This question has caused concern among the business community, and some criticised the selling of JTC land to REITs that seek to maximise their returns. In 2012, Minister for Trade and Industry Lim Hng Kiang defended the government policy of divesting, saying that previously 'JTC tenants have a very unfair advantage in that they're getting subsidised rent from JTC and it's not a level playing field', and adding that the government would not consider taking back JTC land (Chan 2012).

REITs increase the transparency of real estate business. Anyone can walk through a shopping mall owned by a REIT to monitor the performance of his investment. As listed companies, REITs are obliged to publish annual reports showing the development of their portfolios and dividends. REITs diversify their ownership across multiple properties and REITs themselves are owned by multiple shareholders, among which are financial institutions. Thus REITs also offer a glimpse into the real estate possessions of financial institutions. Among the largest share-holders of CapitaMall Trust, for example, are Citibank, DBS, HSBC, NTUC,[5] United Overseas Bank, BNP Paribas, Merrill Lynch, Morgan Stanley, Societe General and Marquarie Capital Securities (CapitaMall Trust Annual Report 2013). In diversifying their ownership across multiple properties, REITs link different slices of real estate under the same management and leverage (debt to asset relation) mechanisms. The requirement to evaluate REIT properties once a year by a professional real estate assessor highlights the role of value in determining the use of land and makes the building cycle shorter.

### Singapore Colonising the World: Sovereign Wealth Funds

Singaporean companies (discussed in Chapter 6) invest and conduct business overseas. Among them is CapitaLand, which in 2008 was Southeast Asia's largest property company, receiving revenue from China, Australia and New Zealand. In addition to private companies, the government's investment corporations are also active players in the world's real estate markets.

In 2008, in the midst of the subprime crisis, the Western world was alerted to 'sovereign wealth funds' (SWFs). These are investment vehicles owned and managed by rich states, like the United Arab Emirates. The fear spread in the media was that 'foreign countries may use their funds to control or influence strategic industries in ways that could be detrimental to national interests' (Robertson 2008). One such fund is the Government of Singapore Investment Corporation (GIC). It is a fund management firm that was established in 1981 to manage Singapore's reserves (i.e. the state's large surplus, arising from a high savings rate). It is a private limited company that is wholly owned by the government of Singapore. The Ministry of Finance sets GIC's investment objectives. The aim of GIC is to invest Singapore's surplus safely and for the long term. The chair of the GIC board was Senior Minister Lee Kuan Yew, emphasising the importance of this institution.

Government funds investing national resources are a rarity in the world. Another country with this kind of global portfolio is Saudi Arabia; it is investing its oil money. Norway invests its oil money likewise, and China deploys its huge surplus along similar lines. In a 2007 list of major sovereign wealth funds, the largest (ranked by assets under management) was Abu Dhabi Investment Authority, and in second place was Government Pension Fund-Global (Norway). Government of Singapore Investment Corporation came third, and Temasek Holding (another sovereign wealth fund owned by the government of Singapore) was ranked 11th (*World Investment Report* 2008: 216). Purchases by sovereign wealth funds, especially of assets with strategic importance (like mines), have fostered national sentiments.

Singapore's sovereign wealth fund, GIC, has investments around the world, both in financial instruments and property. One of GIC's companies is GIC Real Estate. It was formed in 1999 and invests directly and indirectly in real estate worldwide. In 2013, GIC had overseas offices in New York, San Francisco, Tokyo, London, Shanghai, Beijing, Seoul, and Mumbai, managing investments across more than 40 countries.[6]

GIC has a reputation for being secretive about its investments and strategies. The total amount of its investments is unknown 'though it is believed to be in tens of billions of dollars' (GIC's US investments ... 1996). Castells, Goh and Kwok (1990: 181) wrote that it is believed that GIC's investments are 'very large and strategically targeted according to two basic criteria: access to privileged knowledge and contacts in international financial networks; and safe investment with satisfactory levels of return'. Unlike listed real estate investment trusts, sovereign wealth funds are not transparent in their operations. Singapore's Acting Second Finance Minister Raymond Lim defended this secrecy, arguing that 'it is not in Singapore's national interest to disclose the size of the Republic's financial reserves or the returns on them because the information would make it easier for speculators to attack the Singapore dollar' (More info on reserves ... 2004). To measure how much information a sovereign wealth fund discloses, accountability and transparency indices have been calculated (the higher the score, the higher the level of disclosure). One such index gives GIC a score of 39, whereas Alaska Permanent Fund and Norway's Government Pension Fund both score 100, Qatar Investment Authority 2, China Investment Corporation 14, and Russia's Reserve Fund and National Welfare Fund 50 (Loh 2010: 37–38).

The lack of transparency makes it difficult to collect systematic and reliable data on sovereign wealth funds. Sometimes a GIC purchase overseas (in countries where disclosure of information requirements are more onerous than in Singapore) gives a glimpse of GIC's strategy. In 1993, GIC bought stocks in the United States. These purchases triggered US disclosure laws and provided 'a rare peek at the way GIC handles a small piece, at least, of its billions of dollars in overseas assets ... known for conservative strategy' (GIC's US investments ... 1996). 'Prior to these purchases GIC almost never divulged information on its operations. How much the agency manages is also not known' (GIC's US investments ... 1996). Table 7.2 lists some of GIC's investments.

In an interview published in their 2001 Yearbook, Dr Seek Ngee Huat (Director of the Real Estate Department) praised GIC Real Estate for

**Table 7.2** Investments by Singapore's Government Investment Corporation (GIC).

| Year | Investment | City/country |
|------|------------|--------------|
| 2005 | Intercontinental Hotel | Paris |
| 2007 | Sale and leaseback of Merrill Lynch's HQ | London |
| 2008 | Westin Hotel | Tokyo |
| 2008 | Shopping mall (Iso-Omena) (40% ownership) | Espoo (Finland) |
| 2008 | Mall development company (minority stake) | Mexico |
| 2013 | Broadgate, 50% interest | London |

Source: The International Herald Tribune 17 January 2006; The Financial Times 23 March 2007; Morgan Stanley Press Release 26 February 2008; Citycon Pörssitiedote 12 February 2008; Reuters 5 August 2008; GIC home page 23 March 2014.

being one of very few truly global real estate investors. While most real estate investment firms focus on domestic markets, GIC Real Estate invests across America, Asia and Europe (in 2009 it had investments in more than 30 countries). GIC also manages its own fund, unlike most institutional real estate investors that rely on external managers. GIC has invested in different types of properties (offices, retail, industrial, residential and hotels), property companies and real estate investment trusts. GIC uses real estate investments as an instrument to gain access to markets where direct investment opportunities are limited. GIC establishes strategic alliances and joint ventures with local partners to glean information and benefit from local knowledge. GIC's portfolio is geographically diversified. It has investments in Tokyo, Seoul, Hong Kong, Chicago, Madrid, New York, San Francisco, Prague, Sydney, Manila, Beijing, Paris and London.

In contrast to well-known tycoons like Donald Trump and Li Ka-shing, or conspicuous real estate investment acquisitions by Japanese in Los Angeles, GIC is an anonymous investor that does not buy trophy buildings to boost its name and fame but seeks instead to make profitable investments and prefers to keep its investments secret. GIC and REITs base their real estate investment decisions solely on yield. Saskia Sassen (1996) has, as 'a kind of theoretical provocation', introduced the term 'economic citizenship'. Globally operating actors, firms and markets are economic citizens, in the sense that they can have power over individual governments. We may call REITs and SWFs financial citizens. In their search for high yields, they affect the decision-making of the municipality in which they invest. For example, in Espoo (Finland) the decision to open a public library in Iso-Omena partly owned by GIC increased the real estate expenses of the city and thus made it decrease its budget for buying books.

## Real Estate Investment into Singapore

Singapore has attracted foreign real estate investors from Japan, Kuwait, Brunei, Hong Kong, England, Malaysia, Indonesia, the United States and Taiwan. In the early 1990s, there were very few foreign investors in the central business district. The Hong Kong Bank owned the Hong Kong Bank building, and Standard Chartered Bank owned its building. A third of the OUB Centre was owned by the Kuwait Investment Office. In the commercial district of Orchard Road, there were more foreign owners. In 1989, foreigners owned 12 out of 40 buildings there (Chee 1990). The most prominent owners were the Japanese, who owned Delfi Orchard and Palais Renaissance (Yamasin Enterprise), the Promenade (Eammons Investments), the Paragon (Sogo Group) and Orchard Square (22 per cent owned by Takashimaya). There were also investments from Kuwait (Wisma Atria and Forum Galleria), Brunei (Holiday Inn and Hyatt Regency), Hong Kong (Tropicana) and Indonesia (Liat Towers) (Chee 1990). One example of international ownership of commercial property is Bugis Junction. In 1998, 39 per cent was owned by Indonesian businesswoman Endang (daughter of former Pertamine Chief Ibnu Sutowo), 31 per cent by Keppel, 20 per cent by Pidemco and the remaining 10 per cent by the Japanese Saison Group (Ang W M 1998).

Foreigners have also invested in private housing in Singapore, and Singaporean housing is advertised in foreign newspapers. Foreigners can buy apartments in buildings over six storeys in height, and on Sentosa (Singapore's premier resort island) foreigners can buy landed property.[7] Real estate brokers rely on Singapore's liberal investment rules as a selling point. For example in *The Sunday Times* (7 September 1997), developer Seng Realty & Development Pte Ltd advertised: 'Fancy Living in The Aberdeen, Freehold. No Restriction to foreign ownership'. In 2005, 40 per cent of the units in The Sail@Marina Bay were bought by foreigners, and half the houses on Sentosa were sold to foreigners (Wong and Kong 2005).

Why do foreigners buy housing in Singapore? Naturally, the obvious reason is an intention to live there. By international standards, Singapore is seen as an agreeable place to live. In *Asiaweek*'s (Choong 1997) list of the ten most liveable Asian cities, Fukuoka in Japan was the first, followed by Tokyo, then Singapore, Osaka, Georgetown, Hong Kong, Seoul, Bandar Seri Begawan, Kuala Lumpur and Taipei. Singapore is also praised by the business community. One Finnish businessman I interviewed in Indonesia told me that the best locations for transnational companies in Southeast Asia are Penang and Bali. They have good connections, cheap prices and no congestion like Manila or Jakarta. But these locations are not feasible, because a corporate address in Bali or George Town (Penang, Malaysia) does not inspire commercial confidence. Singapore on the other hand, with its reliable legal business environment, is a good address. Another businessman told me that it does not really matter where your base is (because of the time spent travelling), but for spouses and children Singapore is the best place.

In addition to buying a place to live, foreigners investing in housing in Singapore have other motives. Among the motives mentioned by Wan (1995) in his survey were: Singapore's political and economic stability, appreciation of property prices in Singapore, high rental yield, no capital gains tax, low interest rates (most of the foreign investment in Singapore is financed by loans from local banks at cheap rates), stability of the Singaporean dollar and good education opportunities. The motives varied among different nationalities. For Hong Kong citizens (the largest foreign investor group, with 31 per cent of foreign investment) in the early 1990s, the most important reason was uncertainty about Hong Kong's future post-1997 (when the UK handed it back to China); Malaysians (20 per cent) came to do business and needed a place to stay; Indonesians (15 per cent) mentioned political, social and economic reasons, plus better educational opportunities; for the Japanese (12 per cent), the motive was appreciation in the yen and high housing prices in Japan; and similarly the Taiwanese specified high prices in Taiwan (Wan 1995). In 2012, the most prominent investor groups in Singaporean property were the Malaysians (23 per cent), Indonesians (17 per cent), and Indians (12 per cent) (Gafoor 2013: 99). The third largest group in 1995, the Japanese, have been replaced by the Indians, indicating the decline in Japan's economy and the rise of India's fortunes.

Singapore also attracts property investment because of racial discrimination in neighbouring countries. Wealthy Chinese business people have a prominent role in the Indonesian economy and have been a target for rioting Muslims, especially during times of economic crises. Anti-Sinic sentiment and recurrent atrocities against Chinese inhabitants have prompted the Indonesian Chinese to invest in properties overseas in order to have a safe sanctuary in the event of being forced to leave Indonesia. A favourite destination has been Singapore, only a couple of hours by air from Jakarta. An example of this flow was in 1997, when riots protesting against the International Monetary Fund led to the removal of Indonesia's President Suharto. Chinese properties were destroyed in Indonesia and many Chinese inhabitants fled to Singapore. Malaysian property investments in Singapore are also enhanced because of racial discrimination. In Malaysia, the Bumiputera rules (that discriminate against Chinese inhabitants in order to increase economic opportunities for indigenous non-Chinese people) have limited Chinese business people's investment options. This has prompted the Chinese in Malaysia to seek alternative investments, such as property in Singapore.

**Property-minded People**

In addition to institutional investors like GIC, individual Singaporeans also invest in real estate abroad. After moving to Singapore, one pleasure I discovered was reading *The Straits Times*. Among the exotic news, the abundance of real estate advertisements and the real estate section caught my eye; coming from Finland, I did not even realise that newspapers could have a real estate section. A curious feature was the proliferation of full-page advertisements for overseas properties. This was not the type of information found in Finnish newspapers during the early 1990s. *The Straits Times* advertised properties for sale in Australia, London, New Zealand and China. A high yield was promised. One advertisement (*The Sunday Times* 18 June 1995) concerned a strata-title resort hotel in Tasmania with 'rental guarantee 10% net return for 10 + 10 years and free gold card membership to casino and golf course for 10 years'. Properties were and continue to be advertised like commodities. More recently, *The Straits Times* (22 October 2011) featured an advertisement for apartments in London's Canary Wharf, with the caption: 'Entire Stock Release. The Last And Only Canary Corporate Apartments Available Now With Immediate Occupation. All Remaining 1, 2 & 3 Bed Luxury Apartments Must Be Sold Guaranteeing Investors One Of The Last Great Opportunities At Canary Wharf!'. The abundance of real estate advertisements – in a city where more than 80 per cent of people live in public housing – is a mystery, posing questions about the Singaporean homeowner and his housing dream.

   To demonstrate the abundance of property advertisements, I calculated the amount of page space in *The Sunday Times* (23 October 2011) advertising properties for sale. Excluding the classifieds section (that carried property advertisements on 10 pages out of 17), there were 89 pages, and of these 23 carried property advertisements (covering an aggregate total space equating to13 pages). There were, for example, half-page advertisements for properties in London and Bangkok. The Singaporean properties advertised were new projects, like Far East Organization's Waterfront development in Bedok Reservoir Road. With

**Table 7.3**   Property advertisements in *The Sunday Times* 23 October 2011.

| Page | Size (page) | City | Page | Size | City |
|------|------|------|------|------|------|
| 3 | 1/2 | Singapore | 28 | 1/2 | London |
| 5 | 1 | Singapore | 29 | 1/2 | Singapore |
| 6 | 1/2 | London | 31 | 3/4 | Melbourne & Cambridge |
| 7 | 1 | Singapore | 32 | 1/4 | KL |
| 11 | 1/2 | Singapore | 33 | 1/2 | Bangkok |
| 12 | 1 | Singapore | 38 | 1/4 | London |
| 14 | 1/2 | KL | 40 | 1/4 | London |
| 16 | 1/2 | Melbourne | 41 | 1/2 | Singapore |
| 19 | 1 | London | 43 | 1/4 | Melbourne |
| 20 | 1/2 | Melbourne | 46 | 1/4 | Brisbane |
| 26 | 1/2 | New Zealand | Life | 1 | Singapore |
| 27 | 1/2 | London | section 5 | | |

two exceptions (villas in New Zealand and a hotel in London), these advertisements were for housing. I have never seen another newspaper carry so many property advertisements, making *The Straits Times* 'the real estate newspaper'. Table 7.3 lists the relevant page, size and city in respect of property advertisements in *The Sunday Times*.

Who are the readers of these advertisements? Who are the Singaporeans investing in properties abroad and what are their motives? During my years in Singapore, I met one local investor, Mr Chen (not his real name), on several occasions. I met Mr Chen for the first time in 1995. He is a Singaporean (English-educated, ethnically Chinese) investor from a wealthy background. At that time, he had a couple of million-pound investments in properties in central London. Mr Chen did not believe that the property market would ever go down. The reason for this, he thought, was the economy. 'As long as the economy is growing, the market cannot go down.' He typified the Singaporean optimistic spirit, which expresses a firm confidence in the property market and profitability of property investments. Not even the downturn in Singapore during the 1980s seemed to have shaken his confidence.

I asked him whether his reason for investing in London was that prices were lower overseas than in expensive Singapore (an opinion voiced when I interviewed a Singaporean real estate broker). He regarded this as stupid. If investors chase low prices alone, they are unprofessional, Mr Chen said. He did not compare Singapore to London. The reason why he started to invest in London was the economic downturn in the

UK in 1992. It did not affect his investing capability because he was benefitting from the strong Singaporean dollar. He invested in London with
the expectation that prices there would rise – and indeed they did. He
believed that the failure of Japanese investors was proof that low prices
as an investment motive are not enough. He gave me an example of how
low prices are an insufficient reason for real estate investments: prices
in Australia are lower than in Singapore, but this alone is not sufficient
reason to invest in Australia.

Contrary to what is often presented as a key motivation for investors
of Chinese descent, Mr Chen had no nostalgic desire to return to China
or invest in China for 'home' reasons. Economic indicators alone were
important to him. A longing for mystical ancestral land has been presented as a reason behind Asians' particular hunger for land (Goldberg
1985). 'There is also a near mystical value attached to land in Japan,
in contrast with the easy way in which real estate is bought and sold in
America. Land in Japan is like a "family treasure",' said Yukyo Takenak,
a Japanese business expert and continued, 'you don't sell property in
Japan. It's the last thing you do' (Furlong and Yoshihara 1987). It has
been mooted that overseas Chinese investors have sought to assuage
their yearning for the home village of their clan by buying property in
China. Mr Chen did not relate to such cultural explanations, and had
no desire to invest in his ancestral village. In addition, it pleased him
that Singapore was benefitting from political instability in China, as well
as from similar uncertainties in Hong Kong and Taiwan.

Mr Chen regarded the Chinese market as too risky. 'One needs to
have deep pockets if one wants to go to China', he said. And he was
right. Soon after, *The Straits Times* recounted the problems faced by Singaporeans in the Chinese market. A group of Singaporeans had banded
together to pressure a Beijing developer to adhere to the terms of a property contract they agreed for the purchase of office units in Beijing. The
Singaporean buyers said the developer 'had reneged on the net 15 per
cent returns on investment initially guaranteed for the first two years of
ownership' (Chen K 1997).

I met Mr Chen again in 1996. He was by then concentrating his efforts
on the Singapore market, and had also started to develop (instead of just
buying and selling). He was buying old Chinese shop houses, and was
busy redeveloping them as restaurants and hotels. Mr Chen explained to
me that the reason why he had begun developing was because the development business was more satisfying than simply buying and selling. To
buy and sell is irritating, he explained, because one so often realises that
'if one had waited still a little longer one had gained even more'.

Mr Chen was a different kind of property investor than his fellow Singaporean Mrs Fan (not her real name), who I met in Penang, Malaysia.

She had bought a property there. She was at the time renting it out, but thought perhaps of retiring there one day. She told me that, for overseas Chinese, 'to work in Singapore, live in Penang and die in Malacca' is the ultimate ideal. Mr Chen did not think of property along these lines. He was not buying a home when investing in property. He was a 'character mask' (to cite Marx) through and through, and his identity was that of a rationally calculating property investor. Such a calculative attitude towards home is also evident in Singaporean novels. In Daren Shiau's novel *Heartland*, Fifth Uncle from Malaysia visits Wing and his mother Madam Lee who live in Singapore. Fifth Uncle calculates that the flat where Wing and his mother live is worth 300,000 Singaporean dollars, which converts to more than half a million Malaysian ringgit. Fifth Uncle suggests that Madam Lee should sell her flat, move to Malaysia to live with his brother, put the money in the bank and enjoy the interest so that she need no longer work hard. He points out that even in Australia Madam Lee could buy a nice bungalow with a garden if she were to sell her Singapore property.

Some years later I met Mr Chen again. He was still single, and by now well over marriageable age. He invited me to look at his new condo. To visit a Chinese home usually entails enjoying a Chinese dinner with cousins, aunts, uncles, daughters, sons, grandmothers and grandfathers, but he lived alone. He showed me all the rooms and closets in his condo. He showed me his calculations of the income he could receive if he rented out his new condo. To calculate opportunity costs in this way is not only a characteristic of an economic agent, there is also something very Singaporean about this approach to life. After showing me his property and calculations, he took me to a hawker centre for a meal. He was very careful not to spend too much.

A shortage of investment options in a small city-state without a hinterland obliges Singaporeans to search for investment opportunities abroad. The latest place to invest is Iskander in Johor, Malaysia (just over the border from Singapore). In Chapter 2, Batam in Indonesia was discussed as the liminal frontier; now it is Johor's turn. In February 2012, I went to a property show in Singapore marketing properties in Johor. Malaysian developers praised the properties on offer: the infrastructure is in place, with good connections to Singapore and a university in the region. The buying appetite of Singaporeans was whetted with a presentation from a real estate investment expert, who resembled an old-fashioned vacuum cleaner salesman. He engaged the audience with direct questions like 'how many of you think that real estate prices will go up?' and introduced ways of making money in the real estate business. His message was that it is always a good time to buy real estate – there is always someone who has to sell quickly and cheaply – and that the usual real estate rule – location, location, location – did not apply over the border. Seventy per cent of the residential properties in Iskander were bought by foreigners (Gafoor 2013: 355). Many of these have been Singaporeans buying holiday homes, or investing primarily for capital appreciation rather than rental yield (Gafoor 2013).

Foreigners investing in Singapore and Singaporeans investing abroad, real estate investment trusts and sovereign wealth funds (with their internationally diversified real estate portfolios) are phenomena that have evolved in our global era. Money is switched from one real estate investment to another on the basis of expected yields. In recent years, two new symbols of Singapore's global role as the world's wealth management centre have emerged: casinos (that represent the volatile and random nature of global investment flows) and private banking (that cashes in the wealth of the super rich).

### Casinos and Singapore as the World's Wealth Management Centre

In *Gamblers*, Feodor Dostoyevsky compared thrifty Germans to Russians, who needed the game of roulette to accumulate capital. Singapore has it both ways; a high savings rate and a casino industry.

In 2005, two casinos were approved for construction in Singapore, one on Sentosa and the other in Marina Bay. In keeping with the usual Singapore inclination to abbreviate, casinos are called 'the Integrated Resorts' or simply 'IRs'. Their approval was an unexpected decision by the government, which has a reputation for legislating against vices. On the other hand, casinos as a source of revenue perpetuate the colonial government practice of reliance on vices (gambling and liqueur) in taxation policy (see p. 13).

By their very nature, casinos are a contested issue and their arrival on the scene divided opinion among Singaporeans. One concern was the social problems associated with gambling. Derek da Cunha (2010: 48–49) hypothesised a scenario in which a croupier and a gambler might live as neighbours in the same block of HDB flats. Unlike in Macao and Las Vegas, where there are numerous casinos and gamblers flock from abroad, Singapore's two casinos are frequented by locals (at Marina Bay Sands, Singaporeans comprise a third of the visitors; Wong T 2011). Locals visiting casinos need guidance. In Dostoyevsky's novel, the German father tells his children morally uplifting stories about the virtues of saving. In Singapore, the media recount cautionary tales about the dangers of casinos. A typical example tells of a woman who entered a casino in Sydney to collect a free wok (offered to lure gamblers in) and left two days later after losing AUS$30,000 (S$39,000), the bulk of her deceased husband's estate (Pearlman 2011). Another story concerned a property developer who lost AUS$35 million at Melbourne's casino and then sued for 'preying' upon his gambling addiction (Pearlman 2011). Taxi drivers in Singapore tell stories about friends who have became hooked, adding that they themselves only take with them an amount they can afford to lose (which seems to be about S$5000).

Unlike in Las Vegas, where it is impossible to check into a hotel without being channelled through a casino, in Singapore the locals must pay an entry fee (S$100) while overseas visitors gain access via a dedicated 'foreigner' entrance. The government also intervenes and regulates the gambling business. The Casino Regulatory Authority (CRA) is a statutory board empowered to take disciplinary action against casinos. The Casino Control Act (2006) legislates for exclusion of gamblers in three specific scenarios: voluntary exclusion upon a person's own request; family exclusion upon application by another family member; and exclusion of recipients of public assistance and undischarged bankrupts. In 2012 it was suggested to also ban people demonstrating 'weak financial capability', including those with housing arrears or bad credit records (Ong and Tai 2012).

There is no doubt that Marina Bay Sands, designed by Moshe Safdie and developed by Las Vegas Sands, with its iconic triple skyscrapers topped by a ship-form construction (celebrating Singapore's maritime past), is a major new landmark in Singapore. It makes a striking sight on emerging from Changi Airport. While it is a trophy building, visible from almost everywhere in Singapore, it is also a contested landmark. One critical voice is that of artist Chun Kaifeng. His art work *Y, €, $* consists of three 62-cm-high wooden skyscraper figures (depicting Marina Bay Sands) with a connecting roof, representing not a ship as in the case of Marina Bay Sands, but the yen, euro and dollar currency. On the back of his model skyscrapers are drawings resembling the daubs with which loan sharks deface their debtors' doors.

Casinos cash in on the wealth of the rich, and so do the private banks. After the subprime crisis and the ensuing protests against financial greed, the super rich have searched for safe havens to hide their fortunes. 'Swiss's Loss, Singapore's Gain. Forget Swiss bank accounts, having an offshore Singapore bank account is now the range amongst the super rich with private wealth management centres flourishing in the Lion City' headlined Khalil Adis (2009b) in *Property Report*. At a time when investors were deciding where to park their funds, and London and New York were cutting back in the wealth management sector, Singapore prospered as the world's fastest-growing private banking and wealth management centre, enabling its fund management industry to grow from about S$280 billion in 2000 to more than $600 billion by 2007 (Adis 2009b: 30).[8]

## Global Rent and Racism in the Real Estate Market

Property-minded Singaporeans invest in properties in China, Malaysia, UK and Australia and Singaporean newspapers advertise properties overseas. Capital Retail China manages shopping malls in China and Ascendas India Trust science parks in India. Are these signs of increased globalisation and has the real estate market become globalised, like commodities markets and production? Some scholars argue that real estate investors in search of higher yields make local real estate markets dependent on markets in other places (see e.g. Beauregard and Haila 2000; Renaud 1997; Dehesh and Pugh 1999). Real estate scholars in their analyses of the benefits of international diversification of real estate portfolios and estimations of the correlations between yields on real estate securities and shares and bonds take globalisation of real estate markets for granted. Other scholars deny the existence of a global real estate market and argue that there remain wide variations among legal environments, landownership forms and local customs (Corgel et al. 1992), that there are still separate markets for international and local actors (Adair et al. 1999), and regulations and bureaucracies prevent foreigners from entering local markets (Keivani et al. 2001). Both camps are correct; numerous frictions persist in real estate markets, but there are also some trends demonstrating an increasing globalisation.

There is nothing new in the practice of investing surplus produced in one place into properties in another place. In the seventeenth century, profits from the sale of nutmeg imported from the Spice Islands could buy a mansion in Holborn, London (Milton 1999). In the nineteenth century, Chinese merchant Cheong Fatt Tze (1840–1917) invested in properties around the world. In *Sons of the Yellow Emperor* (1990), Chinese author Lynn Pan tells the story of this cosmopolitan man. Cheong was a Mandarin industrialist, originally a Hakka from Kwantung province, who served the Manchu government and then moved to Batavia (today Jakarta) to make his fortune, trading opium, tobacco and spirits, running coconut and rice plantations, and engaging in railway construction, mining and manufacturing. He was the first Chinese Vice-Consul of Penang and the Chinese Consul General in Singapore. In 1915, he went to the United States to attract American investment to China. His 50-day tour received much publicity and *The New York Times* called him

China's Rockefeller (Pan 1990: 144). Cheong was a cosmopolitan man who travelled from city to city and had homes in Java, Sumatra, Penang, Singapore and China. In George Town, Penang, Cheong built the beautiful Cheong Fatt Tze mansion, finished in 1904. It is a courtyard mansion large enough to house nine generations, combining Victorian cast iron with Chinese lattice work, stone lions, wooden birds and flowers (Khoo 1993; Pan 1990).

Since Cheong's time, many new features have evolved in the world's real estate market. These include transnational companies that seek international renown through their trophy buildings, development companies that operate across several countries, REITs and SWFs with their internationally diversified real estate portfolios, and real estate firms collecting and publishing information on real estate yields and vacancies around the world.

An example of a transnational company that gained international recognition is Mitsubishi, which in 1989 purchased New York's landmark Rockefeller Centre. The deal was not necessarily good in cash flow terms, but it may have increased Mitsubishi's revenue indirectly. It brought publicity and brand recognition, and through that perhaps higher profits for Mitsubishi from selling more products. Sharon Zukin (1991, 1995) has called such indirect economic benefits the *symbolic economy*. Ownership of a trophy building can increase a company's fame, and thus its sales and profit. City fathers have been quick to adopt a symbolic economic strategy, and invest in the built environment because they believe that iconic buildings designed by world-famous architects attract investors, transnational companies and tourists. Marina Bay in Singapore, with its S\$4.5 billion government investment, was intended to act as a magnet for global investors seeking premium office space in a prime location.

Critics of symbolic economy strategies question the benefits of real estate investments. Harvard economist Edward Glaeser (2011: 62) has called the belief that new buildings lead to urban success 'the edifice error', and David Harvey (2001) has warned that artificially made places can lose their comparative advantage and distinctiveness after other cities develop even more distinctive buildings. REITs also undermine the benefits of trophy building strategies for companies in channelling the gains of the symbolic economy to real estate companies. The logo of REIT displayed on a building does nothing to help advertise the company that has leased space owned by a REIT.

Singaporean development companies are a good example of companies that operate across several countries (Figure 7.2). They switch investment from one country to another and repatriate profits back to Singapore. These profits may include gains from location (differential

**Figure 7.2**  CapitaLand in Shanghai. Photo: Anne Haila.

rent) or excessive demand (monopoly rent). In order to pay attention to the origin of this revenue I call it global rent. The fruits of land are redistributed globally.

Real estate companies (that collect and publish information of yields and vacancies around the world) and REITs (with their globally diversified portfolios) facilitate the flow of international real estate investments. Comparisons between rental yields, for example, in Indonesia 9.31 per cent, Malaysia 6.21 per cent, the Philippines 8.2 per cent, Singapore 2.95 per cent and Thailand 6.53 per cent (Property Life January 2013) are meant to assist investors in selecting properties abroad.

Despite these phenomena showing increased globalisation, there are still obstacles restraining real estate investment flows. These are connected to explicit restrictions, nationalistic sentiments for land and property and discontent because of inflation in housing prices due to foreign demand. Countries such as Malaysia, Thailand and Indonesia still restrict foreign real estate investments. However, ways have evolved to bypass such restrictions. In Penang (Malaysia), Indonesians invested in the names of their Malaysian relatives. Some countries that restrict foreign individual investment allow ownership by foreign companies, for example by a company incorporated in an offshore tax haven. Such roundabout methods make collecting real estate data laborious and the data unreliable, and suggest that the amount of foreign real estate investment is larger than the statistics show. Foreign investments can also be restricted by treating foreign investors differently from domestic investors, for example by imposing stamp duty for foreigners (this is discussed in the next chapter).

Discrimination in the housing market, whereby landlords select their tenants or banks give loans to customers at different interest rates, is an observed practice. Those discriminated against pay higher prices for housing because they are charged higher interest rates (Harvey 1974), or are excluded on the grounds of ethnicity because of their assumed inability to adhere to market rules (and protect the value of property) (Freund 2007). In the real estate market we can observe similar discrimination. In Los Angeles, Japanese real estate investments created anxiety and during the 1992 riots Korean properties were destroyed. Indonesian Chinese invested in properties in Singapore in order to have a place of refuge in the event of anti-Chinese violence. For Finland, a condition of joining the European Union was that it had to open its real estate market up to foreign buyers. This prompted fears that *nouveau riche* Russians would buy Finland's land and lakes. These examples indicate that Japanese money is not the same as British money, real estate markets in Singapore and Jakarta are not equally attractive to Indonesian Chinese buyers, and Russian and Finnish property buyers are unequally positioned in Finland's real estate market. Although fewer countries today have an openly racialised system when it comes to property (as was the case in South Africa, see Berry 2002 for the racialized system of property rights in South Africa) or discriminate against non-natives and non-locals (like Indonesia and Malaysia), real estate ownership still evokes nationalistic sentiments and there is racial discrimination in property markets.

Foreign property investment can stir up discontent among local inhabitants if it raises housing prices, as it did in Singapore after the subprime and euro crises increased the purchases of foreign buyers or in Hong Kong because of mainland investors. In 2010 prices of private residential properties increased by 17.6 per cent in Singapore (URA Release of 4th quarter real estate statistics 28 January 2011) and in 2011 foreigners purchased 31 per cent of private homes in Singapore (Tan Amy 2012). The government decided to intervene. In Hong Kong it was estimated that more than a third of apartments costing more than HK$12 million were sold to mainland buyers and that Hong Kong property prices rose by about 45 per cent between 2008 and 2010 (Lau J 2010). The influx of Chinese money led to a proposal by legislator Lee Wing-tat that 'the government should consider banning non-locals from buying mass-market homes. Mainlanders and foreigners could be restricted to the luxury market' (Chong 2011).

Unlike rich expatriates or mainland investors in the Singapore and Hong Kong housing markets who are easy scapegoats, real estate investment trusts are anonymous investors who also affect property prices. They are businesses seeking to maximise their yield and distribute their property earnings (global rent) to shareholders around the world. They value their real estate portfolios annually, thus increasing the velocity of real estate investment and shortening the lifecycle of buildings. Their behaviour, as well as the behaviour of expatriate investors and transnational development companies, is affected by interest rates and other investment options in financial markets. These are analysed next.

## Notes

1  Cited in Renaissance City Plan II. Arts and Development Plan 2008.
2  The Bumiputera policy, which aims to protect Malaysia's indigenous and local population and businesses, was introduced after riots in 1968 (Leifer 1995: 65). Expatriate businessmen I interviewed often mentioned the advantages of Singapore, being that it is free from complicated Bumiputera rules restricting free enterprise in Malaysia.
3  A sponsor is a property developer that retains a stake in the REIT.
4  An increasing amount of industrial space is managed by REITs. In 2011, Singapore's seven industrial REITs owned 17 per cent of the total industrial space in Singapore (Jayaraman 2012: 107).
5  NTUC, (the National Trades Union Congress) is Singapore's trade union organisation.
6  GIC home page, http://www.gic.com.sg, 23 March 2014.
7  On Sentosa, 'foreigners can get fast approval – within 48 hours – from the Singapore Land Authority's Land Dealings (Approval) Unit to buy landed property' (Wong and Kong 2005).
8  Among the wealth management banks in Singapore is Macquarie Private Wealth Asia; in order to be eligible, customers (private individuals and families) must have in excess of US$30 million in investment assets (*Property Report*, 2009: 31).

# 8

# Financial Crises and Real Estate

*Anyone who predicted in 1965 when we separated from Malaysia that Singapore would become a financial center would have been thought mad.* (Lee Kuan Yew 2011: 71)

Singapore is a financial centre. Its real estate industry benefits from a high concentration of financial and legal services businesses, a variety of financial institutions (offering loans), and a stock market where securitised real estate can be exchanged. Exposure to international financial markets also has its dangers. Demand by financial sector firms and their employees with high salaries and bonuses increases office and housing prices. The subprime and euro crises made speculative money flow into Singapore and inflated its housing and real estate prices. Chapter 5 introduced the state policies providing public housing and Chapter 6 the provision of public industrial space, this chapter analyses the policies that have made Singapore a financial centre. In particular, this chapter investigates how the government has sought to strike a balance, maximising the benefits and minimising the harmful effects of Singapore being a financial centre.

Historically speaking, once land came to be traded it became a commodity, and feudal rent was monetised. The price of commodified land in the urban land market is not a payment for land as a physical piece of territory or soil, but a payment for anticipated future rents: a payment for a title that confers future revenue. Land price is defined by the equation $p = r \times 100/i$, in which $p$ is the price of land, $r$ is rent

*Urban Land Rent: Singapore as a Property State*, First Edition. Anne Haila.
© 2016 John Wiley & Sons, Ltd. Published 2016 by John Wiley & Sons, Ltd.

and *i* is the interest rate. Thus, time and interest rate affect the price of land. The Singaporean sojourner we met in Chapter 2 understood well the effect of time on house prices and, after returning to Singapore, contemplated whether he should have waited longer for more money. With the introduction of the stock market and the development of financial instruments, land and real estate became securitised and exchanged on the stock market. Securitisation made immobile real estate a liquid investment object. The revolutionary side effect of this was that alternative investment options began affecting the price and use of real estate. Land became a financial asset, thus blurring the boundary between physical assets (land, buildings and equipment) and financial assets (money, bonds, shares and securities). Chapter 2 discussed the commodification of land and monetisation of land rent and Chapter 3 introduced the extension of rent theory by taking into account the possibility of alternative uses of land. This chapter analyses the process of financialisation: land becoming an asset and object of investment; land titles, together with mortgages, becoming securitised, and shares in real estate investment trusts being sold on the stock market; the real estate market becoming intertwined with the financial market, and investment in land being assessed against the potential yield of other asset classes.

Drawing land and real estate deeper into the realms of financial speculation renders urban development vulnerable to financial crises. The history of capitalism is littered with bubbles and crises from as early as the seventeenth and eighteenth centuries (the Tulip Bubble and the South Sea Bubble respectively), followed by railway speculation in the nineteenth century, the Great Depression of the 1930s, the peso meltdown in Mexico in 1994, the Asian crisis in 1997, crises in Russia and Brazil in 1998 and Argentina at the turn of the millennium, the Internet bubble in 2000, the subprime crisis in 2008 and the eurozone crisis in 2011. Economists tend to interpret crises as crises of money, overlooking the role of land and real estate. The question that puzzles me is: when did this focus on money at the cost of land and real estate begin? Was it when the silver mines were discovered in 1545 in South America and mercantalists wrote their theory of the importance of money? Or was it when monetarism won the battle against Keynesianism at the end of the twentieth century? In this chapter I attempt to redress this neglect, analysing the role of land and real estate in financial crises.

The introduction of new financial instruments and the increased importance of financial markets affect real estate development and investment. Securitisation, the packaging of assets and loans into marketable bundles, makes immobile real estate a liquid and comparable investment object, and hence more easily drawn into the yield searching game. The two theories explaining investment comparisons and switches from one option to another are investment switch theory and rent gap theory. The theory of investment switching (Harvey 1978) postulates that investments are switched from the primary circuit of capital (production) to the secondary circuit of capital (real estate) because of crises and conflicts.[1] Rent gap theory (see Chapter 3) compares alternative uses of land and postulates that use is changed when the rent from an alternative use exceeds the rent from present use. My approach differs from these. I am not interested in production and economy as interpretations of switch theory, my interest is rather in the urban and the built environment. I also extend rent gap theory by taking into account the effect of land as an asset value. Like Gotham (2009, 2012), I see the secondary circuit as a historical process in which state policies and regulations have a role, and hence I analyse laws and institutions. Like Gotham I do not see the real estate sector as separate, but investments in real estate and other instruments as intertwined. As we saw in Chapter 6, development companies not only develop but also invest in real estate. I also extend earlier studies on financial centres (Sassen 1991), rankings of financial centres (Leyson and Thrift 1997), and competition between financial centres (Budd 1995) by taking into account financial crises and the role of real estate in them.

I begin by discussing financial centres and their history, with a more detailed look at Singapore and how it became a financial centre. Hong Kong will be briefly introduced as a comparison to demonstrate the distinctive characteristics of Singapore as a financial centre (that is, its government regulation). Two cases illustrate the importance of government regulation: the collapse of Barings and the IMF meeting in Singapore in 2006. In telling the story of Singapore as a financial centre, my focus (in contrast to earlier studies on financial centres) is on real estate. The question I ask is: how has Singapore's role as a financial centre affected its real estate market? To analyse the financial phase in which 'land is treated as a pure financial asset' (Harvey 1982: 347) and land becomes a security (a paper asset) packed together with other assets and mortgage loans into marketable bundles, the yield of which is compared to that of other investments, I introduce the term derivative rent: the yield from land titles securitised, packed together with mortgages and traded on the market as a financial instrument. Packaging real estate titles together with real estate mortgages and selling them in the stock market together with financial instruments obscures the role of land and real estate (an underlying asset). Lastly I analyse the role of real estate in the Asian crisis in 1997 and discuss how Singapore's government policies address crises.

## Financial Centres

A financial centre is 'a place (usually a city) in which there is a high concentration of banks and other financial institutions, and in which a comprehensive set of financial markets are allowed to exist and develop, so that financial activities and transactions can be effectuated more efficiently than at any other locality' (Jao 1997: 3). The International Monetary Fund (IMF) classifies financial centres into three categories: international financial centres, regional financial centres and offshore financial centres. International financial centres are international full-service centres with advanced settlements systems. They support large domestic economies, and have deep and liquid markets where both the sources and uses of funds are diverse, and where legal and regulatory frameworks are adequate to safeguard the integrity of principal–agent relationships and supervisory functions (IMF 2000). Examples are London, New York and Tokyo. Regional financial centres, like Singapore, have a small domestic economy. Offshore financial centres provide limited specialist services. They often have low or zero taxation, moderate or light financial regulation, banking secrecy and anonymity. Financial centres are also classified by reference to the quality of supervision. Singapore and Hong Kong, together with Luxembourg, Switzerland and the Isle of Man, have a high standard of supervision, whereas the Bahamas, the Cayman Islands, Samoa, Vanuatu and Liechtenstein have a low standard of supervision. Financial centres have also been ranked on the basis of willingness to release information and prevent tax evasion. For example, in 2009 OECD announced a blacklist of countries and financial centres that do not release information. Soon afterwards, Costa Rica, Malaysia, the Philippines and Uruguay announced their willingness to cooperate and were transferred to a so-called grey list.

Financial centres go back a long way. Jao (1997) begins his history with the Italian city of Florence in the thirteenth century. Florence's position was founded on international trade and money-lending to monarchs. In the sixteenth century, Genoa emerged as a new financial centre by building a credit system based on gold and silver. In the seventeenth century, Amsterdam succeeded Genoa. Unlike the Italian city-states, Amsterdam was backed by the economic power of a nation state, and was also the commercial and information centre of Europe. Later, Amsterdam lost its position to London. Among the reasons for the rise of London were the industrial revolution (which made Britain the strongest industrial power in the nineteenth century), Britain's victory in the Napoleonic Wars (which made Britain the world's strongest military power), the introduction of new financial instruments (joint-stock banking, merchant banking, central banking, cheques, bills of exchange, bonds and shares), and the city's role as the control centre of the British Empire (Jao 1997: 137–138). After London, New York became the world's financial capital. By 1958, the dollar shortage gave way to the dollar glut, and the United States passed a series of regulations that gave rise to the eurocurrency market in Europe. 'London quickly captured the largest part of this market, thanks to its intelligent and flexible regulatory regime and its financial expertise and experience accumulated over two centuries' (Jao 1997: 138).

Since the 1980s, world financial markets have undergone significant changes (see e.g. Leyson and Thrift 1997). The growth of Japan's economy increased the size and significance of Japanese banks and made Japan the world's leading creditor nation. At the same time, the role of the United States as the global money centre, and the role of commercial banks like Citicorp and Bank of America, declined. Both the debt crises of developing countries and the petrodollars of the oil-producing countries integrated the Third World and Arab countries into the international financial system. Electronic trading, high-frequency trading and fusions between stock exchanges increased the velocity of transfers and competition among centres. The rise of China's economy and the value of yuan, as well as the subprime and euro crises, introduced new problems into the financial architecture.

Why have some financial centres (such as Florence or Amsterdam) lost their position, while the power of others (like London) seems remarkably long-lived? Cassis (2006) proposes that the reason for the rise of a financial centre is the ascendant economic power of the country within which it is situated, and the reason for its fall is war. He concedes that state intervention can have an effect; he doubts, however, that state intervention can determine the destinies of international financial centres. Singapore as a financial centre challenges this opinion (Figure 8.1). Despite the small economy, strong regulatory government has made Singapore an important regional financial centre.

### Singapore and Hong Kong as Financial Centres

Hong Kong and Singapore are classified as second-order financial centres (by Jao 1997), ranking below first-order financial centres like Tokyo, London and New York. Such rankings are based on market value and favour large economies. Rankings by size, though, do not do justice to the financial markets of small economies that can have important functions in transmitting the financial flows of the global economy. Singapore and Hong Kong link the Atlantic, Middle East and Pacific regions for offshore dealings, and bridge the time zone gap

**Figure 8.1**   Republic plaza, Singapore as a financial centre. Photo: Anne Haila.

between the New York/London and Hong Kong/Tokyo markets (Huff 1994: 341).

Hong Kong and Singapore compete with each other for the title of Asia's second-most important financial centre (after Tokyo). Singapore and Hong Kong have fewer entry barriers and regulatory burdens than Tokyo, which has inflexible listing rules, a turnover tax and higher costs (Jao 1997: 102). As a result, the Tokyo stock market has lost companies to the Hong Kong and Singapore markets (Kamo 1995: 36). In 1968, Hong Kong and Singapore vied for supremacy of the Asian dollar market, a battle which Singapore won. Jao (1997) claimed that the slowness of the Hong Kong government to abolish a tax on foreign currency deposits, along with Singapore's incentives for multinational US banks, were important reasons for Singapore's victory. 'Hong Kong lost the Asian dollar market to Singapore in the late sixties because of the government's refusal to abolish the interest withholding tax on foreign currency deposits. By the time the same tax was finally abolished in 1982, Singapore had already established itself as a formidable IFC [International Financial Centre] posing a potential threat to Hong Kong' (Jao 1997: 117).

The Hong Kong stock market is characterised by a multitude of small investors and a large number of public companies involved in the real estate business. There, small investors control their investments and '[a]s a result, even in today's modern market Hong Kong's brokers are in reality holders of individual investor portfolios rather than managers of such portfolios' (Hong Kong Public Companies 1986). Much of the investment in shares in Hong Kong is by the 'man in the street', making this a grassroots market. 'The smaller investor usually manifests a gambling streak, eschewing the so-called blue chip counters in favour of second and third tier companies which appear to offer more attractive rates of return. On the other hand, major brokers, given the large institutional bias of their clients, have little inclination to follow the fortunes of shares of lesser companies' (Hong Kong Public Companies 1986: 16). A market comprising many small investors is susceptible to rumour mongering, producing sudden shifts in market trends and necessitating quick decision-making. Small investors also tend to follow the buying and selling pattern of leading businessmen. Such behaviour is encouraged by the suspicion that a significant amount of trading is insider trading. 'In general it can be said that the real life-blood of the Hong Kong stock market is the small investor, who picks up what rumours he can on the street, always keeps his eye on the local mandarins, and is mindful of international political and economic trends, both of which have a profound effect on the territory's shares. Investment decisions are thus a combination of common sense and an intrinsic love of gambling' (Hong Kong Public Companies 1986: 17).

The other characteristic feature of the Hong Kong stock market is the large number of public companies involved in the property business. In 1985, out of the 247 public companies listed on the Hong Kong Stock Exchange, 161 listed property investment, property development, or ownership or letting of properties among their business activities (Hong Kong Public Companies 1986). The property business is combined with all sorts of other business activities, like food and package cartons (Amoy Canning), shipbuilding (Chung Wah Shipbuilding & Engineering), manufacture and distribution of electronics and plastics (Conic Investment Company), manufacture and sale of garments (Crocodile Garments), manufacture, import, export and sale of carpets (Hong Kong Carpet Manufacturers), generation and supply of electricity (Hong Kong Electric Holdings), manufacture and marketing of pharmaceuticals and Thai silk (Jack Chia International), and the sale and distribution of shoes (Kam Shing Commercial and Industrial Development).

Because of its reliable legal system and *laissez faire* reputation, Hong Kong has been a gateway for Western companies in respect of their operations in China. The handover of Hong Kong to China in 1997 threatened this. In the United States, Chairman of the Select Committee on US National Security, Christopher Cox, claimed in his committee report that Hong Kong had become a major transhipment point for Chinese spies and smugglers. 'Anyone selling to Hong kong, may be selling to China's army' (Iritani 1999). These concerns were denied in Hong Kong. The Hong Kong government labelled the US Congressional report unfair and anti-China (HK slams Cox report… 1999). Such doubts and debates stress the importance of reputation and the fragile position of financial centres. They have to strike a balance between *laissez faire* and regulation. Singapore has excelled at this balancing act, sometimes tightening and at other times relaxing regulations.

Located at a crossroads of trade routes, Singapore's conditions for becoming a financial centre were favourable. Its maritime role drew foreign banks and insurance companies. In addition to the Western and Japanese banks, Singapore also became an important centre for Chinese money. In 1932, three Hokkien banks – the Chinese Commercial Bank, the Ho Hong Bank and the Overseas-Chinese Bank – amalgamated to form Singapore's dominant Chinese bank, the Overseas-Chinese Banking Corporation (OCBC), which in the late 1930s was the largest Chinese-owned bank outside China (Huff 1994: 230). In 2011, the Industrial and Commercial Bank of China (ICBC) (the world's largest bank by market value) opened its first offshore yuan processing centre in Singapore (Tan L 2011). In 1995, an Islamic insurance fund called the Takaful Fund was set up. It gave Muslim Singaporeans the opportunity to invest and obtain insurance cover without compromising their religious principles (Tan C H 1999: 163–164).

Singapore's own banking sector began in 1877, when the Post Office Savings Bank (PosB) was officially opened, and in 1972 the PosB became a statutory board. PosB 'was required to use most of the money deposited with it to buy government securities, or as deposits with the Monetary Authority of Singapore' (Huff 1994: 336), contributing to Singapore's high public sector-driven savings rate. In 1968, the Development Bank of Singapore (DBS Bank) was set up, taking over the function of industrial financing from the Economic Development Board (EDB) (the statutory board discussed in Chapter 5) that had been established in 1961 (Tan 1999: 411). In 1998, the DBS Bank bought the PosBank. Then, the largest shareholders of DBS Bank were MND Holdings and Temasek Holdings, both government holding companies (see Chapter 7). In 1999 the government offered bonds to privatise the DBS shares.

The Monetary Authority of Singapore (MAS), which regulates the financial market, was established in 1971. It functions as Singapore's central bank, and supervises financial markets and institutions. Its mission is to 'promote sustained non-inflatory economic growth, and a sound and progressive financial centre' (MAS Annual Report 2007/2008). The Board of Directors of MAS consists of Ministers (for example the Minister of Trade and Industry and the Minister of Finance in 2008), showing the close relationship between monetary and fiscal policies. In addition to fighting against inflation, developing a sound financial centre and the integration of monetary and fiscal policies, an important policy for MAS has been its exchange rate policy. MAS is appreciated by the financial community for having created a stable financial regime, and has a reputation for implementing conservative and restrictive policy (Mirza 1986: 124). One indicator of the financial system's stability is that, during the post-independence period, no local bank has failed nor have public funds been used to bail out banks (Hamilton-Hart 2003: 96).

In granting permissions to foreign financial institutions, MAS has followed a liberal but selective policy, and has attempted to guarantee equal representation among different countries and regions (Tan 1987: 11). In the 1980s, the tasks of MAS were extended beyond financial markets to include economic policy. MAS took over responsibility for macroeconomic modelling, thereby superseding the Ministry of Finance (MOF) and the Ministry of Trade and Industry (MTI), which had since the early 1970s developed macroeconomic models for Singapore (Peebles and Wilson 1996: 216). MAS 'works closely with the Ministry of Finance to ensure that monetary policy forms an integral part of the overall economic policy for the nation' (Tan 1999: 17). In this sense, MAS differs from central banks in the eurozone (that are independent from political decision-makers). Singapore's practice of recycling politicians and ministers also makes financial decisions less dependent on short-term re-election pressures and cedes less power to financial market actors.

In the late nineteenth century, stockbroking was initiated in the Arcade at Clifford Pier (Tan 1999: 243), where shares in British rubber and tin companies were bought and sold. In 1973 the Stock Exchanges of Malaysia and Singapore were split, and the Stock Exchange of Singapore was incorporated. The Singapore International Monetary Exchange (Simex)[2] was established in 1984 and new financial innovations were introduced, among them sterling futures, the Nikkei Stock index and US Treasury Bond futures. The mission of Simex was to strengthen the position of Singapore as Asia's financial centre. It was connected to the Chicago Monetary Exchange (CME), facilitating worldwide dealing in futures; a deal can be initiated in one country and finished in another (Tan 1987: 15–16). Singapore's financial market encapsulates a wide range of financial instruments, including Asian dollar bonds, negotiable certificates of deposit, fixed rate US dollar certificates of deposit, floating rate certificates of deposit, floating rate notes,

Asian commercial paper, revolving Underwriting Facilities and Notes Issuance Facilities (Tan 1999).

The reasons for Singapore's success as a financial centre – against all the odds and despite the recommendations of international advisors (who recommended an import-substitution strategy) – have been its political stability, reputation as an 'honest' market without corruption, the stability of the Singapore dollar, ease of financial operations, a multiplicity of financial instruments, international institutions, expertise, and above all a flexible and liberal but regulatory government (Mizra 1989; Huff 1994; Peebles and Wilson 1996; Tan 1999). The following two examples illustrate Singapore's difficult balancing act between regulation and financial liberty: the Barings case and the 2006 IMF meeting in Singapore.

### Nick Leeson and the Collapse of Barings

In February 1995, Singapore hit the headlines when one of Britain's oldest banks, Barings, collapsed. The collapse came after one of the bank's employees, Nick Leeson, working in Barings' Singapore office, speculated using futures (the Nikkei 225 index) on the Singapore stock exchange market and incurred a one billion US dollar loss for the bank. After collapse seemed inevitable, Leeson fled Singapore and disappeared. He first went to Kuala Lumpur from where he continued to Kota Kinabalu (Borneo), and then through Brunei to Frankfurt, where he was apprehended. The international media followed the event, amazed at how a 28-year-old working-class lad from Watford had managed to destroy one of Britain's oldest financial dynasties, which had been founded in 1762 and financed the armies that beat Napoleon (McGhie 1995). _The Straits Times_ cited France's Foreign Minister who in the nineteenth century regarded Barings as one of the six great powers in Europe (the five others being Britain, France, Austria, Prussia and Russia) (Tan B B 1995). When Leeson was arrested in Frankfurt, he initially announced that he would not return to Singapore. Later he changed his mind and was extradited to Singapore.

Speculation with Nikkei futures was possible because of rapid electronic transfers. The main markets for Nikkei 225 futures were Singapore and Osaka. On both of these stock markets the value of a future was calculated in a same way, and usually they did not differ from one another. Occasionally, however, the prices were different, and Leeson took advantage of this. He bought futures on the market where the prices were lower and sold them immediately on the other market where the prices were higher.

Rapid and easy transfers made the whole operation, and the sums of money being transferred, largely illusory. The incomprehensible nature of such transfers was evident in Leeson's own account.

> All the money we dealt with was unreal: abstract numbers which flashed across screen or jumped across the trading pit with a flurry of hands ... The real money was our salaries and our bonuses, but even that was a bit artificial: it was all paid by telegraphic transfer, and since we lived off expense accounts, the numbers in our bank balances just rolled up. The real, real money was the $ 100 I bet Danny each day about where the market would close, or the cash we spent buying chocolate Kinder eggs to muck around with the plastic toys we found inside them. (Leeson 1996: 75–76)

The magnitude of the funds that Leeson transferred contributes to the image of this activity as completely unreal. Leeson's own story is full of examples of how the real and unreal became blurred. At the end of 1994, when Leeson was on holiday in Ireland, he received a call from Singapore from his colleague Linda, who was checking the accounts of Barings for the year-end audit. Linda's question concerned the account in which Leeson had hidden the losses.

> What's the balance? Leeson asked, and Linda replied, 'The equity balance this week is 7.78 billion yen'. Linda read it out with as little interest as if it had been the weather forecast or the colour of shoes she was wearing. Leeson asked Linda to 'sell 2,000 December 21,500 puts at a price of 7778 ... print off the normal reports before and after that entry, use the reports before the trade for everything but the trial balance sheet, use the report after that entry for the trial balance itself.' 'Fine' she said, not really understanding what I was saying. (Leeson 1996: 205–206)

The official documents, and Leeson's own memoirs published after the event, show that the Singapore authorities were aware of regulatory violations before the collapse of Barings and that they had warned the bank. After the Singapore International Monetary Exchange found out that something was wrong and had sent a warning letter to Barings, Leeson was called to the office of his superior Simon, who could not understand what the warning letter from Simex meant. Leeson explained:

> 'Oh, they're just banging out about our intra-day funding limits ... I wish they'd just get off our backs and let us do some business'. Simon made a face and said, 'God, they're a pain in the arse. I

mean it's as if they don't want us to trade'. And Leeson added, 'They've gone and muddled out our client accounts with our house position'. Simon agreed and continued, 'They're fucking idiots. And what's this calculation – it looks about £90 million out to me.' Leeson replied, 'Yeah, I know. Look, I'll draft an answer for you ... Don't worry about it'. Simon gave Leeson the offending letter back and the conversation turned to real money. 'Now, what are you betting on Man United? ... Bet you $500 Man United win'. (Leeson 1996: 215)

How did Singapore's rival Hong Kong react to the Barings collapse? Immediately after the news broke, the Hong Kong newspapers *South China Morning Post* and *Hong Kong Standard*, wrote that such an event could never happen on the Hong Kong stock market and that futures were unpopular in Hong Kong. Hong Kong demanded that commercial banks document their assets; a mere 'yes' would not be enough (in Singapore, the losses of Barings were larger than the assets) (Kohli 1995). Soon after, however, *South China Morning Post* and *Hong Kong Standard* supported the position of Singapore officials that the blame lay with Barings in London, which did not intervene despite the warnings of the Singapore authorities. *South China Morning Post* wrote in its editorial 'Certainly it now seems clear that, if only through their negligence, Barings executives in London were at least as much to blame for the bank's collapse as Leeson. Perhaps it is indicative of the all-too-common view in London that Asia is something of a wild east – where different rules apply from back home' (Heavy costs ... 1995).

Leeson was trading futures via the Internet. The use of electronic transfers, however, does not mean that place no longer matters. On the contrary, this case shows that it matters a great deal; it demonstrates the necessity of regulation. The Singapore authorities reacted quickly. After Leeson's disappearance, the authorities began to study the case immediately. Finance Minister Richard Hu led the investigation, and issued a statement ('Collapse of the Barings Group') reiterating the soundness of Singapore's financial system and Simex in particular (Hill 1995). When Leeson was arrested at Frankfurt airport, Singapore demanded his extradition, accusing him of 'forging an accounting document worth seven million yen' (Detained Barings ... 1995). Singapore gave Germany a 1000-page document supporting their extradition claim. It listed 12 accusations against Leeson (Silva 1995). Singapore's extradition request was accepted, and Leeson was sent back to Singapore, where he was sentenced in December 1995 to six and a half years in prison.

Simex not only studied the event in detail, but immediately implemented measures to improve the system. Simex blamed Barings for hiding information concerning Leeson, information that Simex regarded as crucial when it made the decision concerning Leeson's application to trade futures (Chan S M 1995a). Singaporean investigators also asked the question that was ignored in a 337-page report by the Bank of England: Singapore claimed that the key question was why were more than one billion dollars worth of assets entrusted to Leeson after his unauthorised deals were disclosed (Chan S M 1995b). In March 1995 Simex set up an international panel of futures experts with the task of advising the futures exchange and increasing market confidence. The panel was headed by the former head of the Chicago Board of Trade, John Gilmore, who was a partner in American investment company Goldman Sachs & Co. (Simex names... 1995). The detailed report on the Barings case, published by the Singaporean audits office on 7 October 1995, became a bestseller. In November 1995, Simex introduced new measures to control the financial market. Minister of Finance, Dr Hu, announced that, 'Singapore will not bail out banks which are in trouble, but will do everything possible to prevent them from getting into a situation where they could go bust' (Chan S M 1995c). The Barings case shows the importance of monitoring and regulation in a financial centre, and the readiness of the government in Singapore to act. The following example illustrates another type of control from which Singapore as a financial centre benefits.

## The IMF in Singapore

In the early 2000s, anti-globalisation demonstrations had disrupted meetings of the International Monetary Fund and the World Bank in Seattle, Prague and Genoa. In 2006 the IMF and the World Bank arranged their annual meeting in peaceful and well-ordered Singapore. The only disturbance anywhere remotely nearby was to be seen on television: the coup in Thailand. The protesters in Singapore had their own speakers' corner to express their views.

For Singapore the meeting was an opportunity to further boost its reputation as a reliable financial centre. At the opening ceremony, Singapore's Prime Minister Lee Hsien Loong noted Asia's remarkable growth and praised globalisation for fuelling it. He gave credit to Asian governments that, after the 1997 financial crisis, kept their markets open to competition, courted foreign investments and promoted exports (Low I 2006). Afterwards, Prime Minister Lee thanked Singaporeans for making the meeting a success. IMF Chief Rodrigo Rato praised the arrangements for the meeting, specifically mentioning the friendliness that visitors experienced throughout the week (Chan F 2006).

The meeting in Singapore was also an opportunity to rethink the future of emerging markets and international security. Among the topics discussed were aid packages for developing countries and IMF voting rights (with proposals to increase the voting shares of China, South Korea, Turkey and Mexico). The deputy managing director of the IMF, John Lipsky, praised investors' trust in emerging markets: 'Investors' implicit expectations of sustained economic and financial stability in these markets have challenged long-held views about these economies inherent structural weaknesses' (Lipsky 2006: 17). The hosting of the meeting in Asia was also an opportunity to increase cooperation among Asian countries. *The Straits Times* (Tay 2006) reported that Europe and the United States were watching closely as regionalism took shape between ASEAN[3] and its neighbours. Singapore's second Minister for Finance, Tharman Shanmugaratnam, however, suggested that Asia should not follow in the footsteps of the European Union by adopting a common currency (Ng 2006).

*The Straits Times* (S'pore scores high 2006) did not miss the opportunity to praise Singapore's good and efficient governance. It reported on a World Bank study that ranked Singapore high in government effectiveness, regulatory quality, control of corruption, rule of law and political stability, and also mentioned the categories in which Singapore received lower scores (voice and accountability measuring political, civil and human rights). Activists boycotted the Singapore meeting. An Oxfam team leader told *The Straits Times* (Li et al. 2006) that its forum was cancelled 'as part of a boycott of all official IMF-World Bank activities, to register displeasure at Singapore's earlier blacklisting of 27 activists'. Demonstrators were provided a 10 m by 14 m space inside the lobby of the Suntec City Convention Centre where they had to abide by fixed rules. Anti-globalisation activists and other non-governmental organisations held their demonstrations and social forums in Batam, Indonesia (where the authorities initially did not allow these events, but later relented).

The meeting in Singapore went as planned. The only disadvantage was that hotel and airline ticket prices had doubled. There was no tear gas, no cobble-stones thrown at delegates and no armed vehicles. One delegate explained to me that was an unusual experience, to walk alone from hotel to meeting without a police escort changing the route and trying to find an entry point through the fenced perimeter around the meeting place. As Prime Minister Lee pointed out, the Singapore meeting was also recognition of the Asian countries that had survived the Asian financial crisis. The collapse of Barings and demonstrations during the IMF meeting were very minor upsets compared to the Asian financial crisis.

## The Asian Crisis

Singapore's development industry benefits from developed financial markets. Development companies can obtain credit from numerous banks (they are not dependent on just a handful of banks), and borrow from capital and debt markets. However, there are also disadvantages. As a financial and wealth management centre, Singapore draws in speculative money. Whether this money is channelled into real estate depends on the profit of the commodity-producing sector (as the switching theory postulates) and on the interest rate and yield of other investment options (stocks and bonds, for example). When channelled into real estate, speculative money raises prices and increases vacancy. In such situations, the government has intervened to counter the harmful effects of speculative money flowing into real estate.

One such intervention occurred in 1996, when the real estate market was booming and prices escalated. The government decided to intervene and introduced an anti-speculation programme. The measures included taxation of gains from properties sold within three years of purchase, imposition of stamp duty on such sales, and tightening of mortgage credit for residential property purchases (Govt sticks to land ... 1996). Deputy Prime Minister Lee Hsien Loong admitted that 'there was a risk in introducing the property anti-speculation measures ... but the Government acted anyway because the risk of doing nothing was greater' (Govt sticks to land ... 1996). The aims of the government's anti-speculation measures were to cool off and stabilise the market. Curbing speculation was seen as important because 'when speculation becomes excessive a bubble develops. If unchecked, it will eventually burst and seriously damage the rest of the economy, especially the financial sector, and hurt many home owners and small investors' (Govt sticks to land ... 1996). This anti-speculation programme and intervention in the real estate market turned out to be fortunate, as it was introduced just before the real crisis began.

In July 1997, the devaluing of the Thai baht provoked a crisis that spread from Thailand to other countries and from sector to sector. What at the outset was a currency crisis later became an economic, social and political crisis. Only those countries decoupled from the global economy, like Myanmar, were saved from the turmoil. Myanmar's FDI inflows actually increased from 1996 to 1998, from 38 million $US to 40 million (World Investment Report 1999).

At the beginning of the crisis, the worst affected economies were Indonesia, Korea, Malaysia, the Philippines and Thailand. Less affected were Hong Kong, Singapore and Taiwan. The reasons why Singapore suffered less than its neighbours were its high savings rate, fiscal surplus,

**Table 8.1**    FDI inflows and outflows in 1996 and 1998 (million $US).

|                | Inflows | Inflows | Outflows | Outflows |
|----------------|--------:|--------:|---------:|---------:|
| Year           | 1996    | 1998    | 1996     | 1998     |
| Hong Kong      | 5521    | 1600    | 26,531   | 18,762   |
| Singapore      | 7884    | 7218    | 6274     | 3108     |
| Malaysia       | 5078    | 3727    | 4133     | 1921     |
| Western Europe | 115,346 | 237,425 | 203,942  | 406,220  |
| Japan          | 228     | 3192    | 23,428   | 24,152   |
| USA            | 76,453  | 193,375 | 74,833   | 132,829  |

Source: Adapted from World Investment Report 1999.

limited foreign debt, and the fact that it had the world's highest per capita foreign reserves. Also, among Singapore's largest external markets (the European Union, Hong Kong, Japan, Malaysia and the United States), only Malaysia was seriously harmed. The Singaporean government also continued with its Keynesian policy and kept investing in its mass rapid transit system, port facilities, land reclamation and public housing (Asian Development Outlook 1998: 50–52).

Table 8.1 compares FDI inflows and outflows in 1996 and 1998, immediately before and after the crisis. In Hong Kong and Malaysia there was a marked decline of inflows, while in Singapore the decline was smaller. Outflows in these economies fell; in Singapore the outflows in 1998 were half of those in 1996. During the same period, globalisation continued in the Western world. Both inflows and outflows increased, substantially so in Western Europe and the United States. The development of Japan, which experienced the crisis earlier than other Asian countries, resembled that of Western Europe and the United States. Outflows increased slightly, but inflows substantially. The 1997 crisis did not spread globally, but was limited to Asia.

The Asian crisis was not a new phenomenon. There had been several crises before it. The 1997 Asian crisis, however, displayed some new features and has been called 'the mother of all international financial crises' (Johnson and Kwak 2011: 39). Whereas the crises in Latin America in the 1980s were the result of government debt, corruption and bad macroeconomic policies, in East and Southeast Asia there was a climate of low inflation and budget surpluses (or only small deficits), together with stable or rising foreign exchange reserves (Wade and Veneroso 1998). The 'macroeconomic fundamentals' were fine, as was often repeated during the crisis.

The Asian crisis took different forms in different countries. For the Thai economy, based on agribusiness and the exportation of rice, currency stability has been important. According to Phongpaichit and Baker (1998), the technocrats in Bangkok realised too late that the days of a pegged currency were over. In Malaysia, where close relationships between politicians, bureaucrats, party members and entrepreneurs (Searle 1999) are characteristic features of the economy, Prime Minister Mahathir Mohamed's ambitious construction projects did not resolve the crisis, and the situation led to a political crisis too. Taiwan suffered less than other Asian economies because of its large number of family-owned small businesses, which were only modestly globalised and had not received significant amounts of finance from abroad (Cotton 2000: 164). Additionally, the savings rate in Taiwan was one of the highest in the world (40 per cent of GNP in 1988) and the country had the world's second-largest gold reserves after Japan (Dobbs-Higginson 1993: 156).

The most dramatic political effect of the 1997 crisis was the end of Suharto's rule in Indonesia in 1998, following violent riots against cuts in subsidies for the price of rice recommended by the IMF. In Malaysia, Deputy Prime Minister Anwar, who had defended the IMF policy, was fired and imprisoned. Thailand remained politically stable, although workers protested against wage cuts and the middle classes protested against job losses. Some politicians and technocrats became scapegoats, like Prime Minister Chavalit Yongchaiyudh in the Silom Road Business People's protests 'where the rich demanded the resignation of Chavalit' (Ungpakorn 1999: 39). The relationship of the economic crisis to these political upheavals is evident. As Chua Beng Huat (1999) remarked, in countries where the legitimacy of the regime is built 'on a single performance criterion, namely the sustaining of economic growth ... the "legitimacy" of the regime immediately comes under attack' when growth stops (Chua 1999: 783).

In some Asian countries the crisis led to the rise of economic nationalism and protests against globalisation. In Indonesia, the riots were targeted against the IMF. Nobel Prize economist Joseph Stiglitz (2002: 486), who criticised the policies of the IMF for ignoring social consequences, argued that the elimination of food and fuel subsidies for the very poor predictably led to riots. In Malaysia, Prime Minister Mahathir blamed global speculators, particularly George Soros. In Thailand the cause of the crisis was attributed to globalisation, multinational companies and the imperialism of the G7 powers (especially the United States) (Ungpakorn 1999: 44).

Singapore saw the crisis differently. Here the crisis acted as a new impetus for further globalisation. George Yeo, who had served in several ministerial posts (minister for information and the arts, health, trade and industry, and foreign policy) and was regarded as 'the New Guard's most original thinker' by Cherian George (2000: 185), suggested that the Asian financial crisis provided a historic opportunity for Singapore to lure in talent from across the region. 'All over the region now, bright, able, dynamic entrepreneurial people have gone bankrupt or are without jobs' (cited in George 2000: 185), he said in the parliament. He referred to Hong Kong's success, which was based on the influx of entrepreneurial talent from China, suggesting that Singapore should encourage some of this talent to come to Singapore (George 2000: 185).

The Asian crisis was a puzzle for scholars. Different explanations were suggested: negligence on the part of Southeast Asian governments (US federal reserve chairman Alan Greenspan, Asian govts … 1997), a lack of transparency (the IMF), cronyism and rent-seeking, a vicious circle leading to loss of confidence (Krugman 1999), financial panic (Radelet and Sachs 2000), US investors' increased demands for profitability on their Asian investments and the increase of private capital flows (Winters 2000), and the collision of two different financial systems (the Western version with its untrammelled competitiveness versus the Asian version with its opaque price signals) (Rajan and Zingales 2009).

A common feature among these explanations is an underestimation of the role of investments in real estate. Although there is no doubt that speculative real estate investment and conspicuous mega-projects had a role in the Asian crisis, speculative construction projects, excessive investment in real estate (at the cost of productive projects) and the decreased value of real estate as collateral were referred to only in passing. Paul Krugman (1999: 68–90), for example, although noting much pure speculation in real estate, saw the problem as one of reduced confidence and shrinkage in the supply of loans. Like scholars, the region's political leaders did not pay attention to the role of property in the crisis: after the onset of the crisis Indonesia announced plans to build the world's longest bridge, and Malaysia continued with its mega-projects too (which included plans to build the world's biggest dam and longest building) (Winters 2000:46). Such understating of the role of real estate calls for an analysis of the real estate and crises. In what follows, I look first at the case of Bangkok and then at Singapore, where government intervention affected the pace of the crisis.

### Bangkok and Real Estate Speculation

At the outset, Thailand was the epicentre of the economic crisis. In their explanation of the bursting of the Thai economic bubble, Pasuk Phongpaichit and Chris Baker (1998) emphasised the role of finance but also noted the harmful effects of expansion in the property sector. After the government opened up Thailand's financial market to global investors, there was an oversupply of funds. Much of these funds went into property development. 'Between 1991 and 1994, bank lending to property firms doubled from 200 to 400 billion baht or 10 percent of all their loans. By 1996, finance companies had lent 350 billion baht to property, almost a quarter of their total loan business' (Phongpaichit and Baker 1998: 113). Foreign investors were not interested in firms producing commodities, but instead invested in speculative projects offering the prospect of windfall capital gains – property, finance and telecoms. In 1996, 22 per cent of transactions on the stock market were in property and telecoms. The sudden and excessive inflow of foreign money and the oversupply of credit created a situation in which success depended not on selling homes, shops and offices, but on acquiring more and more assets which could be used as collateral for more and more loans (Phongpaichit and Baker 1998: 101–113).

Part of the increased investment in property was needed to meet increased demand for office, industrial and shopping space due to the growth of the Thai economy. But some of the investments were speculative, and in the wrong places. Real estate was bought for speculative purposes, and the excessive buying of housing units led developers to flood the market (Pornchockchai and Perera 2005). Phongpaichit and Baker (1998: 114) claimed that there was no logic applied estimating the amount of space demanded, nor thus to coordinating development. The result was overcapacity and high vacancies. They refer to one development, Muang Thong Thani, as a typical example of a failed project. The largest housing project in Bangkok, Muang Thong Thani was developed by Bangkok Land and modelled on Hong Kong's satellite cities. 'But Bangkok was not Hong Kong. Thais were not yet used to living in high rise and factories did not need to be stacked on top of one another. Only a few of the units were sold and even fewer occupied. Muang Thong became an eerily empty canyon of concrete' (Phongpaichit and Baker 1998: 114).

The devaluation of the Thai baht in 1997 made it difficult for development companies to repay their loans and finish their projects. Bangkok Land, Somprason Land, Sanaviriyana City and Juldis Develop all experienced difficulties (Thailand Country report 4th Quarter 1997). In 1998 almost half of all loans were estimated to be non-performing, and 80 per cent of these were in the property sector (Year-End Economic Review 1998). The closure of financial firms made it impossible for developers to secure funds in order to complete projects. The result was that, as projects were cancelled – including the Hopewells' transit system project in Bangkok – or left unfinished, prices fell and vacancy rates rose. Approvals for development projects plunged to 69 per cent, property prices fell by more than 60 per cent, developers began selling units repossessed from buyers and the office vacancy rate in Bangkok was estimated to be 40 per cent (Year-End Economic Review 1998).

One of the problems in explaining the Asian crisis relates to its timing. The Asian crisis came to a head in July 1997, when the government in Thailand let the Thai baht float. Why did the Asian development state model, that had worked so well, suddenly experience a crisis or, as Chang (1998) asked, why did cronyism suddenly produce a catastrophe in 1997 (Arestis and Glickman 2002: 255)? Jeffrey Winters (2000: 41) asked 'why did the crisis not occur six, twelve, or even eighteen months earlier?' Why did the crisis burst in 1997 although 'all of the problems mentioned for the economies of the region – weak banks, wasteful and non-productive investments, overbuilding in the property sector, excessive borrowing by private sector firms, and speculation in local stocks markets with borrowed funds – have been chronic for years'. His answer is that, on 2 July 1997, investors became aware of the problem, and loss of confidence provoked a herd-behaviour phenomenon.

Why did investors become aware of the problem only in July of 1997? Were there no signals prior to that? In the property market, there had been signs before the crisis. In 1995, 350 small property companies filed for bankruptcy in Bangkok, and 'in early 1995, the authorities sensed the beginning of a bubble and restricted bank lending to property' (Phongpaichit and Baker 1998: 113–114). Table 8.2 shows housing registrations in Bangkok. Housing registrations had already started to decline before 1997. The peak year of housing registrations was 1995, and the number of housing registrations fell dramatically after 1997.

The problems in the housing market (bankruptcies, lending restrictions and a decline in housing registrations) preceding the onset of the crisis give credence to the theory that postulates a causal relationship between the property sector and the productive sector. In his classic study *One Hundred Years of Land Values in Chicago* (1933), Homer Hoyt

**Table 8.2** Housing registrations in greater Bangkok (1991–1998).

| | *1991* | *1992* | *1993* | *1994* | *1995* | *1996* | *1997* | *1998* |
|---|---|---|---|---|---|---|---|---|
| Total (single houses, town houses, condominiums, duplex) | 129,688 | 108,001 | 134,086 | 171,254 | 172,419 | 166,785 | 145,355 | 39,640 |

Source: Adapted from The Land Department, Year-End Economic Review 1998.

investigated trends in land values in Chicago and identified a regular cycle of 18-year duration. Based on Hoyt's study and the hypothesis of land speculation as 'the great initiatory cause' (inspired by Henry George), Fred Harrison (1983) assembled data on peaks in land values, building-cycle peaks and economic recession, arguing that the peak in land values is reached 12 to 24 months prior to the economic recession, and that peaks in the building cycle follow peaks in land values and precede general economic recession (Harrison 1983: 65).

The Hoyt–Harrison hypothesis postulates an order, with firstly the peak in land values, then the building-cycle peak and lastly the economic recession. It is worth checking to see whether this hypothesis is confirmed in the Bangkok data. The housing registrations peak, preceding the crisis, supports the Hoyt–Harrison theory. However, if we take prices into account, there is no evidence that a land value peak preceded the economic recession of 1997. Figure 8.2 shows the development of land index from 1991 to 2000.

The land price index kept rising right up to 1997. Buyers of land kept on paying high prices even after the decline in housing registrations, and banks continued giving loans. Unsold flats and increasing vacancy afterwards show that the demand was speculative, and developers misinterpreted this speculative demand as real demand. Speculators, thus, did not stabilise the market, as some economists believe (see Chapter 6), but

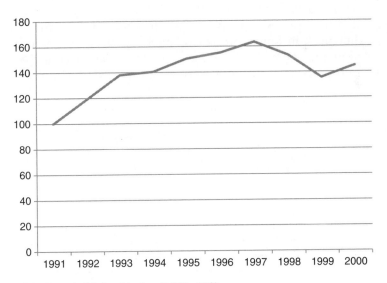

**Figure 8.2**   Bangkok's land index (1991=100).
Source: The Bank of Thailand.

bloated the bubble. Before discussing this irrational behaviour of speculators and belief in rising land prices further, it is worth looking at what
happened in Singapore.

### Singapore and the Financial Crisis

The Asian crisis also affected Singapore. The chairman of MAS, Lee
Hsien Loong, wrote in a statement (MAS Annual Report 1997/1998)
that 'the Asian financial crisis has totally changed the regional landscape, and seriously affected the Singapore economy'. He called for
'a fresh approach' to secure Singapore's position as a major financial
centre. This fresh approach implied the MAS shifting its emphasis from
regulation to supervision (giving more leeway to better-managed institutions), easing its monetary policy and liberalising (allowing market
forces greater freedom). Singapore's problems were not so much in the
banking sector or currency weakness, as experienced by its neighbours
Thailand and Indonesia. There were no failures or bail-outs of banks,
and the Singapore dollar devalued the least among the currencies listed
in Table 8.3, showing changes in exchange rates between 1997 and 1998
(the Hong Kong dollar is pegged to the US dollar, and so left out).

The problems generated by the crisis were not so severe in the banking sector; it was the property sector that suffered more. Figure 8.3 shows
the property price index for residential properties in Singapore.

Prices soared until 1996 and then declined sharply. Compared to
Bangkok, where prices kept rising until the onset of the crisis in 1997,
the earlier peak in Singapore is explained by the government's anti-
speculation programme, introduced in May 1996 to cool the over-
heating property market. The government's intervention also makes it

Table 8.3   Changes in exchange rates.

|                | change (%) 1997–1998 |
|----------------|----------------------|
| Singapore      | −11.6                |
| Taiwan         | −13.8                |
| Malaysia       | −33.6                |
| Korea          | −36.2                |
| Thailand       | −36.0                |
| Philippines    | −33.0                |
| Indonesia      | −73.8                |

Source: Adapted from Hamilton-Hart 2003: 157.

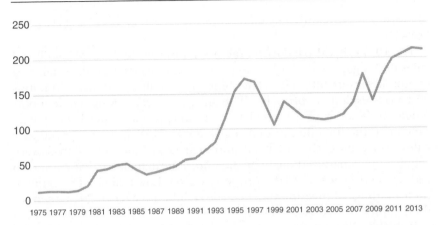

**Figure 8.3** Property price index of residential properties from 1975 to 2014. Source: URA.

difficult to specify effects generated by the crisis. For this reason the Singapore data cannot be used to test the Hoyt–Harrison hypothesis. In the construction sector, the peak was also in 1996. After the crisis, when GDP and the manufacturing sector started to grow, the construction sector recovered more slowly. Manufacturing (total output) declined 3.7 per cent in 1998 but increased 9.9 per cent in the following year; building and construction continued to decline in 1999: −29.6 per cent (written permissions), −52.4 per cent (building plan approvals) and −32.5 per cent (building completions)[4] (Yearbook of Statistics Singapore 2002: 4).

The real estate market and the construction sector might have suffered more had it not been for certain buffers in place at that time. The first buffer was the anti-speculation programme introduced before the crisis (in May 1996). The MAS Annual Report (1999/2000: 17) stated that 'the anti-speculation measures in May 1996 had already dampened sentiments in the property market so that the decline in investments following the Asian financial crisis was somewhat less sharp than would have been the case otherwise'.

The second buffer was public sector housing development. While private residential construction started to decline in 1996, preceding the decline in GDP, public housing construction increased until 1998. The demand for housing was also boosted by Central Provident Fund (CPF) withdrawals for housing. After the crisis, the employers' contribution to the CPF was reduced from 20 per cent to 10 per cent, and homeowners were compensated through a reduced repayment scheme, rescheduling of mortgage loans and deferment of mortgage payments (Tan C H 1999: 368–370).

The 1997 crisis also led to liberalisation policies. In 2000, MAS relaxed rules on Singapore dollar lending. Non-residents (both individuals and companies) were allowed to lend Singapore dollars and invest in bonds and non-residential property. The measures were designed to boost Singapore's status as a financial centre and property market-watchers welcomed the liberalisation (Wong D 2000). MAS also announced new rules concerning the financial and real estate markets. Banks were required to separate their financial and non-financial activities, and to reduce their exposure to the property sector (Low I 2000). The value of their holdings of investment properties could not exceed 20 per cent of their capital funds (Koh 2000).

Post-1997 liberalisation gave some breathing space, but it was not to last for long. The next crisis emerged in 2008. The MAS Annual Report for 2008/2009 stated that 'the past year was extremely challenging for central banks around the world … Singapore, being open and highly dependent on trade, was badly affected by these external developments. After several years of rapid growth, the economy experienced its deepest recession.' In Singapore the main problem was not the financial system; that remained healthy because 'banks have very low non-performing loans (NPLs), minimal exposure to toxic assets, and are well-capitalised and sound' (MAS Annual Report 2008/2009: 4). However, the global financial crisis and economic downturn affected Singapore's global investments, public revenue and the property market.

Singapore's sovereign wealth funds' global investments suffered during the global crisis. Temasek and GIC (the Government of Singapore Investment Corporation) had invested beyond the Asian market – for example, GIC had injected capital (11 billion Swiss francs = S$14.4 billion) into Swiss bank UBS (Ng G 2008). In 2008, the value of Temasek Holdings' portfolio shrank by 31 per cent (Temasek Holdings … 2009). The loss came from investments in Merrill Lynch and Barclays (Temasek Holdings … 2009). Singapore's public revenues also declined. Although government expenditure in Singapore displays limited cyclical behaviour (because of the relative absence of counter-cyclical and unemployment-related payments in government outlays) (MAS Annual Report 1998/1999), tax revenues depend on the business cycle and real estate market. In the late 1990s, MAS estimated that the cyclical response of tax revenue to the business cycle of GDP was 0.28 per cent (i.e. 1 per cent decline in GDP produces 0.28 per cent decline in tax revenue) within which the role of property tax was 0.35 per cent. Land and land-use related taxes are considerable. In 2008, income tax produced S$19.286 billion, and land and land-use related

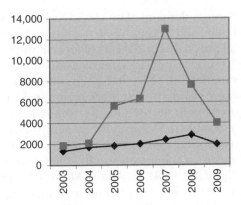

**Figure 8.4** Revenue from property tax (below) and sales of land (above). Millions S$.
Source: Budgets several years.

taxes (property tax, motor vehicle taxes, sales of land and stamp duty) S$13.797 billion (over two-thirds of the amount generated by income tax). Total receipts were S$64.306 billion, of which land and land-related taxes were 21.5 per cent (Budget 2010). Land and land-use related revenues are dependent upon cycles in the property market. Figure 8.4 shows the revenue from the property tax and sales of land between 2003 and 2009.

Revenue from property tax varied from S$1330 million in 2003 to S$2856 million in 2008, subsequently decreasing to S$1979 million in 2009. Revenue from the sales of land varied more markedly, peaking at S$13,000 million in 2007. The benchmark Straits Times Index (STI) is also sensitive to property market cycles. The STI comprises 30 companies, including the following development and real estate companies: CapitaLand, CapitaMall Trust, CapitaMall Asia, City Development, Global Logistics Properties and Hong Kong Land Holdings. When in December 2011 the government introduced an additional stamp duty to cool down the property market, the STI dropped by 2.8 per cent (Kwok 2011).

The property market was affected by the 2008 global crisis, not slumping this time but booming. The property price index (Figure 8.3) soared until 2007, after which it declined but started to rise again in 2009, reaching a record high in 2011. The 2008 subprime crisis, which started with bad housing loans and resulted in foreclosures in the United States, led to a property boom in Singapore. One reason for the record prices was foreign demand. Whereas in 1996 the anti-speculation programme curbed demand, the liberalisation of financial services after the Asian crisis increased foreign demand. The URA (News Releases 7 December 2011) estimated that foreign purchases accounted for 19 per cent of all private residential purchases in 2011. Problems in the United States and Europe, low interest rates and stock market uncertainties made the Singapore property market attractive to foreign investors.

House prices were rising, people were protesting and elections were looming. The government decided to intervene. In February 2010, MAS lowered the loan-to-value (LTV) limit for housing loans from 90 per cent to 80 per cent 'to encourage greater financial prudence among property purchasers and ensure a stable and sustainable property market' (MAS Annual Report 2009/2010: 24). In August 2010, MAS again lowered the LTV from 80 per cent to 70 per cent and increased the minimum cash payment from 5 per cent to 10 per cent. 'The moves were intended to temper sentiments and encourage greater financial prudence among property purchasers' (MAS Annual Report 2010/2011: 28). In January 2011, the LTV was lowered to 60 per cent 'to pre-empt a property bubble from forming' (MAS Annual Report 2010/2011). In December 2011, the government announced an additional buyer's stamp duty for foreigners and corporations (10 per cent), permanent residents already owning one and buying second and subsequent residential properties (13 per cent), and Singapore citizens already owning two and buying third and subsequent residential properties (3 per cent) (URA News Releases 7 December 2011).

In a speech at the Asian Monetary Policy Forum on 24 May 2014, MAS managing director Ravi Menon used the term macroprudential policy to describe Singapore's loan-to-value ratios of 80 per cent for the first property loan, 50 per cent for the second and 40 per cent for the third in respect of loan tenures shorter than 30 years; loan-to-value ratios of 60 per cent for the first property loan, 30 per cent for the second, and 20 per cent for the third in respect of loan tenures longer than 30 years; and a cap on banks' property-related exposure at 35 per cent of total exposures. At a time when crisis-prone Western countries debate new macroprudential policy, Singapore already has experience in this field.

The Hong Kong property market was also affected by the US subprime crisis, and housing prices increased. The Hong Kong government followed Singapore by imposing a stamp duty of 15 per cent. The volume of house sales slowed and prices fell. *South China Morning Post* (McMillan 2012) described the policy as 'chilly' and cast around for alternative investment options, among which were Hong Kong's car parks. Developers Cheung Kong, Wheelock, Sino Land and Sun Hung Properties sold car park spaces in their developments, and prices of car park spaces rose.

Also in Singapore the real estate community was worried and ministers felt the need to defend their intervention policy. At a Redas

Anniversary Dinner in December (29, 2011, cited in Ministry of National Development web page 29 December 2011), Minister of State Tan Chuan-Jin defended government cooling measures. He regarded the diversity of views generated by the matter as natural; the property market has many stakeholders, including homeowners, investors, developers and the wider public. He did not expect developers to welcome the measures, but sought their recognition that the additional stamp duty would ultimately be good for the industry. Also, Prime Minister Lee Hsien Loong (2011), in his New Year message, commented on the additional buyer's stamp duty, saying it would moderate capital inflows and foreign demand, and help stabilise home prices.

The crisis stories in Bangkok and Singapore are different. In Bangkok the banking sector had problems, the proportion of bank lending comprising real estate loans was large and a high vacancy rate had developed. In Singapore the banking sector was healthier, and the government intervened in order to cool an overheated property market. What was similar in Singapore and Bangkok was that the real estate sector was involved in the crisis in several ways. Despite the obvious role of real estate in financial crises, the explanations and remedies of crises have focused on money instead of real estate. What is the origin of such a focus on money, and how does it obfuscate seeing the role of real estate in economic crises?

### The Financialisation of Land and Derivative Rent

Money has long been an easy explanation for crises. The fall of the Ming Dynasty in 1644 has been explained by reference to a shortage of silver (Adshead 1973). The Great Discoveries in the New World have been explained by reference to gold fever in Europe during the fifteenth century. The French Revolution has been explained by reference to the fiscal crisis of 1788 (Sargent and Velde 1995). Changes in political regimes have been explained by reference to inflation in Europe during the 1920s (Polanyi 1944). John Locke was also mesmerised by money, and used it to justify man owning more land than he needs.

The interest in money as an explanation – from physiocrats to monetarism – increased concomitant with the increased importance of the monetary form of wealth. In agrarian societies, land was the main source and form of wealth; physiocrats gave a theoretical interpretation to this and regarded agriculture as the only productive industry. With the commodification of land, land received a monetary value and became traded in the market. The expansion of commerce, and trade and the discovery of silver mines at Potosi (in Peru in 1545), made movable wealth important, and mercantilists advised Europe's governments to store bullion. The next step was the connecting of landed property to paper money and security. In the eighteenth century, John Law, the son of a Scottish gold merchant, proposed monetising landed property; creating paper money guaranteed by land values (Vilar 1984: 249). In the American colonies during the first half of the eighteenth century, banks lent paper money to citizens on the security of their land, farms and town houses (Thayer 1953). A relationship between production and speculative real estate projects had already developed by the eighteenth century when investments were being switched from production in Europe into real estate in America. This happened because European markets provided insufficient opportunities to adventurous Dutch bankers, who established the Holland Land Company to speculate on land in America (Evans 1924).

The rise of the money economy, as Simmel (1978: 277) wrote, reduced qualitative determinations to quantitative ones. Land was reified into the monetary value of real estate thus blurring the boundary between physical and financial assets. Today real estate is used as collateral for loans, rendering bank lending, the health of banks and the fate of homeowners dependent on the assessed value of real estate and vulnerable to real estate cycles. Declining values of properties used as collateral can bankrupt banks when their proportion of (unperforming) real estate loans is high, and bankrupt households when a loan exceeds the value of the property (negative equity).[5] Ever more complicated relations between real estate and finance have been created through modern investment instruments. Securitisation of real estate, REITs, options, derivates and investing in real estate as an alternative to other investment objects (as was the case when the dotcom bubble burst, and investors piled *en masse* into the real estate sector (Overveldt 2009: 218)) have made land and real estate not only fictitious capital but fictitious financial investments (fictitious in the sense of breaking the connection to the use of land). I propose calling this form of rent derivative rent. It is payment for a real estate security derived from real estate as an underlying asset, but is also affected by the prices of other investment options.

Explanations for economic crises have ignored this complicated intertwining of the real estate and financial markets. Irving Fisher (1933) introduced the debt–deflation theory of great depressions (the reason for depression is too much debt). Milton Friedman and Anne Schwarz's (1963) *A Monetary History of the United States 1867-1960* explained the 1929 depression as the result of inappropriate monetary policy (too small a supply of money). John Kenneth Galbraith (1955), in *The Great Crash of 1929,* blamed investors' belief in rising land prices as a reason for the crisis. Daniel Kahneman and Richard Thaler (Thaler 1980; Kahneman et al. 1990) introduced the concept of the endowment effect (people value more the things that they own), explaining too high prices demanded by real estate owners. In his famous *Irrational Exuberance* (2000), Robert Shiller explained real estate bubbles by referring to irrational overpricing (because of a strong psychological element) leading to a social epidemic. Akerlof and Shiller (2009) called the irrational belief that land prices always go up 'animal spirits'. The bubble continues to evolve until a loss of confidence (Krugman and Wells 2010).

These accounts reduce the cause of crises to money (debt) or the irrational beliefs and behaviour of agents (land prices go up until loss of confidence takes over). Real estate speculation, despite its obvious role in financial crises, has been ignored. One recent example of economists' lukewarm interest in analysing real estate is *The Economists' Voice* (edited by Stiglitz et al. 2008) in which top economists (Kenneth Arrow, Joseph Stiglitz, Paul Krugman, Martin Feldstein, Richard Posner, Gary Becker, Paul Rubin and Robert Schiller) discuss modern problems such as global warming, the Iraq war, capital control, currency crises, government debt, social security and terrorism. The issue of land is not addressed. The topic of real estate, though, is so obvious in today's economic crisis that it cannot be ignored completely, and is discussed in the final three articles. How, then, do top economists suggest fixing the current real estate bubble? They see it as an external phenomenon; the only question that interests them is when and how the bubble will burst so the economy may get back on track. Yale economist Robert Shiller provided empirical data for the United States, Amsterdam and Norway, and claimed that these three examples show no long-term upward trend in home prices – bubbles will always end and homeowners will always be at risk of a drop in property prices.

In acknowledging the emotionally susceptible nature of human beings (irrational belief that real estate prices always go up), instead of presuming the ubiquity of rational economic man, behavioural economists contradict the Hayekian idea that prices are signals that allocate resources through the market – the idea that forms the basis of property rights theory. In blaming individuals' irrational behaviour, they, however, do not seek to criticise the market model, but to suggest finding financial instruments to make the market work. Shiller (2008: 284), for example, has proposed 'creating liquid international markets for real estate price risk' that would allow people to 'manage their exposure to the real estate market' (Shiller 2008: 283). 'Investment banks may offer real estate index-linked notes and hedge the risk that they incur in offering them by taking a position in the futures markets' (Shiller 2008: 285). Insurance companies and mortgage lenders may create new products that will protect homebuyers from changing house prices, suggested Shiller. Real estate economists (some of which have analysed the relation between property and financial markets, see

Coakley 1994, and the role of real estate in crises, see Mera and Renaud 2000) share the belief in the market mechanism and suggest improving appraisal methods and opening real estate markets to prevent economic crises and real estate bubbles (see e.g. Quigley 2001). Land price indices are constructed to provide information of 'correct' prices that can work as signals and guide the behaviour of agents. Behind these proposals of hedging real estate investment risks and developing better appraisal methods and indices is the Hayekian belief that prices carry information about preferences, valuations and expectations, affect the behaviour of agents and prices as signals allocate resources through the market (wherein the government should not intervene).

Is the Hayekian belief valid in the real estate market? Is opening real estate markets, developing a real estate index and hedging real estate investment risk a solution to real estate bubbles and the housing question? What are the effects of such drawing of real estate deeper into financial speculation? First, land and houses as visible forms of wealth are rendered invisible. Who owns securitised real estate titles and mortgages, and how much in the way of derivatives is accumulated on top of property, is not seen. Second, REITs as landlords are inflexible negotiators, thinking only about yield. This has an effect of accelerating land use changes and displacing those users who cannot afford paying high rents. Third, these new instruments make land, real estate and housing even more vulnerable to speculation and financial cycles, even more fictitious. Fourth, we can question the existence of equilibrium real estate prices implied in the idea of prices as signals. Real estate prices are not simply determined by demand and supply. Real estate prices can hide bribes (connected to the granting of development permission, for example) and money laundering and be manipulated (in accounts). This undermines the capacity of the real estate market to coordinate, even if real estate prices could be valued correctly. Real estate prices also depend on the valorisation of industries that change over time. An example is the overvalorisation of the output of firms and workers in the financial sector in global cities (Sassen 1994: 37) that led to an increase in the value of land and rent used for financial services. Such accidental overvalorisation was also noticed by real estate brokers. A managing director of CB Richard Ellis said: 'It's astounding what this whole dotcom, telecom industry is doing to real estate. It's the modern equivalent of the California gold rush' (Bagli 2000: 29). Agents can also misinterpret real estate prices as signals. In Bangkok developers misinterpreted speculative demand as real demand and developed too much space, and in the United Kingdom during the 1970s, when property investors mistook the growth in the property sector as an indicator of economic growth (Smyth 1985: 207).

Instead of drawing real estate deeper into financial speculation another type of solution to economic crises and real estate bubbles is to evaluate the use value of the projects produced. Hiroshi Yoshikawa (2008) has criticised monetary policy as a means of restraining increases in asset prices. Instead of implementing monetary policy, what should be done is to screen the development projects that are financed. Not all asset price inflation is bad, observed Yoshikawa (2008: 72), and as an example referred to the sharpest postwar rise in Japanese land and stock prices (in 1960 and 1961): 'The 90% annual increase in the price of manufacturing land at that time simply reflected a change in the economic fundamentals.' And, Yoshikawa continued, 'If the monetary authorities had peevishly attempted to restrain this land price rise through monetary stringency, they would have accomplished nothing more than unnecessarily restraining Japan's high economic growth' (Yoshikawa 2008: 72).

The experience of recent financial crises and the role of real estate in them show that behavioural economists are correct: there is something irrational in people's behaviour in the real estate market; land and real estate prices keep on rising until a loss of confidence takes over (as in Bangkok) or until the intervention of the government (as in Singapore). Instead of blaming people for holding irrational beliefs or banks for granting excessive loans, or believing that correctly assessed real estate prices make real estate markets work, there is a need to examine the real estate black box, to ascertain the reasons for harmful price fluctuations and how they might be prevented. Monopoly rents (together with bribes hidden in real estate prices and manipulation of real estate values), the irrational volatility of real estate prices and random valorisation disprove the assumption that real estate prices act as signals and real estate markets function as postulated by property rights theorists. The experience of recent crises shows that the real estate market does not work – prices can give wrong signals, and real estate markets need government intervention to prevent crises, regulate prices, appropriate monopoly rents, bail out homeowners and save the urban landscape from the harmful effects of financial crises. Derivative rents draw land and real estate into a financial game. When Nick Leeson speculated with Nikkei futures, Leeson himself and Barings were hurt. Speculative real estate derivatives also hurt homeowners and the built environment.

### Notes

1   See the debate about switching investment from commodity production to the built environment: Harvey 1978, 1985, 2008; King 1989; Beauregard 1994; Charney 2001; Gotham 2006; Aalbers 2008; Christophers 2011.

2  In 1999 the Stock Exchange of Singapore (SES) and Simex merged.
3  ASEAN, the Association of Southeast Nations, was established in 1967 to accelerate economic growth, social progress and cultural development in the region.
4  Figures exclude hostels, HDB flats, tenement houses, parsonages and executive condominium.
5  Libertarians – like Douglas French, in his book *Walk Away: The Rise and fall of the Home Ownership Myth* (2010) – have suggested that, in negative equity situations, borrowers should abandon 'underwater' homes: ownership as such is not defended. In countries like Finland, walking away like this is impossible since loans follow the borrower even after the property is lost (this happened to many households during the recession of the early 1990s).

# 9

# Conclusion
## *The Land, Urban and Rent Question*

### The Regime of Regulating Public Land

The prolonged financial crisis at the beginning of the twenty-first century has called capitalism's future into question. The Occupy Wall Street Movement criticised capitalists for their greed, and economists are busy searching for alternative models to Western capitalism. One that has been suggested is the Chinese model of state capitalism – the Beijing Consensus – to replace the Washington Consensus. Another proposed model is the Singapore consensus (involving a blend of state and market, with the government deliberately positioning the country in the global economy) (see e.g. Skilling 2012; Miklehwait and Wooldridge 2014).

In this book I have analysed the blend of state and market in Singapore. I have not claimed that this blend is the model that other cities should adopt, although so-called 'best practices' are popular in town planning today. I have argued, however, that Singapore's blend of state and market has a lot to do with land. Surprisingly, the role of land and real estate has been neglected in the accounts of Singapore's economic success and resolution of the housing question. This book is an attempt to correct this neglect and analyse the path taken after the passing of Land Acquisition Act in 1966. To emphasise the important role of real estate in Singapore's economy, the wealth of its people and government, and the success of its companies, I have called Singapore a property state, and in this book analysed the various functions of land and real estate.

*Urban Land Rent: Singapore as a Property State*, First Edition. Anne Haila.
© 2016 John Wiley & Sons, Ltd. Published 2016 by John Wiley & Sons, Ltd.

**Table 9.1** Singapore's land regime.

| Land treated as | Form of property | Relationship | Justification | Rent | Development mode |
|---|---|---|---|---|---|
| Use value and source of revenue | State | SLA, URA, HDB, JTC Expiring leases and auctions | Economic growth and increase of asset value | Public revenue | Successive rounds of land acquisitions, collective sales, public housing and industrial space |

Discussions of forms of capitalism have identified various types, for example liberal market economies and coordinated market economies (see Hall and Suskice 2001). I wanted to include in these discussions the crucial factor of land and real estate, thus far neglected in this debate. In Chapter 2, I introduced historical land regimes and assigned tasks for the subsequent chapters in seeking to decode Singapore's land regime. Table 9.1 summarises Singapore's land regime. I call it *the regime of regulating public land.*

Today the state owns 90 per cent of the land in Singapore. The origins of the state's land ownership were in the treaty Raffles agreed with the local chieftain Temenggon Abdur-Ranman of Johor, and the land left by the British colonial administration. The state's land bank was accumulated gradually, reaching 90 per cent of all Singapore's land by 2002 (thanks to the appropriating powers of Land Acquisition Act passed in 1966). Land-acquisition power is vested in the state, and land acquisitions may occur whenever land is needed for the public good.

State ownership is a crucial factor in Singapore's land regime. It is a necessary condition, although not an entirely sufficient one. States can use their land resources in various ways. A state can use its landed property for the public good or trying to maximise fiscal rent. State property, as Macpherson (1978) noted, is a form of corporate private property. States can use their land resources like private enterprises, and today, when governments face pressure to cut their expenses and find alternative sources for collecting revenues other than increasing taxes, they are increasingly tempted to sell their landed properties and charge the market rent for the use of their land and real estate.

The state of Singapore has used its land resources to provide public housing for the majority of the population, and public industrial space for the economy to grow. Despite placing public needs first, the state has still received significant revenues from its landed property and left space for the private development industry to grow and prosper. State land is treated as use value (public housing and industrial space) and exchange value (leased for private developers) and as a source of public revenue. The Urban Redevelopment Authority has leased the land by means of public, transparent and fair land auctions, and defined conditions for its use in leases that create obligations for developers. Land-development power has been kept in the hands of the state, exercised by the state land institutions: the Singapore Land Authority (SLA), Urban Redevelopment Authority (URA), Housing Development Board (HDB) and Jurong Town Corporation (JTC).

The development market is shared between private and government developers. Fair land auctions make developers compete and hone their competitiveness. This has made Singaporean development companies successful with projects overseas. Government-linked companies (Surbana and Ascendas) export their experience in the fields of town planning and business parks. This, together with international real estate development ventures on the part of CapitaLand and other government-linked companies, has brought land-related revenue into Singapore from abroad.

The legitimation of the state land regime was assured by giving Singaporeans a stake in economic growth, making them homeowners and asset holders. This was easy when housing prices increased at a moderate rate, making people wealthier while still allowing new generations to become homeowners. The situation changed when the financial crises in the US and Europe led to rapidly increasing housing prices in Singapore, making it difficult for first-time buyers to get a flat. This called for intervention in the real estate market: the Monetary Authority of Singapore (MAS) introduced cooling measures, lowered the loan-to-value (LTV) limit for housing loans and increased the minimum cash payment in respect of housing purchases.

What can the Singaporean land regime model offer other cities? How does this inquiry into land and rent contribute to our understanding of the land question, the urban question, and the rent question?

## The Land Question

The eminent land economist Richard Ely noted that 'under all is the land' (Wurtzebach and Miles 1987: 8). Over the centuries, the land question has changed. In peasant societies, the land question concerned the enclosure of common lands and peasants revolting against it. In the days of industrialisation, the land question involved speculation with railway lands. In the age of urbanisation, the land question revolved around housing the masses. In the time of suburbanisation, the land question concentrated on speculation with fringe land. Now, in the era of financialisation, the land question is about real estate derivatives ruining the built environment.

At the beginning of the twenty-first century, land has once again become a social problem and a controversial issue. In Mexico, collective *ejido* lands have been privatised. Indigenous people have demanded their land rights in Canada, Australia, Africa, Australia and Northern Europe. Vietnam introduced a new land law in 1993, Cambodia did the same in 2001 and Indonesia passed the Land Acquisition Law in 2011. In China, land disputes have led to property rights activism. Land grabs are a problem across Africa. China has leased land and bought raw materials in Africa. South Korea and the United Arab Emirates have purchased land in Sudan. Finnish companies are cultivating tree plantations in Indonesia and China. A French company, Cogema (an affiliate of state-owned Areva), applied for the right to search for uranium in Southern Finland, taking advantage of Finland's antiquated liberal laws allowing mining rights on private land. In other words, in the twenty-first century the land question has become a global question, and the global enclosure movement concerns not only the global South, but also post-socialist countries and the developed West.

This study of Singapore's land regime shows that: first, the land question is not only a rural question but also an urban question; second, the land question is not only an economic question concerning the use of land as a thing in the most efficient way, but also a moral, social and political question; and third, the land question is the real estate question. Land does not only have a use value but can be mobilised in various ways: horizontal (extending the use of land, subdivision of land and suburbanisation), vertical (intensifying the use of land), global (international flows and places), redevelopment (densification and repeated land acquisitions) and valorisation (financialisation and securitisation of land).

In urban areas the land question differs in format from the countryside, where land reform (discussed in Chapter 4) implemented just once is enough to give land to the tiller. *The land question in urban areas* (with ever-expanding populations) is about densifying land use and redevelopment. This calls for repeated rounds of land acquisitions. Land in urban Singapore is scarce. The task of the government has been to find the best and most efficient way of using the land. The vision of the Singapore Land Authority (SLA), as laid out in Limited Land, Unlimited Space, demonstrates the determination to densify, redevelop and intensify the use of Singapore's scarce land resources. The second round of land acquisitions started when the growing population needed land for housing and transport. This new round of land acquisitions was possible because, according to the common law principles adhered to in

Singapore, land ownership is not absolute: both land and buildings revert to the government on the expiry of leases (discussed in Chapter 5). Recurrent land acquisitions can be justified by appealing not to John Locke, but to Immanuel Kant, as does modern pragmatist Daniel Bromley (2006: 190), who argues that when conditions change, land justly acquired may evolve into land unjustly held (discussed in Chapter 2). Collective sales legislation in Singapore was meant to encourage people to participate in the densification process.

The land question is not only an economic question concerning the efficient use and management of land as property rights scholars assume, it is also a *moral, social, political and ideological question.* Land can be used either for the public good or to maximise rental income, and its use, management and ownership necessitate justification.

A popular belief in our time is that private and secure property rights lead to economic growth and democracy. This Locke–North myth (discussed in Chapter 2) is justified by appealing to specific and fortuitous European history. Today the justification story does not revolve around ploughing, sowing and reaping, as in Locke's time, but is more abstract. Following the property rights doctrine of Douglas North and Ronald Coase, it claims that ambiguous property rights lead to waste and the dissipation of valuable resources. To enable an economy to grow, cities to prosper and the wellbeing of people to increase, the contemporary justification story recommends defining ambiguous property rights and letting the market decide the allocation of land. This story has been universalised and applied not only to land, but also to intellectual property rights, plants, genes, natural medicine and cultural artefacts.

In Singapore, landed property rights are clear and simple. Land is either held leasehold or freehold, and the leases define the use of land. Compared to countries where politically contested changes of ownership and land reforms tore classes apart and left scars on society, in Singapore the government gradually appropriated land using powerful land acquisition laws (discussed in Chapter 4). Singapore was an immigrant city where no indigenous group claimed land rights, and no rural landowner class existed to be exploited. Singapore followed the pragmatist model of Henry George in disregarding ideological battles of just ownership, but differed from the Georgist model in that land became the property of the state. The dilemma for the government was how to combine a free market economy with state ownership of land, and how to convince foreign investors that Singapore is a free market economy despite the state ownership of land. Combining public landownership and a free market economy is a unique Singaporean pragmatist solution that has been beneficial for transnational companies locating there

(obtaining access to cheap labour), Singaporean development companies (becoming global actors, discussed in Chapters 6 and 7) and Singaporeans themselves (becoming homeowners, discussed in Chapter 5).

State land used for public housing is a good example of how in Singapore land use decisions are not motivated by economic interests alone.
Accommodating squatters in public housing (instead of simply evict-
ing them) subsequent to land acquisitions demonstrates the state's concern for social consequences. Privatising government-linked companies
and decreasing the share of public housing show the policy principle
Singapore applies: when the market can do the job, the government
withdraws.

In addition to having a use value, land is also an investment object
and asset, increasingly so today. The land question is a *real estate question.*
In *The Urban Revolution*, Henri Lefebvre (2003: 160) conjectured: 'As
the percentage of overall surplus value formed and realized by industry begins to decline, the percentage created and realized by real estate
speculation and construction increases. The second circuit supplants
the first, becomes essential.' This is what happened in Finland, for example, when the state and municipalities centralised real estate management and began demanding maximum rent from the tenants of their
corporatised real estate.

Securitisation made real estate a liquid investment object. The
bundling of real estate titles and real estate mortgages into new financial instruments (derivatives rent), and their financialisation (analysed
in Chapter 8), made yields on real estate investment dependent upon
yields on other investment options, and rendered the real estate market vulnerable to financial crises. The new financial actors – the real
estate investment trusts (REITs) and sovereign wealth funds (SWFs) –
are anonymous landlords answerable to shareholders, seeking the highest yield from their real estate investment and valuing their property
portfolios regularly, thus making exchange value and asset value more
important criteria than use value in land-use decisions.

In the feudal world of landlords and tenants, a rent relation was a
social relation. Enclosures and the parcelling up of land made it into
a commodity and created a land market that, in place of customs,
allocated the use of land; land became treated as a thing, and earlier
land-based social relations were broken. Securitisation, financialisation
and the dispersal of ownership among real estate investment trusts and
sovereign wealth funds make it difficult to know who is accountable for
land use decisions. Through its REITs and government investment corporations, the state of Singapore is participating in this new real estate
game, yet the Monetary Authority of Singapore (MAS) seeks to regulate
and check the harmful effects of financialisation.

## The Urban Question

Andy Merrifield (2014: xii) has defined the new urban question, not the urban as a spatial unit of reproduction (as Manuel Castells (1972) defined it), but as 'a space which capital *productively* plunders: capital now actively dispossesses collective consumption budgets and upscales land by valorizing urban space as a commodity, as a pure financial asset, exploiting it as well as displacing people'. The urban as a space which capital plunders implies fewer possibilities for peoples' participation in urban development. Thus it is no wonder that the radical claim at the turn of the millennium was 'the right to the city'. This claim, however, left unanswered questions like whose rights, what kinds of rights, and what is the city? It is, thus, unsurprising that David Harvey (2012: xv) has described the right to the city as 'an empty signifier'. This study of Singapore's urban land regime has tackled these unanswered questions: by analysing the rights of one group of citizens, the working class; by analysing one type of rights (development rights) crucial in cities but surprisingly neglected by urban scholars; and by analysing the relationship between between the state and the municipality.

The Fabian socialist-inspired PAP government of Singapore decided to resolve the housing question, and respected *the right of the urban working class* to the city. Urban squatters were accommodated in public housing and made homeowners (discussed in Chapter 5). It is an irony that both the left and right have missed this radical quality of Singapore's housing policy. After the working class was housed and made homeowners, the provision of public housing was extended to the urban middle class. Comprising both middle and working class, the propertied class (87 per cent of Singaporeans are homeowners) has stabilised society through a common interest in the value of homes.

It is surprising how little urban scholars have analysed *development rights* that are crucial in urban development. This book has filled this research gap by analysing the city in which the state as a significant landowner controls the development and demands a development charge from developers. Throughout this book the today dominant ideology has been contrasted to rent theory. One difference between these concerns development rights. One of the arguments of property rights scholars is that 'if a person owns a resource, he takes better care of it'. This may be true in respect of individuals, but in cities individual action creates externalities, and growing populations require redevelopment and densification of land use. Thus, development rights in urban areas should not be individuals' rights to do as they please with their land, or developers' rights to speculate. Development rights are different types of rights than, for example, the right to plant an apple tree or the right to sell land. They concern not only an owner of land, but also others and the wider community, and therefore should be coordinated by the municipality. Further, assigning development rights affects the value of real estate and treats site owners unequally. This incites some to speculate and lobby. In Singapore, the conditions of land leases and premiums keep control in the hands of government and prevent land speculation. En bloc legislation incites collective behaviour and nullifies the power of the minority.

Cities between the state and the individual have puzzled liberal theorists (see Chapter 5). Singapore is a city-state where the tasks of *the state and the municipality* are not always easy to separate. Land reformers (discussed in Chapter 4) were perplexed by the difference between the state and the municipality. Marx proposed the nationalisation of land, and in Mao's China land became state property. Thomas Spence distrusted remote government and suggested that parishes should own the land, collect rent and provide services. The Fabians recommended that municipalities should appropriate and lease land.

A state's appropriating powers usually apply only to specific macro priorities – such as national defence, highways and national parks – not in order to build housing. For their part, municipalities are often reluctant to use their expropriation powers (that is if they have any) because of potentially conflicting interests of the decision-makers involved. I called this the dilemma of land acquisitions (discussed in Chapter 5): the state is too far removed and the municipality is too close. Singapore's solution was government land acquisition powers to appropriate private land for housing development, and responsibility for town planning in the hands the Ministry of National Development. The statutory boards dealing with housing (HDB), industrial land (JTC) and town planning (URA) may have conflicting interests as to land use. However, the government (ministries, MND and MAS) above these boards has a coordinating and regulating role. Thus, the state does more than protect and enforce property rights, and construct the legal environment for the market (the minimum tasks assigned to governments by property rights theorists). The land-owning government of Singapore appropriates land for private developers, leases land to developers through public auctions (making private developers compete), provides public housing and industrial space, and intervenes in the real estate market to prevent speculation and to cool or stimulate the property market (see Chapters 6 and 8).

For municipalities owning land, it can be a significant source of revenue (fiscal rent). In both Singapore and Hong Kong, the government receives a large amount of revenue from land leases. How land is valued is, therefore, an important question. Is there a 'natural, real, or correct price' of public land (see Chapter 5)? The price of land on the land market is the capitalised rent, and thus depends on the rent that the land is expected to produce. If the rent from an alternative use is counted as a cost, the price is different from a price based on present use. From the point of view of society, land is provided free and the whole rent is surplus. From the point of view of an individual, the whole rent is a cost of production (see Chapter 3). In short, there is no one or 'natural value' of public land, but the value of public land depends on the point of view taken, and also on the strategy the city or state assume as landowners. If they decide to make money through their real estate and maximise rent revenue – becoming players in the real estate market – the price is different from the price calculated based on use (residential or recreational, for example). In the neoliberal era, states and municipalities face the pressure of maximising rent revenue. Singapore shows an alternative model; the state land is also used for public good.

In Singapore, state land is valued both as use value and exchange value. The building of public housing was possible because land was not assessed according to market value. In other words, public housing is subsided thanks to 'land subsidy' (see Chapter 5). The JTC's attempt to measure land productivity by calculating the productivity of various industrial uses was a method based on use (see Chapter 6). In land acquisitions, market value was used. Peculiar to Singapore was the fact that market value used in compulsory land acquisitions was, until 2007, pegged at the price level of a certain year (see Chapter 4). This gave the government the unearned increment of land value due to, for example, increased development rights and building infrastructure. Development charges are another measure in Singapore to give society the increase in land value due to increased density or change of land use.

## The Rent Question

Throughout its history, rent theory has been applied to address contemporary social problems. In the nineteenth century, the issue was corn duties; in the 1970s, high house prices; and in the 1980s, land speculation. Today, the global enclosure movement and the neoliberal aspiration to price everything have made rent theory relevant once again. This book is an attempt to update rent theory and make it applicable to present conditions. Labour and capital have changed greatly since the days of the classical economists, and there are new theories and explanations concerning these factors of production. Land has also changed, but there has not been much progress in its study since the days of David Ricardo. One reason for the underdeveloped nature of rent theory is that when people talk about rent they mean different things. I suggest standardising the rent vocabulary (in Chapter 3) by connecting rent to land, calling economic rent in property rights language 'manipulated rent' and adding the prefix 'political' to rent-seeking.

The rent concepts (or forms of rent) applied in this study are differential rent, monopoly rent, absolute rent, fiscal rent, global rent and derivative rent. Distinguishing between these various forms of rent is not just a nominal act – as Guido Martinotti said: social scientists are not shamans who have the power to name things. All forms of rent are monopoly rent in the sense that their cause is exclusive ownership of land. However, it is useful to distinguish various forms of rent because origins and conditions for different forms of rent vary, and therefore the measures taken to affect them must be different. For example, rises in house prices due to foreign demand (global rent) can be checked by restricting or taxing foreign demand, and separating public and private housing markets. Words matter as well. Using the vocabulary of rent-seeking blames corrupt cronies for lobbying the government and obtaining monopoly privileges. Thus, policy recommendations have been about cleaning up government, without evaluating the development projects that 'cronies' lobbied for. Such evaluation could have saved the Asian economies from those speculative projects that contributed to the Asian financial crisis (see Chapter 8).

The analysis of Singapore's state land regime tests land rent theory in three ways: first, it shows that it is possible to abolish absolute rent, and provide both affordable housing and the conditions to permit a private (capitalist) development industry to prosper (just as classical economists and Marx argued); second, it shows that land prices as market signals are deceptive and can exacerbate crises; and third, it shows that real estate has a role in economic and financial crises, and the real estate market requires regulation to prevent the harmful effects of financialisation.

High land prices and zoning authorities are often blamed for *unaffordable housing*. However, house prices are not high because land is expensive, but vice versa: house prices determine land prices, as rent theory explains (see Chapter 3). The reason for insufficient land supply and high house prices is not planning authorities zoning too little residential land, but that the monopoly of land makes land scarce and invites speculation. The absence of hoarding of land by private developers, absolute rent and land speculation explains why the provision of affordable housing for the majority of Singapore's population was possible (see Chapter 5).

Preventing the hoarding of land is beneficial to the development industry. Land banks tie up capital and thus prevent construction firms from improving productivity. Land banks (hoarded land) also make development companies vulnerable to market cycles and fluctuations in asset prices (as shown in Chapter 6). As well as acting to prevent land hoarding, the Singapore government has encouraged developers and lessees to upgrade their buildings. In 2008, the building premium was removed (discussed in Chapter 5). This Georgian two-rate tax creates an incentive for developers to use land efficiently (see Chapter 4).

Economists (discussed in Chapter 8) view real estate bubbles as external and anomalous phenomena, and the only question that interests them is when the bubble will burst in order to get the economy back on track again. They believe that in the long run bubbles always end, and house prices will come down. In the short term, however, irrational overpricing due to 'animal spirit' (Akerlof and Shiller 2009) or 'herd behaviour' can provoke a social epidemic. In acknowledging the emotionally susceptible nature of human beings, instead of presuming the ubiquity of rational economic man (and thus contradicting the idea of Hayek and property rights scholars that prices are *signals* that allocate resources through the market), the new behavioural economists resemble land economists who assign land and landowners a special role. The behavioural economists, however, do not seek to criticise market allocation, but to blame irrational behaviour for disturbing the economy. Their proposed solution is to create 'hedging instruments for real estate price risk' (Shiller 2008: 284). 'Investment banks may offer real estate index-linked notes... insurance companies may expand their home-owners insurance offerings into home equity insurance... mortgage lenders may create new mortgage products', wrote Shiller (2008: 285). This solution draws land deeper into financial speculation, and would make land, real estate and housing more vulnerable to financial crises.

Singapore offers a different policy recommendation. The analysis of the role of real estate in the financial crises in Bangkok and Singapore (Chapter 8) showed that real estate prices did not work as signals to guide behaviour to make the market work. Irrational overpricing of real estate continued until a loss of confidence took over in Bangkok and until anti-speculation measures were introduced by the government in Singapore. Singapore's anti-speculation programmes show that regulating the market works, helping not just homebuyers but also saving the commodity-producing economy.

At the time when the crisis-prone Western world discusses the possibility of introducing new initiatives, called 'macroprudential policy', the property state of Singapore can already offer relevant experience. In his speech at the Asian Monetary Policy Forum (14 May 2014), MAS managing director Ravi Menon described Singapore's property market cooling measures (loan-to-value ratio limits and caps on banks' property related exposures) as macroprudential policy. Thus, as to this latest proposed remedy to the global financial crisis, Singapore has valuable advice to give.

The land question has been a persistent and recurrent question through history. Today, the global enclosure movement and urbanisation have once again made the land question and the rent question very real. Who gets rent, why and how it is distributed? To resolve these questions is to find out what prevents us from making our cities better. This study of Singapore has shown that producing affordable housing for the majority of people is possible. The key is preventing land speculation, which can be done when land is in public ownership and not used on the basis of its market value or rent from alternative use. Furthermore, this need not be at the exclusion of a successful private development industry. On the contrary, the private sector also benefits from containment of land speculation. The leasing system makes it possible to use the contractual terms of leases in order to regulate development. Whether such restrictive regulations are used, or whether developers are free to appropriate rent, is up to the government leasing out the land. Public landownership makes it possible to prevent speculation and render housing affordable. Whether a land owning government makes use of such conditions is a matter of policy choice.

# Annex
## *Note on Data*

I began collecting empirical material for this study in 1993 when I moved to Los Angeles as a visiting scholar at the Lewis Center for Regional Policy, at the University of California. In Los Angeles I interviewed members of three Japanese real estate companies (real estate departments of Mitsubishi, Mitsui and Nomura) and one Korean realty firm. From 1994 to 1996, I lived in Singapore and taught urban economics at the National University of Singapore's Department of Building and Real Estate Management. During this time I interviewed Singaporean investors, planners, businessmen and expatriates. Since then, I have supplemented the empirical material during several trips to Asia including longer study periods, for example in Hong Kong.

Two valuable sources of data have been the Singaporean newspapers *The Straits Times* and *The Business Times*. The close relationship between the government and these newspapers makes them reliable sources of information about government policies. As a commentator on Singapore's politics, Cherian George notes the role of the national press as an establishment institution: 'the PAP [the People's Action Party, in power since 1959] has never been content with national institutions that are merely cowed into submission: it wants them to support positively its policies and programmes' (George 2000: 66). In addition to Singaporean newspapers, others, like the *South China Morning Post*, are useful because Asian developers do not readily give interviews, but they do speak to the media.

*Urban Land Rent: Singapore as a Property State*, First Edition. Anne Haila.
© 2016 John Wiley & Sons, Ltd. Published 2016 by John Wiley & Sons, Ltd.

Collecting information about real estate projects and real estate prices can sometimes be difficult. Susan Fainstein (1994: xi) tells of her experience interviewing people in the real estate industry: 'I was extremely impressed by graciousness, articulateness, and cogent analyses of many of the individuals within the real estate industry and the public sector to whom I talked.' At least in the West, there must be something in the built environment and buildings that make developers feel proud and personally attached to their work that explains their talkativeness. My experience in interviewing Asian companies was not always as encouraging. I once asked a developer in Hong Kong to tell me about his quite conspicuous development project. He replied, perhaps half-joking, 'If I tell you, they will kill me.' Interviews with Japanese executives were formal occasions with the presence of the company lawyer. On one occasion, a Japanese corporate president proposed that we take off our jackets, a gesture I interpreted to be symbolic. What followed was a quite honest confession that Japanese companies had losses in Los Angeles in 1993 (information the other interviewees did not disclose).

I have interviewed businessmen, civil servants, property investors and brokers. Most interviews were prearranged. In addition, a valuable source of information has been informal discussions. An especially good source of information was the many long flights from Helsinki to Singapore. During the 14 hours, I was occasionally fortunate enough to have a chatty businessman sitting next to me, and after a couple of glasses of good wine I was provided insights into the world of Finnish businessmen in Asia. Especially fruitful was the night I spent, because of the cancellation of the Finnair flight, at the Bangkok airport sitting in a bar with two Finnish currency traders working in Singapore. One worked for a bank as a seller and the other worked for a Finnish multinational company as a buyer. Five days before the collapse of the Thai baht in 1997, these two money dealers had a hunch about it.

Because this is an urban studies book, observation has also been used as a method of collecting data. The events and forces analysed in this study were readable in the built environment. For example, walking in the summer of 1997 in Surabaya, Indonesia, I was surprised to see that almost every second house was a bank. Obviously it was easy to establish a bank in Indonesia. This was a couple of weeks before the burst of the Asian crisis and the signs of it were already visible in the landscape. Less than a year later in Bangkok, a sign I saw over and over again was 'office space for rent'. As Claude Lévi-Strauss wrote in *Tristes Tropiques*, sometimes a short glimpse can capture the essence of a city. In March, 1998, the essence of Bangkok was a crisis in the property market.

# References

'A land law to re-house squatters'. 1965. The Straits Times, 17 June, p. 6.

Aalbers, Manuel. 2008. 'The financialization of home and the mortgage market crisis'. Competition and Change, 12, 148–166.

Adair, Alastair, Tim Berry, Stanley McGreal et al. 1999. 'Globalisation of real estate markets in central Europe'. European Planning Studies, 7, 295–305.

Addae-Dapaah, Kwame. 1999. 'Utilization of urban residential land: a case study of Singapore'. Cities, 16, 93–101.

Adis, Khalil 2009a. 'REITs, property funds or stocks'. Property Report, Singapore, Malaysia, Indonesia. Singapore: Ensign media. February, 40–41.

Adis, Khalil. 2009b. 'Swiss's loss, Singapore's gain'. Property Report Singapore, Malaysia, Indonesia. Singapore: Ensign Media. February, 30–31.

Adshead, S.A.M. 1973. 'The seventeenth century general crisis in China'. Asian Profile 1, 271–280.

Aiyar, Swaminathan, Andrew Parker and Johan van Zyl. 1995a. Market-assisted land reform: a new solution to old problems. Agriculture and Natural Resources Department. The World Bank.

Aiyar Swaminathan, Andrew Parker and Johan van Zyl. 1995b. Market-assisted land reform: helping solve a debt crisis. Agriculture and Natural Resources Department. The World Bank.

Akerlof, George and Robert Shiller. 2009. Animal Spirits: How Human Psychology Drives the Economy and why it Matters for Global Capitalism. Princeton, NJ: Princeton University Press.

Alatas, Syed Hussein. 1974. 'The captive mind and creative development'. International Social Science Journal, 26, 695–700.

Alchian, Armen. 1961. Some Economics of Property. Santa Monica, CA: Rand Corporation.

Alonso, William. 1960. 'A theory of the urban land market'. Papers and Proceedings. Regional Science Association 6, 149–157.

Alonso, William. 1964. Location and Land Use: Toward a General Theory of Land Rent. Cambridge, MA: Harvard University Press.

Ambrose, Peter. 1986. Whatever Happened to Planning? London and New York: Methuen.

Anan, Ganjanapan. 2001. The issue of community: how to think about locality in terms ofrights, power and resource management [in Thai]. Bangkok: Thailand Research Fund.

Anderson, Benedict. 1983. Imagined Communities. London: Verso.

Anderson James. 1777. An Enquiry into the Nature of Corn Laws. Edinburgh.

Ang, Lilian. 1997. 'PM's letter to Heng dated November 21, 1997'. The Business Times, 6 December.

Ang, Wan May. 1997. 'Redas to be less vocal from now on, says new head, Real Estate Developers' Association of Singapore, Redas'. The Business Times, 10 December.

Ang, Wan May. 1998. 'Indonesia's Endang to sell her 39% stake in Bugis Junction'. The Straits Times, 5 August, p. 1.

Ang, Yiying. 2009. 'People's Park Complex ... or hostel?' The Straits Times, 8 May, p. C1.

ARA. 2010. Asunnottamat, Selvitys. Helsinki: Asuntorahasto.

ARC Report. 1977. The role of the property developers in Singapore. Prepared for Singapore Land and Housing Developers Association. ARC Project No 59/77/24.

Arestis, Philip and Murray Glickman. 2002. 'Financial crisis in Southeast Asia: dispelling illusion the Minskyan way'. Cambridge Journal of Economics, 26, 237–260.

Arneil, Barbara. 1994. 'Trade, plantation and property: John Locke and the economic defence of colonialism'. Journal of the History of Ideas, 55, 591–609.

Arneil, Barbara. 1996. John Locke and America: The Defence of English Colonialism. Oxford: Clarendon Press.

Arrighi, Giovanni. 2007. Adam Smith in Beijing: Lineages of the Twenty-first Century. London and New York: Verso.

Asian Development Outlook: Population and Human Resources. 1998. Manila: Asian Development Bank.

'Asian govts to blame for currency crisis, says Greenspan', 1997, The Business Timesonline, 15 October.

Badcock, Blair. 1989. 'An Australian view of the rent gap hypothesis'. Annals of the Association of American Geographers, 79, 125–145.

Badcock, Blair. 1990. 'On the nonexistence of the rent gap, a reply'. Annals of the Association of American Geographers, 80, 459–461.

Bagli, Charles V. 2000, 'For upstarts of cyberspace, a scramble for rental space', The New York Times, 2 April.

Balchin, Paul and Jeffrey Kieve. 1977. Urban Land Economics. London and Basingstoke: The Macmillan Press.

Ball, Michael. 1977. 'Differential rent and the role of landed property'. International Journal of Urban and Regional Research, 1, 380–403.

Ball, Michael. 1985a. 'The urban rent question'. Environment and Planning A, 17(4), 503–525.

Ball, Michael. 1985b. 'Land rent and the construction industry'. In: Land Rent, Housing and Urban Planning: A European Perspective, edited by M. Ball, V. Bentivegna, M. Edwards and M. Folin. London: Croom Helm.

Ball, Michael. 1988. Rebuilding Construction: Economic Change in the British Construction Industry. London: Routledge.

Ball, M., V. Bentivegna, M. Edwards and M. Folin (eds). 1985. Land Rent, Housing and Urban Planning: A European Perspective. London: Croom Helm.

Balzac, Honore de. 1832. Colonel Chabert. New York: New Directions. 1997.

Bandyopadhyay, Pradeep. 1982. 'Marxist urban analysis and the economic theory of rent'. Science and Society, 46, 162–196.

Baring Securities. 1991. Hong Kong Property Market Review, Vol. II: Company Analysis, April. London.

Barlow, James. 1993. 'Controlling the housing land market: some examples from Europe'. Urban Studies, 30, 1129–1149.

Barlow, James and Simon Duncan. 1994. Success and Failure in Housing Provision: European Systems Compared. Oxford: Pergamon.

Barrett, Wayne. 1992. Trump: The Deals and the Downfall. New York: HarperCollins.

Barthes, Ronald. [1956] 1989. Myth today. In: Barthes Selected Writings. Glasgow: William Collins Sons & Co.

Baumol, William and Alan Blinder. 1985. Economics: Principles and Policy. Third edition. New York: Harcourt Brace Jovanovic Publishers.

Beamish, Jane and Jane Ferguson. 1989. A History of Singapore Architecture: The Making of a City. Singapore: Graham Press.

Beatley, Timothy. 1994. Ethical Land Use. Baltimore, MD: The Johns Hopkins University Press.

Beauregard, Robert. 1994. 'Capital switching and the built environment: United States 1970–89'. Environment and Planning A, 26, 715–732.

Beauregard, Robert and Anne Haila. 2000. The unavoidable continuities of the city. In: Globalizing Cities: A New Spatial Order? edited by P. Marcuse and R. van Kempen. Oxford: Blackwell Publishers.

Becker, Lawrence. 1977. Property Rights: Philosophic Foundation. New York: Henley and Boston.

Behnke, Evers and Möller. 1976. Grundrente und Bodenspekulation: Fallstdudien zum Städtischen Veränderungsprozess in Hamburg 1948–1975. Berlin: Verlag für das Studium der Arbeiterbewegung.

Benjamin, Geoffrey. [1976] 1997. The cultural logic of Singapore's 'multiculturalism'. In: Understanding Singapore Society, edited by Ong Jin Hui, Tong Chee Kiong and Tan Ern Ser, 67–85. Singapore: Times Academic Press.

Berry, Sara. 2002. 'Debating the land question in Africa'. Comparative Study of Society and History, 44(4), 638–668.

Blaug, Mark. 2000. 'Henry George: rebel with cause'. The European Journal of the History of Economic Thought, 7, 270–288.

Blaug, Mark. 2001. 'No history of ideas, please, we're economists'. Journal of Economic Perspectives, 15, 145–164.

Bourassa, Steven. 1993. 'The rent gap debunked'. Urban Studies, 30, 1731–1744.

Bradley, Preston. 1980. 'Henry George, biblical morality and economic ethics: some conclusions from a lifetime's study of the relation between ethics and economics'. The American Journal of Economics and Sociology, 39, 209–215.

Bragdon, Kathleen. 1996. Native People and Southern New England 1500–1650. Norman, OK: University of Oklahoma Press.

Braudel, Fernand. [1967] 1973. Capitalism and Material Life 1400–1800. New York: Harper & Row.

Brede, Helmut, Barbara Dietrich and Berhard Kohaupt. 1976. Politsiche Ökonomie des Bodens und Wohnungsfrage. Frankfurt am Main: Suhrkamp.

Brede, Helmut, Berhard Kohaupt and Hans-Joachim Kujath. 1975. Ökonomische und Politsche Determinanten der Wohnungsversordgung. Frankfurt am Main: Suhrkamp.

Brenner, Neil. 2003. 'Stereotypes, archetypes, and prototypes: three uses of superlatives in contemporary urban studies'. City and Community, 2, 205–216.

Brenner, Neil. 2004. New State Spaces: Urban Governance and the Rescaling of Statehood. Oxford: Oxford University Press.

Brenner, Robert. 1977. The origins of capitalist development: a critique of neo-Smithian Marxism. New Left Review, 104, 25–93.

Bromley, Daniel. 2006. Sufficient Reason: Volitional Pragmatism and the Meaning of Economic Institutions. Princeton, NJ: Princeton University Press.

Bromley, Daniel. 2008. 'Formalising property relations in the developing world: the wrong prescription for the wrong malady'. Land Use Policy, 26, 20–27.

Brook, Timothy. 2009. Vermeer's Hat: The Seventeenth Century and the Dawn of Global World. London: Profile Books.

Brounen, Dirk and Sjoerd de Koning. 2012. '50 years of real estate investment trusts: an international examination of the raise and performance of REITs'. Journal of Real Estate Literature, 20, 197–223.

Brown, Harry Gunnison. 1924. 'Is a tax on site values never shifted?' The Journal of Political Economy, 32, 375–382.

Buchanan, James. 1980. Rent seeking and profit seeking. In: Towards a Theory of the Rent Seeking Society, edited by J.M. Buchanan, R.D. Tollison and G. Tullock. College Station, TX: Texas University Press.

Buchholz, Todd. 1989. New Ideas from Dead Economists. New York: Penguin Books.

Budd, Leslie. 1995. 'Globalisation, territory and strategic alliances in different financial centers'. Urban Studies, 32, 345–336.

Buitelaar, Edwin and Barrie Needham. 2007. 'Property rights and private initiatives: an introduction'. The Town Planning Review, 78, 1–8.

Bunnell, Tim, Lisa Drummond and K.C. Ho. (eds). 2002. Critical Reflections on Cities in Southeast Asia. Singapore: Times Academic Press.

Cannadine, David. 2002. Ornamentalism: How the British saw their Empire. London: Penguin Books.

CapitaMall Trust. 2013. Annual Report. Singapore.

Carell, Erich. 1948. Bodenknappheit und Grundrentenbildung. Berlin: Wissenschaftliche Editionsgesellschaft.

Caruth, Cathy. 2002. 'The claims of the dead: history, haunted property, and the law'. Critical Inquiry, 28, 419–441.

Cassis, Youssat. 2006. Capitals of Capital: A History of International Financial Centres, 1780–2005. Cambridge: Cambridge University Press.

Castells, Manuel. [1972] 1977. The Urban Question: A Marxist Approach. London: Edward Arnold.

Castells, Manuel, L. Goh and R Y-W Kwok. 1990. The Shek Kip Mei Syndrome. London: Pion.

Chan, Fiona. 2006. 'Many thanks and well done Singapore, say delegates', The Straits Times, 21 September, p. H10.

Chan, H.C. and H.D. Evers. 1978. National identity and nation building in Southeast Asia. In: Studies in ASEAN Sociology, edited by Chen and Evers. Singapore: Chopmen.

Chan, Kam Wing. 1994. Cities with Invisible Walls: Reinterpreting Urbanization in Post 1949 China. Singapore: Oxford University Press.

Chan, Robin. 2012. 'Industrial land prices and rents still competitive', The Straits Times, 17 November, p. B16.

Chan, Sue Meng. 1995a. 'Barings may be fined for withholding 'material' information from Simex', The Straits Times, 15 March.

Chan, Sue Meng. 1995b. 'Question of why funds were released to Leeson unanswered', The Straits Times, 22 July.

Chan, Sue Meng. 1995c. 'S'pore will not bail out banks in trouble, says Dr Hu', The Straits Times, 7 November, p. 1.

Chang, T.C. 2000. 'Renaissance revisited: Singapore as a "global city for the arts"'. International Journal of Urban and Regional Research, 24, 818–831.

Chang, H-J. 1998. 'Korea: the misunderstood crisis'. World Development, 26, 1555–1561.

'Change to avoid public confusion: PM moves Horn Kee to another GPC post'. 1997, The Straits Times, 10 December.

Charney, Igal. 2001. 'Three dimensions of capital switching with the real estate sector: a Canadian case study'. International Journal of Urban and Regional Research, 25, 740–758.

Chatterjee, P. 2004. The Politics of the Governed: Reflections on Popular Politics in Most of the World. New York: Columbia University Press.

Chee, Piang Yoong. 1990. Foreign investment in Singapore property market. Dissertation BEM. National University of Singapore.

Chen, Cheng. 1961. Land Reform in Taiwan. Taipei: China Publishing Company.

Chen, Kao. 1997. 'Dispute over Beijing office units', The Straits Times, 24 October.

'Cheung Kong's S'pore reit sale could hurt HK', 2003, The Business Times, online edition, 10 July.

Chiew, Seen Kong. 1985. Socio-cultural framework of politics. In: Government and Politics of Singapore, edited by Jon Quah, Chan Heng and Seah Chee Meow. Singapore: Oxford University Press.

Ching, Tuan Yee and Benjamin Ng. 2008. 'Realising the Marina Bay vision', The Business Times, 22 March.

Chiu, Stephen Wing-kai. 1992. The state and the financing of industrialization in East Asia. Historical origins of comparative divergences. PhD, Princeton University.

Chong, Dennis. 2011. 'Take mainland sting out of housing market, Exco member urges'. South China Morning Post, 15 May.

Choong, Tet Sieu. 1997. 'The best cities in Asia'. Asiaweek, 5 December, p. 38–42.

Christophers, Brett. 2011. 'Revisiting the urbanization of capital'. Annals of the Association of American Geographers, 101, 1–8.

Chu, J.J. 1996. Taiwan: a fragmented 'middle' class in the making. In: The New Rich in Asia: Mobile Phones, McDonalds and Middle-class Revolution, edited by Richard Robison and David Goodman. London and New York: Routledge.

Chua, Beng Huat. 1995. Communitarian Ideology and Democracy in Singapore. London and New York: Routledge.

Chua, Beng Huat. 1997. Political Legitimacy and Housing: Stakeholding in Singapore. London and New York: Routledge.

Chua, Beng Huat. 1999. 'The attendant consumer society of a developed Singapore'. In: Singapore: Towards a Developed Status, edited by Linda Low. Singapore: Oxford University Press.

Chua, Beng Huat. 2000. 'Public housing residents as clients of the state'. Housing Studies, 15, 45–60.

Chua, James. 2013. Investing in Singapore real estate. Singapore: James Chua Way Huang.

Chua, Lee Hoong. 1997. 'Suzhou homes all snapped up', The Straits Times, 4 December.

Chua, Mui Hoong. 1996. 'Why S'pore cannot assume it has arrived: SM Lee', The Straits Times, 8 December, p. 45.

Chua, Mui Hoong. 1997. 'Textbooks need injection of Asian perspective', The Straits Times, 27 October, p. 39.

Clammer, John. 1985. Singapore: Ideology, Society, Culture. Singapore: Chopman Publishers.

Clark, Eric. 1987. The Rent Gap and Urban Change: Case Studies in Malmö 1860–1985. Lund: Lund University Press.

Clark, Eric. 1988. 'The rent gap and transformation of the built environment: Case studies in Malmö 1860–1985'. Geografiska Annaler, 70, 241–254.

Clark, Eric. 1995. 'The rent gap re–examined'. Urban Studies, 32, 1489–1503.

Clark, Eric and Andreas Gulberg. 1991. 'Long swings, rent gaps and structures of building provision: the postwar transformation of Stockholm's inner city'. International Journal of Urban and Regional Research, 15, 492–504.

Clarke, Simon and Norman Ginsburg. 1976. 'The political economy of housing'. Kapitalistate 4–5. Working Papers on the Capitalist State. The San Francisco Bay Area Kapitalistate Group.

Coakley, Jerry. 1994. 'The integration of property and financial markets'. Environment and Planning A, 26, 697–717.

Coase, R.H. 1991. 'The institutional structure of production. The 1991 Alfred Nobel Memorial Prize Lecture in Economic Sciences'. In: R.H. Coase Essays on Economics and Economists. 1994. Chicago: The University of Chicago Press.

Coedes, G. 1968. The Indianized States of Southeast Asia. Honolulu: University of Hawai'i Press.

Colchester, Marcus. 1989. Pirates, Squatters and Poachers. The Political Ecology of Dispossession of the Native Peoples in Sarawak. London: Survival International.

Collins, Catherine. 1989. 'Could Japanese realty holdings hurt U.S.?' Los Angeles Times, 7 May, p. VIII 3.

Collis, Maurice. 2000. Raffles: The Definitive Biography. Singapore: Graham Brash.

Corgel, John, Austin Jaffe and Robert Lie. 1992. 'Modeling the economics of leasing provision: some cross–cultural comparisons of European contracts'. Paper presented at the American Real Estate and Urban Economics Association Meeting. January.

Cotton, James. 2000. The Asian crisis and the perils of enterprise association: explaining the different outcomes in Singapore, Taiwan and Korea. In: Politics and Markets in the Wake of the Asian Crisis, edited by Richard Robinson, Mark Beeson, Kanishka Jayasuriya and Hyuk-Rae Kim. London and New York: Routledge.

Cruikshank, Julie. 1998. The Social Life of Stories: Narrative and Knowledge in the Yukon Territory. Vancouver: UBC Press.

Cullen, Jim. 2003. The American Dream: A Short History of an Idea that Shaped a Nation. Oxford: Oxford University Press.

Cunha, Derek da. 2010. Singapore Places its Bets: Casinos, Foreign Talent and Remaking a City-state. Singapore: Straits Times Press.

Curthbert, Alexander. 1991. 'For a few dollars: urban planning and the legitimation process in Hong Kong'. International Journal of Regional Research, 15, 575–593.

Dale, Ole Johan. 1999. Urban Planning in Singapore: The Transformation of a City. Oxford: Oxford University Press.

Dambrosch, Leo. 2005. Jean-Jacques Rousseau: Restless Genius. Boston and New York: Houghton Mifflin.

Davies, Margaret. 2007. Property: Meanings, Histories, Theories. New York: Routledge-Cavendish.

Davis, Mike. 1990. City of Quartz: Excavating the Future in Los Angeles. London and New York: Verso.

DBS Annual Report. 1994. Singapore.

Dehesh, Alireza and Cedric Pugh. 1999. 'The internationalization of post 1980 property cycles and the Japanese "bubble" economy, 1998–96'. International Journal of Urban and Regional Research, 23, 147–164.

De Lorme, Charles, David Kamerschen and John Mbaku. 1986. 'Rent seeking in the Cameroon economy: Krueger's analytic technique helps to account for development lag in colonial states'. The American Journal of Economics and Sociology, 45, 413–423.

Defoe, Daniel. 1719. Robinson Crusoe. Sterling: Penguin Classics. 2006.

Demsetz, Harold. 1967. 'Towards a theory of property rights'. American Economic Review, 57, 347–359.

Denman, D. R. 1957. Estate Capital: The Contribution of Landownership to Agricultural Finance. London: Allen and Unwin.

'Detained Barings trader in attempt to reach London'. 1995, South China Morning Post, 3 March, p. 1.

Deyo, F. C. (ed.). 1987. The Political Economy of the New Asian Industrialism. Ithaca, NY: Cornell University Press.

Diehl, Karl. 1921. David Ricardos grundgesetzen der volkswirtschaft und besteuerung. Leipzig.

Directory of Registered Contractors. 2001. Singapore.

Dobb, Maurice. 1946. Studies in the Development of Capitalism. London: Routledge & Kegan Paul.

Dobbin, Christine. 1996. Asian Entrepreneurial Minorities: Conjoint Communities in the Making of the World Economy: 1570–1940. London: Routledge Curzon.

Dobbs-Higginson, M.S. 1993. Asia Pacific: Its Role in the New World Disorder. Hong Kong: Longman.

Dodge, Richard Irving. [1882] 1970. Our Wild Indians: Thirty-Three Years' Personal Experience among Red Men of the Great West. Freeport, NY: Books for Libraries Press.

Dunkerley, Harold. 1983. Urban Land Policy: Issues and Opportunities. Oxford: Oxford University Press.

Eckardt, James. 2006. Singapore Girl. Singapore: Monsoon.

Economic Review Committee Report. 2003. Singapore: Ministry of Trade and Industry.

Edel, Matthew. 1976. 'Marx's theory of rent: urban applications'. Kapitalistate, 4–5, 100–24.

Edel. Matthew, Elliott Sclar and Daniel Luria. 1984. Shaky Palaces: Homeownership and Social Mobility in Boston's Suburbanization. New York: Columbia University Press.

Edensor, Tim and Mark Jayne. (eds). 2012. Urban Theory Beyond the West. London and New York: Routledge.

Edgeworth, F.Y. 1925. Papers Relating to Political Economy. London: Macmillan.

Ely, Richard. 1920. 'Land speculation'. Journal of Farm Economics 2, 121–135.

Elyachar, Julia. 2005. Markets of Dispossession: NGOs, Economic Development, and the State in Cairo. Durham: Duke University Press.

Eng, Kuah Khun. 1994. Bugis Street in Singapore: development, construction and the reinvention of cultural landscape. In: Cultural Identity and Urban Change in Southeast Asia, edited by M. Askew and W. Logan. Geelong: Deakin University Press.

Engels, Friedrich. [1887] 1979. The Housing Question. Moscow: Progress Publishers.

Engels, Friedrich. 1884. The Origin of the Family, Private Property and the State. Chippendale: Resistance Books.

Esping-Andersen, Gösta. 1990. The Worlds of Welfare Capitalism. Princeton, NJ: Princeton University Press.

Evans, Alan. 1999. 'On minimum rents: Part 1. Marx and absolute rent'. Urban Studies, 36, 2111–2120.

Evans, Paul. 1979 (original 1924). The Holland Land Company. Fairfield: Augustus M. Kelley Publishers.

Evers, Hans–Dieter. 1984. 'Urban landownership, ethnicity and class in Southeast Asian Cities'. International Journal of Urban and Regional Research, 8, 481–96.

Evers, Hans-Dieter and Rüdiger Korf. 2000. Southeast Asian Urbanism: The Meaning and Power of Social Space. Münster: Lit Verlag.

Fainstein, Susan. 1994. The City Builders: Property, Politics and Planning in London and New York. Oxford: Blackwell.

Faure, David. 2002. What Weber did not know: towns and economic development in Ming and Qing China. In: Town and Country in China: Identity and Perception, edited by Faure David and Tao Tao Lui. Basingstoke and New York: Palgrave.

Feagin, Joe. 1987. 'The secondary circuit of capital: office construction in Houston, Texas'. International Journal of Urban and Regional Research, 11, 172–192.

Feldstein, Martin. 1977. 'The surprising incidence of a tax on pure rent: A new answer to an old question'. Journal of Political Economy, 85, 349–360.

Ferguson. Nial. 2011. Civilization: The West and the Rest. Harmonbdsworth: Allen Lane, Penguin Books.

Fernandez, Walter and Hsueh Yun Tan. 1997. 'PM moves Horn Kee to another GPC post: change to avoid public confusion', The Straits Times, 10 December.

Fine, Ben. 2002. 'Economics imperialism and the new development economics as Kuhnian paradigm shift'. World Development, 30, 20057–70.

Finley, M.I. 1981. Economy and Society in Ancient Greece. London: Chatto and Windus.

Fischel, William. 1987. The Economics of Zoning Laws. A Property Rights Approach to American Land Use Controls. Baltimore: The John Hopkins University Press.

Fisher, Irving. 1933. 'The debt-deflation theory of great depressions'. Econometrica, 1, 337–357.

Foley, Duncan. 2006. Adam's Fallacy: A Guide to Economic Theology. Cambridge, MA: The Belknap University Press.

Forbes, Dean. 1996. Asian Metropolis: Urbanization and the Southeast Asian City. Melbourne: Oxford University Press.

Frank, Hartmut and Hans-Henning Joares. 1973. 'Planungspolitik'. In: Architektur und Kapitalverwertung Veränderungstendenzen in Beruf und Ausbildung von Architekten in der BRD. Frankfurt am Main: Brake.

Frantz, Douglas. 1989. 'Great Japanese land rush', LA Times, 8 March, p. 15.

Frantz, Douglas and Catherine Collins. 1989. Selling Out: How we are Letting Japan Buy Our Land, Our Industries, Our Financial Institutions and Our Future. New York: McGraw-Hill.

Fraser, W.D. 1984. Principles of Property Investment and Pricing. Basingstoke and London: Macmillan.

French, Douglas. 2010. Walk Away: The Rise and Fall of the Home Ownership Myth. Auburn, AL: Ludwig von Mises Institute.

Freund, David. 2007. Colored Property: State Policy and White Racial Politics in Suburban America. Chicago and London: The University of Chicago Press

Friedman, Milton. 1953. Essays in Positive Economics. Chicago: The University of Chicago Press.

Friedman, Milton and Anne Schwartz. 1963. A Monetary History of the United States 1867–1960. Princeton, NJ: Princeton University Press.

Friedmann, John. 2005. China's Urban Transition. Minneapolis and London: University of Minnesota Press.

Friedmann, John and Goetz Wolff . 1982. 'World City formation: an agenda for research and action'. International Journal of Urban and Regional Research, 6, 69–83.

Frug, Gerald. 1984. City as a legal concept. In: Cities of the Mind: Images and Themes of the City in the Social Sciences, edited by L. Rodwin and R. Hollister. New York and London: Plenum Press.

Furlong, Tom and Nancy Yoshihara, 1987, 'The Japanese land rush in America', LA Times, 1 February, p. 5.

Furuboth, Eirik and Rudolf Richter. 1991. The new institutional economics: an assessment. In: The New Institutional Economics, edited by Eirik G. Furubotn and Rudolf Richter. Tübingen: J.C.B. Mohr.

Fustel, Coulanges de Numa Denis. 1891. The Origin of Property in Land. Swan Sonnenschein.

Gaertner, Wulf. 2005. 'De jure naturae et gentium: Samuel von Pufendorf's contribution to social choice theory and economics'. Social Choice Welfare, 25, 231–241.

Gafoor, Ismail. 2013. The Ultimate Guide to Real Estate Investment in Singapore. Singapore: Ismail Gafoor.

Galbraith, John Kenneth. 1954. The Great Crash 1929. New York: Houghton Mifflin Harcourt Publishing Company.

Gates, Paul Wallace. 1942. 'The role of the land speculator in western development'. Pennsylvania Magazine of History and Biography, 66, 314–333.

George, Cherian. 2000. Singapore. The Air-conditional Nation. Singapore: Landmark Books.

George, Henry. [1879] 1920. Progress and Poverty. New York: Doubleday, Page & Co. 'GIC's US investments give a glimpse of its strategy', 1996, The Business Times, 11 May. Bloomberg Business News.

Giddens, Anthony. 1984. The Constitution of Society. Cambridge: Polity.

Glaeser, Edward. 2011. Triumph of the City: How our Greatest Invention makes us Richer, Smarter, Greener, Healthier, and Happier. New York and London: Penguin Books.

Goh, Chok Tong. 1997. 'Letter from Mr Goh to Mr Heng', The Straits Times, 6 December, p. 56.

Goh, Keng Swee. 1994. Foreword. In: Stepping out: The Making of Chinese Entrepreneurs, by Chan Kwok Bun and Claire Chiang See Ngoh. Singapore: Prentice Hall.

Goldberg, Michael. 1985. The Chinese Connection: Getting Plugged into Pacific Rim Real Estate, Trade and Capital Markets. Vancouver: University of British Columbia Press.

Goodman, Roger and Ito Peng. 1996. The East Asian welfare states: peripatetic learning, adaptive change and nation building. In Welfare States in Transition: National Adaptations in Global Economies, edited by Gösta Esping-Andersen. London: Sage.

Gotham, Kevin Fox. 2006. 'The secondary circuit of capital reconsidered: globalization and the U.S. real estate sector'. American Journal of Sociology, 12, 231–275.

Gotham, Kevin Fox. 2009. 'Creating liquidity out of spatial fixity: the secondary circuit of capital and the subprime mortgage crisis'. International Journal of Urban and Regional Research, 33, 355–371.

Gotham, Kevin Fox. 2012. Creating liquidity out of spatial fixity: the secondary circuit of capital and the restructuring of the US housing finance system. In: Subprime Cities, edited by M. Aalbers, 25–52. Wiley-Blackwell.

Gottdiener, Mark. 1985. The Social Production of Urban Space. Austin TX: University of Texas Press.

Government of Singapore Investment Corporation. 2001. Yearbook 2001. Singapore. Government of Singapore Investment Corporation.

'Govt sticks to land release scheme', 1996, The Straits Times, 7 December.

Grey, Thomas. 1969. 'The disintegration of property'. Property: Nomos, 86, edited by J. Roland Pennock and John Chapman. New York: New York University Press.

Grundy-Warr, Carl, Karen Peachey and Martin Perry. 1999. 'Fragmented integration in the Singapore-Indonesian border zone: Southeast Asia's "growth triangle" against the global economy'. International Journal of Urban and Regional Research, 23, 304–328.

Guo, Sujian. 2003. 'The ownership reform in China: what direction and how far?' Journal of Contemporary China, 36, 553–573.

Hadhi, Abdul. 1997. 'JTC freezes factory, land rents for one year', The Business Times, 29 June, p. 1.

Haila, Anne. 1990. Land as a Financial Asset. Otaniemi: Kiinteistöopin laitoksen julkaisuja.

Haila, Anne. 1999. 'City building in the east and west'. Cities, 16, 259–267.

Haila, Anne. 2000. 'Singapore and Hong Kong as property states', Urban Studies, 37, 2241–2256.

Haila, Anne. 2007. 'The market as the new emperor'. International Journal of Urban and Regional Research, 31, 3–20.

Hall, P. and D. Suskice. 2001. Varieties of Capitalism: The Institutional Foundations of Comparative Advantage. Oxford: Oxford University Press.

Hallett, Graham.1979. Urban Land Economics. London and Basingstoke: The Macmillan Press.

Halper, Stefan. 2010. The Beijing Consensus: Legitimizing Authoritarianism in our Time. New York: Basic Books.

Hamilton-Hart, Natasha. 2003. Asian States, Asian Bankers: Central Banking in Southeast Asia. Singapore: Singapore University Press.

Hammel, Daniel. 1999. 'Re-establishing the rent gap: an alternative view of capitalized rent'. Urban Studies, 36, 1283–1293.

Harding, Garrett. 1968. 'The tragedy of the commons'. Science, 162, 1243–1248.

Harrington, Shannon. 2007. "Queen of mean' made millions but stiffed tradesmen and terrorized staff'. The Globe and Mail, 21 August.

Harrison, Fred. 1983. The Power in the Land. London: Shepheard-Walwyn.

Hart, Gillian. 2002. Disabling Globalization: Places of Power in Post-apartheid South Africa. Pietermaritzburg: University of Natal Press.

Harvey, David. 1973. Social Justice and the City. Baltimore: The Johns Hopkins University Press.

Harvey, David. 1974. 'Class-monopoly rent, finance capital and the urban revolution'. Regional Studies, 8, 239–255.

Harvey, David. 1978. 'The urban process under capitalism: a framework for analysis'. International Journal of Urban and Regional Research, 2, 101–131.

Harvey, David. 1982. The Limits to Capital. Oxford: Basil Blackwell.

Harvey, David. 1985. The Urbanization of Capital: Studies in History and Theory of Capitalist Urbanisation. Oxford: Basil Blackwell.

Harvey, David. 2001. Spaces of Capital. New York: Routledge. New York.

Harvey, David. 2012. Rebel Cities. London and New York: Verso.

Harvey, David and Lata Chatterjee. 1974. 'Absolute rent and the structuring of space by government and financial institutions'. Antipode, 6, 22–36.

Hase, Patrick. 2013. Custom, Land and Livelihood in Rural South China. Hong Kong: Hong Kong University Press.

Häussermann, Hartmut and Anne Haila. 2005. The European city: a conceptual framework and normative project. In: Cities of Europe, edited by Y. Kazepov. Oxford: Blackwell Publishing.

Hayden, Dolores. 1984. Redesigning the American Dream: The Future of Housing, Work and Family Life. New York: W.W. Norton & Company.

Hayek, Friedrich. 1945. 'The use of knowledge in society'. The American Economic Review, 35, 519–530.

HDB Sample Household Survey. 2013. Public housing in Singapore: residents' profile, housing satisfaction and preferences. Singapore: Housing Development Board.

Healey, Patsy. 1994. Urban policy and property development: the institutional relations of real estate development in an old industrial district. Environment and Planning A, 26, 177–198.

'Heavy cost of ignoring warning signals', 1995, South China Morning Post, 5 March, p. 12.

Heilbroner, Robert. 1992. The Worldly Philosophers. New York: Simon & Schuster.

Heller, Michael. 1998. 'The tragedy of the anticommons: property in the transition from Marx to markets'. Harvard Law Review, 111, 621–688.

Henderson, Jeffrey. 1991. 'Urbanization in Hong Kong – South China region: an introduction to dynamics and dilemmas'. International Journal of Urban and Regional Research, 15, 169–179.

Henderson, Hubert. [1921] 1947. Supply and Demand. Cambridge: The University Press.

Henderson, Vernon. 1994. 'Externality and industrial development'. Cityscape: A Journal of Policy Development and Research 1, 75–93.

Heng, Chye Kiang. 1999. Cities of Aristocrats and Bureaucrats: Development of Medieval Chinese Cityscapes. Singapore: National University of Singapore Press.

Heng, Chiang Meng 1997. 'Mr Heng's reply to Mr Goh', The Straits Times, 6 December, p. 56.

Hill, C. 1995. 'Singapore closes down remaining businesses', South China Morning Post, 2 March, p. 14.

Hill, Michael and Kwen Fee Lian. 1995. The Politics of Nation Building and Citizenship in Singapore. London and New York: Routledge.

Hindess, Barry and Paul Hirst. 1975. Mode of Production and Social Formation. London: Macmillan

'HK developers deny cartel plot to force down property prices', 1994, The Straits Times, 31 May.

'HK slams Cox report on high-tech theft', 1999, The Straits Times, 15 June, p. 21.

Ho, Chi Wing and Loo Lee Sim. 1992. Studies on the Property Market. Singapore: University Press of Singapore.

Ho, K.C. 1993 Issues on industrial and urban development in local literature: public housing in Singapore. In: Malaysia and Singapore: Experiences in Industrialization and Urban Development, edited by Lee Boon Hiok and K. S. Susan Oorjitham. Kuala Lumpur: University of Malaya Press.

Ho, Kong Chong and Valerie Lim Nyuk Eun. 1992. Backlanes as contested regions: construction and control of physical space. In: Public Space: Design, Use and Management, edited by Chua Beng Huat and Norman Edwards. Singapore: Singapore University Press.

Hodgson, Geoffrey. 2001. How Economics Forgot History. London and New York: Routledge.

Hoenig Guide to the companies of Hong Kong. 1998. Hong Kong.

Holland, D.M. (ed.). 1970. The Assessment of Land Value. Madison, WI: University of Wisconsin Press.

Hong Kong Public Companies. 1986.

Hong, Yu-Hung. 1998. 'Transaction costs of allocating increased land value under public leasehold system: Hong Kong'. Urban Studies 35, 1577–1595.

Hoyt, Homer. 1933. One Hundred Years of Land Values in Chicago. Chicago: Chicago University Press.

Hsiung, Bingyuang. 1992. 'On resolving the problems entailed by the rent reduction Act of Taiwan's land reform'. The Development Economies, 30, 198–214.

Huff, W. G. 1994. The Economic Growth of Singapore: Trade and Development in the Twentieth Century. Cambridge: Cambridge University Press

Hume, David. 1739. A Treatise of Human Nature. Originally Oxford: Oxford University Press. 2000.

IMF. 2000. Background Paper: Offshore Financial Centers. Washington, DC: IMF

International Directory of Company Histories. 1991, Vol IV, edited by Adele Hast. Chicago and London: St James Press.

Iritani, Evelyn. 1999. 'U.S.-China spy dispute casts Hong Kong as a weak point in security', International Herald Tribune, 23 June, p. 6.

Irwan, Alexander. 2005. Institutions, discourses, and conflict in economic thought. In: Social Sciences and Power in Indonesia, edited by Vedi Hadiz and Daniel Dhakidae. Jakarta and Singapore: Equinox Publishing

Ischboldin, Boris. 1957. Zur rundlegung der moderner Grundrententheorie. Schmollers Jahrbuch für Gesetzgebung. Verwaltung und Volkswirchaft, 77, 671–92.

Jacobs, Jane. 1969. The Economy of Cities. New York: Vintage.

Jaffe, Austin and C.F. Sirmans. 1986. Fundamentals of Real Estate Investment. Englewood Cliffs, NJ: Prentice-Hall.

Jäger, Johannes. 2003. 'Urban land rent theory: a regulationist perspective'. International Journal of Urban and Regional Research, 27, 223–249.

Jao, Y.C. 1997. Hong Kong as an International Financial Centre: Evolution, Prospects and Policies. Hong Kong: City University of Hong Kong Press.

Jayaraman, Bobby. 2012. Building Wealth through REITs. Singapore: Marshall Cavendish.

Jefferson, Anna. 2011. Narratives of moral order in Michigan's foreclosure crisis. Working Paper.

Jevons, Stanley. [1871] 1970. The Theory of Political Economy. London: MacMillan.

Johnson, Simon and James Kwak. 2011. 13 Bankers: The Wall Street Takeover and the Next Financial Meltdown. New York: Vintage Books.

Jomo, K.S. 1986. A Question of Class: Capital, the State and Uneven Development in Malaya. Singapore: Oxford University Press.

Jomo. K S. 1997. Southeast Asia's Misunderstood Miracle: Industrial Policy and Economic Development in Thailand, Malaysia and Indonesia. Boulder: Westview Press.

Jomo, K.S. 2000. Comment: crisis and the developmental state in East Asia. In: Politics and Markets in Wake of the Asian Crisis, edited by R. Robinson, M. Beeson, K Jayasuriya and H-R. Kim. London and New York: Routledge.

'JTC sets out to make every square inch count', 1999, The Straits Times, 4 November.

Junka, Teuvo. 1988. Kilpailu ja keskittyminen talonrakennusalalla.

Jutikkala, Eino. 1958. Suomen talonpojan histroai. Helsinki: Suomalaisen kirjallisuuden seura.

Kahneman Daniel, Jack Knetsch and Richard Thaler. 1990. 'Experimental tests of the endowment effect and the Coase theorem'. The Journal of Political Economy, 98, 1325–1348.

Kamo, Toshio. 1995. 'The change of Tokyo's economic functions in a global city'. Hogaku Zasshi Journal of Law and Politics, 41, 28–42.

Karlsen, Carol. 1989. The Devil in the Shape of a Woman: Wirtschraft in Colonial New England. Vintage Books. New York.

Katz, Steven. 1986. 'Towards a sociological definition of rent: notes on David Harvey's "The limits to capital"'. Antipode, 18, 64–78.

Keivani, Ramin, Ali Parsa and Stanley McGreal. 2001. 'Globalisation, institutional structures and real estate markets in central European cities'. Urban Studies, 38, 2457–2476.

Kelly, John. 1981. 'The new barbarians: the continuing relevance of Henry George'. American Journal of Economics and Sociology, 40, 299–308.

Keppel Land Annual Report. 1994. Singapore.

Kerr, Alex. 1996. Lost Japan. Melbourne, Oakland, CA, London, Paris: Lonely Planet Publications.Keynes, J.M. 1926. The End of Laissez-faire. London: Hogarth Press.

Keynes, John Maynard. 1935. The General Theory of Employment, Interest and Money. London: Palgrave MacMillan.

Khan, Mushtaq. 1996. 'An input–output framework for the analysis of rent-seeking'. Paper presented at the international workshop on rent-seeking in Southeast Asia. University of Malaya, Kuala Lumpur, August.

Khondker, Habibal Haque. 2002. The sociology of development in Singapore. In: The Making of Singapore Sociology, Society and State, edited by Tong Chee Kiong and Lian Kwee Fee. Singapore: Times Academic Press.

Khoo, Su Nin. 1993. Streets of George Town. Penang: Janus Print & Resources.

King, R. 1989. 'Capital switching and the role of ground rent: theoretical problems'. Environment and Planning A, 21, 445–62.

Kivi, Aleksis. 1870. *Seitsemän veljestä.* Porvoo: WSOY 1966.

Khublall, N 1988. Singapore Property Tax. Law and Valuation. Singapore: Longman.

Ko, Kenneth and Sandy Li. 1998. 'Suspending land sales welcomed', South China Morning Post, 23 June.

Koh, Edna. 2000. 'Singapore bankers support reforms', The Straits Times, 22 June, p. 78.

Kohli, Sheel. 1995. 'Barings on brink of closure after $5b loss', South China Morning Post, 27 February, p. 1.

Kong, Lily. 2000. Values, conflicts, identity construction and urban change. In: A Companion to the City, edited by Gary Bridge and Sophie Watson. Oxford: Blackwell.

Kong, Lily L.L. and Jasmine S. Chan. 2000. 'Patriarchy and pragmatism: ideological contradictions in state policies'. Asian Studies Review, 24, 501–531.

Koninck, de Rodolphe. 1992. Singapore: An Atlas of the Revolution of Territory. Montpellier: Reclus.

Konrad, George and Ivan Szelenyi. 1977. Social conflicts of underurbanization. In: M. Harloe (ed.) Captive Cities: Studies in the Political Economy of Cities and Regions. Chichester: John Wiley & Sons.

Kosonen, Pekka. 1995. Eurooppalaiset Hyvinvointivaltiot. Gaudeamus.

Kotkin, Joel. 1993. Tribes: How Race, Religion and Identity Determine Success in the New World Economy. New York: Random House.

Krabben, Erwin van der. 2009. 'A property rights approach to externality problems: planning based on compensation rules'. Urban Studies, 46, 2869–2890.

Krätke, Stefan. 1992. 'Urban land rent and real estate market in the process of social Restructuring'. Environment and Planning D, 10, 245–264.

Krech III, Shepard. 1999. The Ecological Indian: Myth and History. New York and London: W.W. Norton & Company.

Krueger, Anne. 1974. 'The political economy of the rent-seeking society'. The American Economic Review, 64, 291–309.

Krugman, Paul. 1994. 'The myth of Asia's miracle'. Foreign Affairs, Nov/Dec, 62–78.

Krugman, Paul. 1999. The Return of Depression Economics. New York and London: W.W. Norton & Company.

Krugman, Paul and Robin Wells. 2010. 'The slump goes on: why?' The New York Review, LVII, 57–60.

Ku, Genvieve and Chris Yeung. 1998. 'Tung meets tycoons as flat price war bites', South China Morning Post, 21 May.

Kung, J.K. 2002. 'Choice of land tenure in China: the case of a country with quasi–private property rights'. Economic Development and Cultural Change, 50, 793–817.

Kwa, Chong Guan. 2007. Writing Singapore's history: from city-state to global city. In: S. Rajaratnam on Singapore: From Ideas to Reality, edited by Kwa Chong Guan. Singapore: World Scientific.

Kwok, Jonathan. 2011. 'S'pore shares inch up after EU agreement', The Straits Times, 13 December, p. B13.

Kwok, Kian Woon, C.J. Wee Wahn-ling and Karen Chia (eds) 2000. Rethinking Chinatown and Heritage Conservation in Singapore. Singapore Heritage Society.

Lafargue, Paul. 1890. The Evolution of Property: From Savagery to Civilization. London: Swan & Sonnenschein & Co.

La Grange, Adrianne, Chin-oh Chang and Ngai Ming Yip. 2006. 'Commodification and urban development: a case study of Taiwan'. Housing Studies, 21, 53–76.

Lai, Lawrence. 1998. 'The leasehold system as a means of planning by contract: the Hong Kong case'. Town Planning Review, 69, 245–71.

Lai, Lawrence and Marco Yu. 2001. 'The rise and fall of discriminatory zoning in Hong Kong'. Environment and Planning B, 28, 295–314.

Lam, Peng Er and Kevin Yl Tan. 1999. Lee's Lieutenants: Singapore's Old Guard. St. Leonards: Allen & Unwin.

Lamarche, Francois. 1976. Property development and the economic foundations of the urban question. In: Urban Sociology: Critical Essays, edited by C. Pickvance. London: Tavistock Publications.

Latif, Asad-ul Iqbal. 2009. Lim Kim Son: A Builder of Singapore. Singapore: ISEAS.

Lau, Justine. 2010. 'Investors from mainland snap up HK property', Financial Times, 14 October, p. 3.

Lau, Siu-Kai. 2003. 'Confidence in Hong Kong's capitalist society in the aftermath of the Asian financial turmoil.' Journal of Contemporary China, 35, 373–386.

Layard, P.R.G. and A.A. Walters. 1978. Microeconomic Theory. London and New York: McGraw Hill Book Company.

Lazear, Edward. 2000. 'Economic imperialism'. The Quarterly Journal of Economics, 115, 99–146.

Lee, Hsien Loong. 2011. 'Singapore needs to be confident, clear about priorities: PM Lee', The Straits Times, 31 December.

Lee, Joanne 1997, 'Act now to prevent property collapse, Redas urges Govt', The Straits Times, 18 November.

Lee, Kuan Yew. 2000. The Singapore Story: Memoirs of Lee Kuan Yew. Abridged edition. Singapore: Times Media.

Lee, Kuan Yew. 2011. From Third World to First. New York: Collins.

Lee, Soo Ann. 1976. Property taxation and land use policy in Singapore. In: The Cities of Asia: A Study of Urban Solutions and Urban Finance, edited by John Wong, 357–373. Singapore: Singapore University Press.

Leeson, Nick. 1996. Rogue Trader. New York: Little Brown.

Lefebvre, Henri. 2003. The Urban Revolution. Minneapolis, MN. University of Minnesota Press.

Le Galès, Patrick. 2002. European Cities. Oxford: Oxford University Press.

Leifer, Michael. 1995. Dictionary of the Politics of Southeast Asia. London and New York: Routledge.

Leifer, Michael. 2000. Singapore's Foreign Policy: Coping with Vulnerability. London: Routledge.

Leong, Ching. 2000. 'Eviction a must for killer-litter bugs', The Straits Times, 18 July, p. 35.

Leung P.C. and E.E. Ooi (eds). 2003. SARS War: Combating the Disease. Singapore: World Scientific.

Leung, Yew Kwong. 1987. Development Land and Development Charge in Singapore. Singapore: Butterworths.

Ley, David. 1987. 'Reply: The rent gap revisited'. Annals of the Association of American Geographers, 77, 465–468.

Leyshon, Andrew and Nigel Thrift. 1997. Money/Space: Geographies of Monetary Transformation. London: Routledge.

Li, Conghua. 1998. China: The Consumer Revolution. Singapore: John Wiley & Sons.

Li, Lin Hing. 1999. Urban Land Reform in China. Basingstoke: Macmillan Press.

Li, Xueying, Tracy Sua and Devi Asmarani. 2006. 'Activists cancel forums to show Displeasure', The Straits Times, 17 September, p. 17.

Lie, John. 1998. Han Unbound: The Political Economy of South Korea. Stanford, CT: Stanford University Press.

Lim, Lydia. 2000. 'Killer menace', The Straits Times, 18 July, p. 34.

Lim, Lan Yuan. 1987. Development Charge. Singapore: Singapore National Printers.

Lindqvist, Johan. 2010. Singapore's Borderlands. Tourism, Migration and Anxieties of Mobility. Singapore: NUS Press.

Linebaugh, Peter. 2008. The Magna Carta Manifesto. Oakland, CA: University of California Press.

Lipietz, Alan. 1985. Marxist approach to urban ground rent: the case of France. In: Land Rent, Housing and Urban Planning: A European Perspective, edited by M. Ball, V. Bentivegna, M. Edwards and M. Folin. London: Croom Helm.

Lipsky, John. 2006. 'A virtuous circle of success in sight', The Straits Times, September 18, p. 17.

Lo, Fu-Chen and Yue-Man Yeung. 1996. Globalization and the World of Large Cities. Tokyo: United Nations Press.

Locke, John. 1689. Second treatise of government. In: Two Treatises of Government: A Critical Edition with an Introduction and Apparatus Criticus, by Peter Laslett. Cambridge: Cambridge University Press, revised edition 1964.

Lodge, George and Ezra Vogel. 1987. Ideology and National Competitiveness: A Study of Nine Countries. Boston: Harvard Business School.

Logan, John. 2002. (ed.) The New Chinese City: Globalization and Market Reform. Oxford: Blackwell.

Logan, John and Harvey Molotch. 1987. Urban Fortunes. Berkeley: University of California Press.

Loh, Lixia. 2010. Sovereign Wealth Funds. Singapore: Talisman Publisher.

Long, Simon. 1997. 'The family firm', The Economist, 26 July, pp. 12–14.

Looney, Robert. 1989. 'The economic impact of rent seeking and military expenditures: A comparison of third world military and civilian regimes'. The American Journal of Economics and Sociology, 48, 11–29.

Low, Gail Ching-Liang. 1993. 'White skins/black masks: the pleasures and politics of imperialism'. In: Space and Place: Theories of identity and Location, edited by Erica Carter, James Donald and Judith Squires, p. 241–266. London: Lawrence & Wishart.

Low, Ignatius. 2000. 'Banks must spin off non-financial businesses', The Straits Times, 22 June, p. 1.

Low, Ignatius. 2006. 'New trade barriers, oil prices top list of IMF concerns', The Straits Times, 20 September, p. 1.

Low, Linda. 1990. State entrepreneurship. In: Local Entrepreneurship in Singapore: Private and State, edited by Lee Tsao Yuan and Linda Low. Singapore: Times Academic Press.

Low, Linda. 1998. The Political Economy of a City-State. Government-made Singapore. Singapore: Oxford University Press

Luithlen, Lutz. 1994. Office Development and Capital Accumulation in the UK. Aldershot: Ashgate.

Luria, Sarah. 2006. Capital Speculations: Writing and Building of Washington D.C. Hanover and London: University Press of New England.

MacFarlane, Alan. 1978. The Origins of English Individualism. Oxford: Blackwell.

Macpherson, C.B. 1978. The meaning of property. In: Property: Mainstream and Critical Positions, edited by C B. Macpherson. Oxford: Basil Blackwell.

Mah, Bow Tan. 2011. Reflections on Housing a Nation. A Collection of Commentaries by Mah Bow Tan. Singapore: Ministry of National Development.

Mäkinen, Virpi. 2008. 'Oikeus ja politiikka'. In Keskiajan Filosofia, edited by V. Hirvonen and R. Saarinen. Helsinki: Gaudeamus.

Malthus, Thomas. 1815. An Inquiry on the Nature and Progress of Rent. London: J.F. Dove.

Marangos, John. 2008. 'Thomas Paine (1737–1809) and Thomas Spence (1750–1814) on land ownership, land taxes and the provision of citizens' dividend'. International Journal of Social Economics, 35, 313–325.

Marriot, Oliver. 1967. The Property Boom. London: Hamish Hamilton.

Marshall, Alfred. 1890. Principles of Economics. London: Macmillan and Co.

Martin, David. 1981. John Stuart Mill and the Land Question. University of Hull. Occasional Papers in Economics and Social History no 9.

Martinez, Mark. 2009. The Myth of the Free Market. Sterling, VA: Kumarian Press.

Martinotti, Guido. 2005. Social morphology and governance in the new metropolis. In: Cities of Europe, edited by Y. Kazepov. Oxford: Blackwell Publishing.

Marx, Karl. [1863] 1968. Theories of Surplus Value. Part II. Moscow: Progress.

Marx, Karl. [1894] 1981. Capital, vol. 3. Harmondsworth: Penguin.

Marx, Karl and Friedrich Engels. [1848] 2002. The Communist Manifesto. London: Penguin Classics.

Marx, Karl and Friedrich Engels. 1975. Selected Correspondence. Moscow: Progress Publishers.

MAS Annual Report 1998/1999. Singapore: Monetary Authority of Singapore.

MAS Annual Report 1999/2000. Singapore: Monetary Authority of Singapore.

MAS Annual Report 2007/2008. Singapore: Monetary Authority of Singapore.

MAS Annual Report 2008/2009. Singapore: Monetary Authority of Singapore.
MAS Annual Report 2009/2010. Singapore: Monetary Authority of Singapore.
MAS Annual Report 2010/2011. Singapore: Monetary Authority of Singapore.
Massey, Doreen and Alejandrina Catalano. 1978. Capital and Land, Landownership by Capital in Great Britain. London: Edward Arnold.
Matondi, Prosper. 2012. Zimbabwe's Fast Track Land Reform. London: Zed Books.
McBriar, A.M. 1966. Fabian Socialism and English Politics 1884–1918. Cambridge: Cambridge University Press.
MCCY. 2013. Progress of the Malay Community in Singapore since 1980. Singapore: Ministry of Culture, Community and Youth.
McFarlane, Colin. 2012. 'The entrepreneurial slum: civil society, mobility, and the co-production of urban development'. Urban Studies, 49, 2795–2816.
McGee, Terry. 1967. The Southeast Asian City: A Social Geography of the Primate Cities of Southeast Asia. London: Bell.
McGee, Terry. 1989. Urbanisasi or kotadesasi? Evolving patterns of urbanization in Asia. In: Urbanization in Asia: Spatial Dimensions and Policy Issues, edited by F. Costa, A. Dutt, and A. Noble. Honolulu: University of Hawai'i Press.
McGhie, Tom. 1995. 'Man who broke the royal bank', International Express, 2–6 March, p. 1.
McIntosh, Angus P.J. and Stephen Sykes. 1985. A Guide to Institutional Property Investment. Basingstoke: Macmillan.
McKinnon, Malcom. 2011. Asian Cities: Globalization, Urbanization and Nation-building. Copenhagen: NIAS Publishers.
McMillan, Alex. 2012. 'Choices almost as safe as houses', South China Morning Post, 10 December, p. 6.
Medema, Steven. 2009. The Hesitant Hand. Princeton, NJ: Princeton University Press.
Mera, Koichi and Bertrand Renaud (eds). 2000. Asia's Financial Crisis and the Role of Real Estate. New York and London: M.E. Sharpe.
Merrifield, Andy. 2014. The New Urban Revolution. London: Pluto Press.
Merrington, John. 1975. 'Town and country in the transition to capitalism'. New Left Review I/93.
Miklethwait, John and Adrian Wooldridge. 2014. The Fourth Revolution: The Global Race to Reinvent the State. New York: The Penguin Press.
Miksic, John. 2013. Singapore and the Silk Road of the Sea 1300–1800. Singapore: NUS Press.
Milgrom, Paul and Robert Weber. 1982. 'A theory of auctions and competitive bidding'. Econometrica, 50, 1089–1122.
Mill, John Stuart [1848] 1909. Principles of Political Economy. 7th edition. London: Longmans, Green and Co.
Milton, Giles. 1999. Nathaniel's Nutmeg, or, The True and Incredible Adventures of the Spice Trader who Changed the Cause of History. London: Hodder & Stoughton.
Ministry of National Development. 2007. Press Release, 18 July. Singapore.
Minsky, Hyman. 1986. 'The evolution of financial institutions and the performance of the Economy'. Journal of Economic Issues, xx, 2, 345–353.

Mirza, Hafiz. 1986. Multinationals and the Growth of the Singapore Economy. Singapore: McGraw-Hill.

Mitchell, Clyde. 1949. 'Land reforms in South Korea.' Pacific Affairs, 22, 144–154.

Mitchell, Timothy. 2007. The properties of markets. In: Do Economists Make Markets? Edited by D. MacKenzie, F. Muniesa and L. Siu. Princeton, NJ: Princeton University Press.

Mitsubishi Corporate Profile. 1992. Tokyo: Mitsubishi.

Molotch, Harvey. 1976. 'The city as a growth machine'. American Journal of Sociology, 82, 309–330.

Montesquieu, Charles-Louis De S Baron. The Spirits of Laws. Original 1748. New York: Cosimo 2007.

'More info on reserves not in nation's interest', 2004, The Straits Times, 20 October, p. H7.

Morgan, Lewis. 1877. Ancient Society: Or, Researchers in the Lines of Human Progress from Savagery, through Barbarism to Civilization. London: Macmillan and Co.

Motha, Philip and Belinda Yuen. 1999. Singapore Real Property Guide. Singapore: Singapore University Press.

Müller, Herbert. 1952. Die Städtisch Grundrente und die Bewertung von Baugrundstücken. Tübingen.

Müller, Walter. 1933. Das Problem der Grundrentein der Neueren Literatur des Sozialökonie. Göttingen.

Muth, Richard. 1969. Cities and Housing. Chicago: Chicago University Press.

Nas, P.J.M. 1986. The Indonesian City. Dordrecht – Holland: Foris Publications.

Nas, P.J.M. 1989. 'Town and countryside in Indonesia.' SOJOURN, 4, 20–33.

Nathan, Dominic 1994' 'Most hawkers opt to buy their stall', The Straits Times, 24 June p. 1.

Naughton, Barry. 1999. Between China and the world: Hong Kong's economy before and after 1997. In: Cosmopolitan Capitalists: Hong Kong and the Diaspora at the End of the Twentieth Century, edited by Gary Hamilton. Seattle and London: University of Washington Press, 80–99.

Neef, Rainer. 1974. Die ökonomische verwertung städtische bodens und ihre wirkung auf die stadentwicklung. Dissertation, University of Marburg.

Nell-Breuning, von Oswald. 1965. Die Preisbildung am Bodenmarkt. So Planen und Bauen.

Ness, Gayl D and Prem P Talwar. 2005. Asian Urbanization in the New Millennium. Singapore: Marshall Cavendish.

Netzer, Dick. 1966. The Economics of the Property Tax. Washington, DC: Brookings.

Ng, Grace. 2006. 'Common currency not suitable for Asia says Tharman', The Straits Times, 18 November, p. H6.

Ng, Grace. 2008. 'GIC to proceed with $14b funding for UBS', The Straits Times, 29 February.

Ng, Kang-chung 2011, 'Elite clubs may have to open doors wider', South China Morning Post, 10 May, p. C1.

North, Douglas. 2005. Understanding the Process of Economic Change. Princeton NJ: Princeton University Press.

North, Douglas and Robert Thomas. [1973] 1999. The Rise of the Western World: A New Economic History. Cambridge: Cambridge University Press.

O'Connor, Richard. 1995. 'Indigenous urbanism: class, city and society in southeast Asia'. Journal of Southeast Asian Studies, 26, 30–34.

Ogborn, Miles. 2007. Indian Ink: Script and Print in the Making of the East India Company. Chicago and London: The University of Chicago Press.

Ong, Hwee and Janice Tai. 2012, 'Casino ban to include thousands on aid schemes', The Straits Times, 18 May, p. B2.

Ooi, Jin-bee. 1959. 'Rural development in tropical areas with special reference to Malaya', The Journal of Tropical Geography, 12.

Oon, Diana. 1997. 'OPH's Leong Horn Kee steps aside as head of nat'l devt GPC', The Business Times, 10 December.

Oon, Diana. 1998: 'Recent industrial land sales upset developers', The Business Times, 22 October, p. 3.

Oon Diana and A Hadhi. 1997. 'Redas blasted over appeal to curb govt land sales', The Business Times, 31 July.

Oppenheimer, Franz. 1909. David Ricardos Grundrententheorie. Darstellung und Kritik. Berlin: Druck und verlag von Georg Reimer.

Oser, Jacob. 1970. The Evolution of Economic Thought. New York: Harcourt, Brace & World

Overtveldt Johan van. 2009. Bernanke's Test: Ben Bernanke, Alan Greenspan and the Drama of the Central Banker. Chicago: Agate.

Paine, Thomas. [1776] 2003. Common sense. In: Common sense, rights of man, and other essential writings of Thomas Paine. New York: Signet Classics.

Paine, Thomas. [1791] 2003. Rights of man. In: Common Sense, Rights of Man, and Other Essential Writings of Thomas Paine. New York: Signet Classics.

Paine, Thomas. [1797] 2003. Agrarian justice. In: Common Sense, Rights of Man, and Other Essential Writings of Thomas Paine. New York: Signet Classics.

Palmer, Michael. 1987. 'The surface-subsoil from divided ownership in late imperial China: some examples from the new territories of Hong Kong'. Modern Asian Studies, 21, 1–19.

Pan, Lynn. 1990. Sons of the Yellow Emperor: The Story of the Overseas Chinese. London: Mandarin.

Pearlman, Jonathan 2011, 'Aussie casinos under scrutiny', The Straits Times, 11 December.

Peebles, Gavin and Peter Wilson. 1996. The Singapore Economy. Cheltenham: Edward Elgar.

Pejovic, Steve. 1982. 'Karl Marx, property rights school and the process of social Change'. Kyklos, 35, 383–397.

Perry, M.L., L. Kong and B. Yeoh. 1997. Singapore: A Developmental City State. Chichester: John Wiley & Sons.

Petty, William. 1662. A treatise of taxes and contributions. In: The Economic Writings of Sir William Petty, together with the observations upon bills of mortality, more probably by Captain John Graunt.1891, edited by C.H. Hull. Cambridge: Cambridge University Press.

Phang, Sock-Yong. 1995. George, economic development, and the distribution of land rents in Singapore. Lincoln Institute of Land Policy Research Papers.

Phang, Sock-Yong. 2001. 'Housing policy, wealth function and the Singapore economy'. Housing Studies, 16, 443–459.

Phongpaichit, Pasuk and Chris Baker. 1998. Thailand's Boom and Bust. Chiang Mai: Silkworm Books.

Pipes, Richard. 1999. Property and Freedom: The Story of How the Centuries of Private Ownership has Promoted Liberty and the Rule of Law. New York: Alfred Knopf.

Pirenne, Henri. [1936] 1972. Economic and Social History of Medieval Europe. London: Routledge & Kegan Paul.

Pisani, Ralph and Robert Pisani. 1989. Investing in Land: How to be a Successful Developer. New York: John Wiley & Sons.

Polanyi, Karl. [1944] 2001. The Great Transformation. Boston: Beacon Press.

Poon, Alice. 2005. Land and the Ruling Class in Hong Kong. Richmond: Alice Poon.

Pornchokchai, Sopon and RanjithPerera. 2005. 'Housing speculation in Bangkok: lessons for emerging economies'. Habitat International, 29, 439–452.

Powell, Robert. 1989. Innovative Architecture of Singapore. Singapore: Select Books.

Prime Minister's Speeches, Press Conferences, Interviews, Statements. Republic of Singapore.

Pritchard, Evan T. 2007. Native New Yorkers: The Legacy of the Algonquin People of New York. San Francisco and Tulsa: Council Oak Books.

Proudhon, Pierre-Joseph. [1840] 1994. What is Property? Cambridge: Cambridge University Press.

Pye, Lucian. 1985. Asian Power and Politics: The Cultural Dimensions of Authority. Cambridge, MA and London: The Belknap of Harvard University Press.

Quah, Jon S.T. 1987. 'Public bureaucracy and policy implementation in Singapore'. Southeast Asian Journal of Social Science, 15, 77–95.

Quak, H.W. 1998, ' Talk of HK repatriations should be treated with caution', The Business Times, 27 June.

Qing, S. 1995. An introduction to the real estate legal system in the People's Republic of China. In: Legal Aspects of Real Property Investment in the Asia Pacific Region, by Inter Pacific Bar Association. Singapore: Butterworths.

Quigley, John. 2001. Real estate and Asian crisis. Working paper. Institute of Business and Economic Research. University of California, Berkeley.

Radelet, Steven and Jeffrey Sachs. 2000. The onset of the East Asia: Asian financial crisis. In: Currency Crisis, edited by P. Krugman. Chicago: University of Chicago Press.

Rajan, Raghuram and Luigi Zingales. 2009. 'Which capitalism? Lessons from the East Asian crisis'. Journal of Applied Corporate Finance, 11, 40–48.

Rajaratnam, S. 1972. 'Singapore: Global City'. Speech to the Singapore Press Club on February 6, 1972. In S. Rajaratnam on Singapore: From Ideas to Reality, edited by Kwa Chong Guan. Singapore: World Scientific Publishing.

Ramirez, Carlos and Ling Hui Tan. 2003. 'Singapore, Inc. versus the private sector: are government-linked companies different', IMF Working Paper, July.

Reid, Anthony. 1988. Southeast Asia in the Age of Commerce 1450–1680. Volume one: The Lands below the Winds. Chiang Mai: Silkworm Books.

Reid, Anthony. 1993. Southeast Asia in the Age of Commerce 1450–1680. Volume two: Expansion and Crisis. Chiang Mai: Silkworm Books.

Reid Anthony. 1999. Charting the Shape of Early Modern Southeast Asia. Chiang Mai: Silkworm Books.

Reid, Anthony. 2010. Violence at sea: unpacking 'piracy' in the claims of states over Asian seas. In: Elusive Pirates, Pervasive Smugglers: Violence and Clandestine Trade in the Greater China Seas, edited by R. Antony. Hong Kong: University Press of Hong Kong.

Renard, Vincent. 2007. 'Property rights and the "transfer of development rights"'. The Town Planning Review, 78, 41–60.

Renaud, Bertrand. 1997. 'The 1985 to 1994 global real estate cycle: an overview'. Journal of Real Estate Literature, 5, 13–44.

Report of the Cost Review Committee 1996. Singapore: Ministry of Trade and Industry.

Ricardo, David. 1815. An essay on the influences of a low price of corn on the profit of stock. London: Printed for John Murray.

Ricardo, David. [1817] 1974. The Principles of Political Economy and Taxation. London: J. M. Dent & Sons.

Richardson, Harry. 1977. The New Urban Economics and Alternatives. London: Pion.

Richardson, Harry, M.J. Vipond and R.A. Furbey. 1974. Housing and Urban Spatial Structure: A Case Study. Farnborough: Saxon House.

Riggs, F. 1996. Thailand: The Modernization of a Bureaucratic Polity. Honolulu: East-West Centre Press.

Riikonen, Hannu. 1985. James Joycen Odysseus. Kielen ja kerronnan sokkelo. Juva: Gaudeamus.

Robbins, Lionel. 1932. An Essay on the Nature and Significance of Economic Science. London: Macmillan.

Robertson, David 2008, 'Singapore to act on sovereign wealth funds', Times online, 19 March.

Robinson, Jennifer. 2002. 'Global and world cities: a view from off the map'. International Journal of Urban and Regional Research, 34, 265–285.

Robinson, Jennifer. 2006. The Ordinary City: Between Modernity and Development. London: Routledge.

Robinson, Joan. [1933] 1959. The Economics of Imperfect Competition. London: Macmillan.

Robinson, R. 1986. Indonesia: The Rise of Capital. Sydney: Allen & Unwin.

Rosdolsky, Roman. 1968. Zur Entstehungsgeschichte des Maxschen Kapital. Der Rohentwurt de Kapital 1857–1858. Frankfurt am Main.

Rose, Carol. 1994. Property and Persuasion. Essays in the History, Theory, Rhetoric of Ownership. Boulder, CO: Westview.

Rousseau, Jean Jacques. [1755] 1994. Discourse on the Origin of Inequality. Oxford: Oxford University Press.

Rowe, Peter. 2005. East Asian Modern: Shaping the Contemporary City. London: Reaktion Books.

Roy, Ananya. 2003. 'Paradigms of propertied citizenship: transitional techniques of Analysis'. Urban Affairs Review, 38, 463–491.

Roy, Ananya. 2005. 'Urban informality: towards an epistemology of planning'. Journal of the American Planning Association, 71, 147–158.

Said, Edward. 1978. Orientalism. Routledge & Kegan Paul.

Sakolski, Aaron Morton. 1932. The Great American Land Bubble. New York: Harper Brothers.

Samuels, Warren. 2003. 'Why the Georgist movement has not succeeded: a speculative memorandum.' The American Journal of Economics and Sociology, 62, 583–592.

Samuelson, Paul. 1970. Economics. 8th edition. McGraw Hill.

Sardar, Ziauddin. 2000. The Consumption of Kuala Lumpur. London: Reaktion Books.

SarDesai, D.R. 1994. Southeast Asia: Past and Present. Third edition. Boulder, CO and San Francisco, CA: Westview Press.

Sargent, Thomas and Francois Velde.1995. 'Macroeconomic features of the French revolution'. Journal of the Political Economy, 103, 474–518.

Sassen, Saskia. 1991. The Global City: New York, London, Tokyo. Princeton, NJ: Princeton University Press.

Sassen, Saskia. 1994. Cities in a World Economy. Thousand Oaks, CA: Pine Forge Press.

Sassen, Saskia. 1996. Losing Control? Sovereignty in an Age of Globalization. New York: Columbia University Press.

Saunders, Peter. 1990. A Nation of Home Owners. London: Unwin Hyman.

Sayer, Andrew. 1992. Method in Social Science. London: Routledge.

Schiffer, Jonathan. 1991. 'State policy and economic growth: a note on the Hong Kong Model'. International Journal of Urban and Regional Research 15, 180–196.

Schiffrin, H. 1956/1957. 'Sun Yat-sen's early land policy'. Journal of Asian Studies, 16, 549–564.

Schoenberger, Karl 1989, 'Japan's odd man out', LA Times, 20 August, p. 1.

Scott, Allen J. 1980. The Urban Land Nexus and the State. London: Pion.

Searle, Peter. 1999. The Riddle of Malaysian Capitalism: Rent-Seekers or Real Capitalists? St. Leonards: Allen & Unwin.

Selby-Bigge and P.H. Nidditch (eds). 1978. A Treatise of Human Nature. Oxford: Clarendon Press.

Seligman, Edwin. 1910. The Shifting and Incidence of Taxation. 3rd edition. New York: Columbia University Press.

Seligman, Edwin. 1915. Essays in Taxation. London: Macmillan.

Sen, Amartya. 1997. 'Human rights and Asian values: what Lee Kuan Yew and Le Peng don't understand about Asia', The New Republic, July 14.

Sen, Amartya. 2009. The Idea of Justice. London: Penguin Books.

Seow, Kah Ping. 1998. 'Planning for quality living in Singapore'. Paper presented at Quality of Life in Cities Conference, 4–6 March Singapore.

Sesser, Stan. 1994. The Lands of Charms and Cruelty. New York: Vintage Books.

Shachtman, Tom. 1991. Skyscraper Dreams: The Great Real Estate Dynasties of New York. Boston: Little, Brown and Company.

Sherraden, Michael, Sudha Nair, S. Vasoo, Ngiam Tee Liang and Margaret Sherraden. 1995, 'Social policy based on assets: the impact of Singapore's Central Provident Fund'. Asian Journal of Political Science, 3, 112–133.

Shiau, Daren. 2002. Heartland. Singapore: Ethos Books.

Shields, Rob. 1992. Places on the Margin: Alternative Geographies of Modernity. London: Routledge.

Shiller, Robert. 2000. Irrational Exuberance. Economic Affairs, 2000, 20, 59–63.

Shiller, Robert. 2008. Long-term perspectives on the current boom in home prices. In: The Economists' Voice: Top Economists Take on Today's Problems, edited by J. Stiglitz, A. Edlin and J. De Long. New York: Columbia University Press.

Siddique, Sharon. 1990. 'The phenomenology of ethnicity: a Singapore case study'. Sojourn, 5, 35–62.

Silage, Michael. 1984. 'Land reform in Kiaochow, China'. The American Journal of Economics and Sociology, 43, 167–178.

Silagi, Michael. 1989. 'Henry George and Europe: as dissident economist and path-breaking philosopher, he was a catalyst for British social reform'. American Journal of Economics and Sociology, 48, 113–122.

Silva de, Gerry. 1995. 'S'pore has strong extradition case: Frankfurt prosecutor', The Straits Times, 29 April, p. 48.

Sim, Loo Lee, Sau–Kim Lum and Lai Choo Malone Lee. 2002. 'Property rights, collective sales and government intervention: averting a tragedy of the anticommons'. Habitat International, 26, 457–470.

'Simex names chairman of global experts' panel', 1995, The Straits Times, 21 March.

Simmel, George. 1978. The Philosophy of Money. London: Routledge and Kegan Paul.

Simon, Herbert. 1943. 'The incidence of a tax on urban real property'. The Quarterly Journal of Economics, LVII, 398–420.

Simone, AbdouMaliq. 2010. City Life from Jakarta to Dakar: Movements at the Crossroads. New York and London: Routledge.

Singapore Cooperation Enterprise New Release, September 15, 2008.

Singapore Government Press Statement 1964 Text of Speech by the Prime Minister, Mr. Lee Kuan Yew, in Moving the Second Reading of the Land Acquisition (Amendment no. 2) Bill 1964 in the Legislative Assembly on Wednesday June 10.

Singapore Parliament Report 1966, 26 October. Parliament of Singapore.

'Singapore Redas worried about property market slump report', 1997, Dow Jones International News, 30 July.

'Singapore's success achieved by being pragmatic: SM Lee', 1996, The Straits Times, 2 January.

Sito, Peggy. 1998. 'Developers deny auction boycott plan to protest for change to land policy', South China Morning Post, 22 June.

Sito, Peggy. 2013. 'Li retains lead in Hong Kong rich list with US $30b fortune', South China Morning Post, 11 June.

Skilling, David. 2012. 'Debate on capitalism', The Straits Times, 11 February.

Skinner G.W. (ed.). 1977. The City in Late Imperial China. Stanford CT: Stanford University Press.

Skouras, A. 1978. 'The neutrality of land taxation'. Public Finance, 33, 113–134.

SLA Annual Report 2010/2011. Singapore: Singapore Land Authority.

SLA Press Release 2008a Waiver of building premium. Singapore: Ministry of Law.

SLA Press Release 2008b Supplementary. Singapore: Ministry of Law.

Smirnow, I. K. and J. A. Winogradown. 1973. Die Grundrente. In Geschichte der politischen Ökonomie des Sozialismus, edited by D. K. Trifonow and L. D. Schirokorad. Berlin.

Smith, Adam. [1776] 1904. An Inquiry into the Nature and Causes of the Wealth of Nations. London: Methuen.

Smith, Michael Peter. 2001. Transnational Urbanism. Oxford: Blackwell.

Smith, Neil. 1984. Uneven Development: Nature, Capital and the Production of Space. Oxford: Basil Blackwell.

Smith, Neil. 1987. 'Gentrification and the rent gap.' Annals of the Association of American Geographers, 77, 462–465.

Smith, Neil. 1992. New city, new frontier: the lower east side as wild, wild west. In Variations on a Theme Park, edited by M. Sorkin. New York: The Noonday Press.

Smith, Neil. 1996. The New Urban Frontier: Gentrification and Revanchist City. London: Routledge.

Smyth, Hedley. 1985. Property Companies and the Construction Industry in Britain. Cambridge: Cambridge University Press.

Soja, Edward. 2010. Seeking Spatial Justice. Minneapolis, MN: University of Minnesota Press.

Soto, de Hernando. 2000. The Mystery of Capital: Why Capitalism Triumphs in the West and Fails Everywhere Else. New York: Basic Books.

Spence, Thomas. [1797] 1982. The rights of infants. In: The Political Works of Thomas Spence, edited by Dickinson H.T. Newcastle upon Tyne: Avero.

'S'pore scores high on governance', 2006, The Straits Times, 17 September, p. 16.

'S'pore land bill goes to select committee', 1966, The Straits Times, 23 June, p. 5.

Steinhardt, Nancy. 1990. Chinese Imperial City Planning. Honolulu: University of Hawai'i Press.

Stevenson, Katherine Cole and H. Ward Jand. 1986. Houses by Mail: A Guide to Houses from Sears, Roebuck and Company. The Preservation Press.

Stiglitz, Joseph. 2002. 'Information and change in the paradigm in economics'. The American Economic Review 92, 460–501.

Stiglitz, Joseph, Aaron Edlin and Bradford DeLong. (eds) 2008.The Economists' Voice: Top Economists Take on Todays' Problems. New York: Columbia University Press.

Stonier, Alfred and Douglas Hague. 1967. A Textbook of Economic Theory. Edinburgh: Longmans.

Sturgeon, Janet. 2005. Border Landscapes: The Politics of Akha Land Use in China and Thailand. Chiang Mai: Silkworm Books.

Sunstein, Cass. 1997. 'Behavioral analysis of law'. The University of Chicago Law Review, 64, 1175–1195.

Sweezy, Paul. 1950. 'A critique', Science and Society, Spring.

Tan, Amanda .2012. 'Mountbatten condo up for collective sale', The Straits Times, 10 October, p. B10.

Tan, Amy. 2012. 'Foreign buyers retreat from luxury segment', The Edge Singapore, 13 February, p. CC3.

Tan, Bah Bah. 1995. 'The Watford kid – smart player or somebody's patsy', The Straits Times, 4 March, p. 6.

Tan, Colin. 1997. 'JTC to rent HDB flats out to foreigners', The Straits Times, 28 August, p. 1.

Tan, Chwee Huat. 1987. Financial Markets and Institutions in Singapore. 5th edition. Singapore: Singapore University Press.

Tan, Chwee Huat. 1999. Financial Markets and Institutions in Singapore. 10th edition. Singapore: Singapore University Press.

Tan, Lorna. 2011. 'ICBC opens first offshore Yuan processing centre here', The Straits Times, 12 March.

Tan, Sai Siong. 1997. 'Govt intervention is unavoidable', The Straits Times, 24 November.

Tan, Say Tin, Leong Foong Lin, Basil Chan Aik Leong, et al. 2009. Economics in Public Policies: The Singapore Story. Singapore: Marshall Cavendish.

Tan, Sook Yee. 1998. Private Ownership of Public Housing in Singapore. Singapore: Times Academy Press.

Tang, Yunbin. 1989. 'Urban land use in China'. Land Use Policy, 6, 53–63.

Tay, Erica. 2006. 'Asian chief: more work for group to become trade block', The Straits Tines, 17 September, p. 13.

Tay, Simon. 2009. City of Small Blessings. Singapore: Landmark Books.

Taylor, Antony. 2004. Lords of Misrule: Hostility to Aristocracy in Late Nineteenth- and Early Twentieth Century Britain. Basingstoke: Palgrave Macmillan.

Tee, Edmund. 1999. 'Info com the next key sector', The Straits Times, 23 June, p. 1.

Teh, Hooi Ling. 1998. 'DBS land-led shanghai project delayed amid glut', The Business Times, 18 February, p. 11.

'Temasek Holdings takes a severe hit', 2009, Bangkok Post, 11 February.

Teo, Anna. 2005. 'S'pore 2nd easiest place to do business report', The Business Times, 14 September, p. 3.

Teo, Joyce. 2008. 'Some Gillman Heights owners fight on for their homes', The Straits Times, 14 March.

Thailand Country Report. 1997. 4th quarter. London: Economist Intelligence Unit.

Thaler, Richard. 1989. 'Toward a positive theory of consumer choice'. Journal of Economic Behavior and Organization, 1, 39–60.

Thant, Myint-U. 2007. The River of Lost Footsteps: A Personal History of Burma. London: Faber and Faber.

Thayer, Theodore. 1953. 'The land-bank system in the American colonies'. The Journal of Economic History, xiii, 145–159.

The Hoenig Guide to the Companies of Hong Kong. 1998. Hong Kong: E F P International.

Thünen, Johann Heinrich von. 1826. Der isolierte staat in beziehung auf landwirtschaft und nationalökonomie. Rostock.

Tideman, Nicolaus. 2004. 'George on land speculation and the winner's curse'. The American Journal of Economics and Sociology, 63, 1091–1095.

Torrens, Robert. 1815. An Essay on the External Corn Trade. London: J. Hatchard.

Tullock, Gordon. 2005. The Rent-seeking Society. Indianapolis: Liberty Fund.

'Tung constrained'. 1998. The Economist, 28 March.

Turnbull, C.M. 1982. A History of Singapore 1819–1975. Oxford: Oxford University Press.

Tyabji, Amina and Lin Kuo Ching. 1989. 'The financing of public housing in Singapore'. Southeast Asian Journal of Social Science, 17, 21–43.

Unger, Danny. 1998. Building Social Capital in Thailand: Fibers, Finance, and Infrastructure. Cambridge: Cambridge University Press.

Ungpakorn, Ji Giles. 1999. Thailand: Class Struggle in an Era of Economic Crisis. Hong Kong: Asia Monitor Resources Centre.

URA. 1995. Changing the face of Singapore through the URA sale of sites. Singapore: Urban Redevelopment Authority.

URA. 2011 Release of 4th quarter real estate statistics, 28 January.

Vasil, Raj. 2000. Governing Singapore: A History of National Development and Democracy. St. Leonards: Allen & Unwin.

Vilar, Pierre. 1984. A History of Gold and Money 1450–1920. London: Verso.

Vygodski, V. S. 1976. Miten Marx teki suuren keksintönsä: 'Pääoman' syntyhistoria. Helsinki.

Wade, Robert and Frank Veneroso. 1998. 'The Asian Crisis: The High Debt Model Versus the Wall Street-Treasury-IMF complex'. New Left Review.

Wagner, Adolf. 1926. Grundrente und preishöhe: ein kritische beitrag zur nationalökonomischen theorie. Marburg.

Wake, C.H. 1975. 'Raffles and the Rajas: the founding of Singapore in Malayan and British colonial history'. Journal of the Malayan Branch of Royal Asiatic Society, 48, 47–73.

Walker, Andrew. (ed.) 2009a. Tai Lands and Thailand: Community and State in Southeast Asia. Singapore: NUS Press.

Walker, Andrew. 2009b. Modern Tai community. In: Tai lands and Thailand: Community and State in Southeast Asia, edited by A. Walker. Singapore: NUS Press.

Walker, Anthony and Roger Flanagan. 1991. Property and Construction in Asia Pacific, Hong Kong, Japan, Singapore. Oxford: BSP Professional Book.

Walker, Richard. 1974. 'Urban ground rent: building a new conceptual framework'. Antipode, 6, 51–58.

Walters, A. A. 1974. Land speculator – creator or creature of inflation? In: Government and the Land, edited by A. A. Walters, F.G. Pennance, W.A. West, et al. Lancing: The Institute of Economic Affairs.

Wan, Adrian. 2010. 'Priest wrong to single out Li as a 'devil' admits leader', South China Morning Post, 15 November.

Wan, Wei Lin. 1995. Foreign buyers of private residential properties in Singapore. Dissertation. Department of Building and Real Estate. National University of Singapore.

Wapshott, Nicholas. 2011. Keynes. Hayek. The clash that Defined Modern Economics. New York and London: W.W. Norton & Company.

Ward, Kevin. 2008. 'Editorial – Toward a comparative (re)turn in urban studies? Some Reflections'. Urban Geography, 29, 405–410.

Watson, James. 2011a. Hereditary tenancy and corporate landlordism in traditional China: a case study. In: Village life in Hong Kong: Politics, Gender and Ritual in the New Territories, by James Watson and Rubie Watson. Hong Kong: The Chinese University Press.

Watson, James. 2011b. Agnates and outsiders. Adoption in a Chinese lineage. In: Village Life in Hong Kong: Politics, Gender and Ritual in the New Territories, by James Watson and Rubie Watson. Hong Kong: The Chinese University Press.

Watson, James and Rubie Watson. 2011a. Village Life in Hong Kong: Politics, Gender and Ritual in the New Territories. Hong Kong: The Chinese University Press.

Watson, James and Rubie Watson. 2011b. (ed.) Fieldwork in the Hong Kong New Territories (1965–1987). In: Village Life in Hong Kong: Politics, Gender and Ritual in the New Territories, by James Watson and Rubie Watson. Hong Kong: The Chinese University Press.

Watson, Rubie. 2011. The Creation of Chinese Lineage. The Teng of Ha Tsuen, 1669–1751. In: Village Life in Hong Kong: Politics, Gender and Ritual in the New Territories, by James Watson and Rubie Watson. Hong Kong: The Chinese University Press.

Weatherford, Jack. 1997. The History of Money. New York: Three Rivers Press.

Weber, Max. 1966. The City. Translated and edited by Don Martindale and Gertrud Neuwirth. New York: The Free Press.

Webster, Chris. 2007. 'Property rights, public space and urban design'. The Town Planning Review, 78, 81–101.

Wee, Agnes. 1988. 'Three property giants in billion-$ battle', The Straits Times, 17 August, p. 11.

Wei, Julie, Ramon Myers and Donald Gillin (eds). 1994. Prescriptions for Saving China: Selected Writings of Sun Yat-Sen. Stanford, CA: Hoover Institutions Press.

Weiss, Marc. 1987. The Rise of the Community Builders: The American Real Estate Industry and Urban Land Planning. New York: Columbia University Press.

Wenzer, Kenneth. 1997. 'Tolstoy's Georgist spiritual political economy (1897–1910): anarchism and land reform'. American Journal of Economics and Sociology, 56, 639–667.

Werczberger, Elia and Eliyahu Borukhov. 1999. 'The Israel land authority: relic or neccessity'. Land Use Policy 16, 129–138.

Wertheim, W.F. (ed.). 1958. The Indonesian Town: Studies in Urban Sociology. The Hague and Bandung: W. van Hoeve.

West, Edward. 1815. Essay on the Application of Capital to Land. London: T. Underwood.

White, Ben. 2005. Between apologia and critical discourse: agrarian transitions and scholarly engagement in Indonesia. In: Social Science and Power in Indonesia, edited by Vedi Hadiz and Daniel Dhakidae. Jakarta and Singapore: Equinox Publishing.

White, Morton and Lucia White. 1962. The Intellectual versus the City. New York and Toronto: New American Library.

Who's Who in Real Estate. Redas Directory. 1997. Singapore.

Whyte, Martin King and William L. Parish. 1984. Urban Life in Contemporary China. Chicago: Chicago University Press

Widodo, Johannes. 2009. Regionalism/localism: learning from vernacular-cosmopolitan sustainable constructs in Southeast Asia. Paper presented at ARI workshop Constructing Sustainability – Ethics, Techniques and Aesthetics, February 13. Singapore.

Wieser, Friedrich von. 1929. Die theorie der städtischen grundrente. In: Friedrich von Wieser: Gesamte Abhandlungen. Tübingen.

'Will Britain become a nation of coolies?' 1996, The Straits Times, 14 January.

Williams, Raymond. 1975. The Country and the City. St. Albans: Paladin.

Williams, Howard. 1977. 'Kant's concept of property'. Philosophical Quarterly 27, 32–40.

Wingo, Lowdon. 1961. Transportation and Urban Land. Washington, DC: Resources for the Future.

Winters, Jeffrey. 2000. The financial crisis in southeast Asia. In: Politics and Markets in the Wake of the Asian Crisis, edited by Robison R, Beeson M, Jayasuriya K, Kim H. London: Routledge.

Wittfogel, Karl. 1957. Oriental Despotism. New Haven, CT: Yale University Press.

Wong, A. K. and Ooi G.L. 1989. Spatial reorganization. In: Management of Success: The Moulding of Modern Singapore, edited by Sandhu K.S and Wheatley P. Singapore: Institute of Southeast Asian Studies.

Wong, Douglas. 2000. 'Govt relaxes rules on Sing dollar lending', The Straits Times, 7 December, p. 1.

Wong, Foster and Ernest Kong. 2005. 'Lion City is a bit of a gamble', South China Morning Post, 15 June, p. 6.

Wong, T. 2011.'Casino novelty 'wearing off', The Straits Times, 13 March, p. 16.

Woodruff, A.M. 1980. Five lessons for land reformers. Land & Liberty.

World Development Report. 1996. From Plan to Market. Washington: The World Bank.

World Development Report. 2009. Reshaping Economic Geography. Washington: The World Bank.

World Investment Report. 1995. Transnational Corporations and Competitiveness. New York and Geneva: United Nations.

World Investment Report. 1999. Foreign Direct Investment and the Challenge of Development. New York and Geneva: United Nations.

World Investment Report. 2008. Transnational Corporations and the Infrastructure Challenge. New York and Geneva: United Nations.

Wu, C.L. 1989. Taxation of land and buildings. In: The Economic System of Hong Kong, edited by H.C.Y. Ho and L.C. Cheu. Hong Kong: Asian Research Service.

Wu, Fulong (ed.). 2005. Globalization and the Chinese City. London and New York: Routledge.

Wu Fulong and Chris Webster (eds). 2010. Marginalization in Urban China. Basingstoke: Palgrave Macmillan.

Wu, Tang Hang. 2007. 'The legal representation of the Singaporean home and the influence of the common law'. Hong Kong Law Journal, 32, 81–102.

Wurtzebach, Charles and Mike Miles. 1987. Modern Real Estate. New York: John Wiley & Sons.

Wyckoff, William. 1988. The Developer's Frontier: The Making of the Western New York Landscape. New Haven, CT and London: Yale University Press.

Yearbook of Statistics Singapore. 2002. Singapore: Department of Statistics.
Yearbook of Statistics Singapore. 2013. Singapore: Department of Statistics.
Yearbook of Statistics Singapore. 2014. Singapore: Department of Statistics.
Year-end Economic Review. 1998. The Land Department Thailand, Bangkok Post. www.bangkokpost.com 7 January 2000.
Yee, Shirley and Chua Beng Huat. 1999. 'Sociological research: following the contours of social issues'. In: Singapore Studies II: Critical Surveys of the Humanities and Social, edited by Chua Beng Huat. Singapore: National University of Singapore. Centre for Advanced Studies.
Yeh, A. and F. Wu. 1996. 'The new land development process and urban development in Chinese cities'. International Journal of Urban and Regional Research, 20, 330–353.
Yeh, Stephen. 1995. Public Housing in Singapore: A Multi-disciplinary Study. Singapore: Singapore University Press.
Yeoh, Brenda. 1996. Contesting Space: Power Relations and the Urban Built Environment in Colonial Singapore. Kuala Lumpur: Oxford University Press.
Yeoh, Brenda and T. C. Chang. 2001 'Globalising Singapore: debating transnational flows in the city'. Urban Studies, 38, 1025–1044.
Yeow, Pei Lin. 1998. 'High-tech facilities at factory prices', The Straits Times, 11 December.
Yeung, Henry and Kris Olds (eds). 2000. Globalization of Chinese Business Firms. Basingstoke: Palgrave Macmillan.
Yeung Yue-man and Stephen Yeh. 1971. 'Commercial pattern in Singapore's public housing estates'. The Journal of Tropical Geography, 33, 73–86.
Ylikangas, Heikki. 1977. Nuijasota. Helsinki: Otava.
Yoshihara, K. 1988. The Rise of Ersatz Capitalism in Southeast Asia. Singapore: Oxford University Press.
Yoshikawa, Hiroshi. 2008. Japan's Lost Decade. Tokyo: House Press, The International House of Japan.
Yuen, Belinda. 2007. 'Squatters no more: Singapore social housing'. Global Urban Development Magazine 3. http://www.globalurban.org/GUDMag07Vol3Iss1/Yuen.htm [Accessed June 2015].
Zhu, Jieming. 2002. 'Urban development under ambiguous property rights: A case of China's transition economy'. International Journal of Urban and Regional Research, 26, 41–57.
Zukin, Sharon. 1991. Landscapes of Power: From Detroit to Disney World. Berkeley and Los Angeles, CA: University of California Press.
Zukin, Sharon. 1995. The Cultures of Cities. Cambridge, MA and Oxford: Blackwell.

# Index

References to illustrations are in italics: references to tables and notes have 't' or 'n' after the page number, e.g. 148t, 157n.

absolute rent, xix, 23, 47–48, 60, 75, 104, 119, 148–152, 154, 157n, 224
Abu Dhabi Investment Authority, 167
actual rent, xix, 57, 59
Adair, Alastair, 178
Addae-Dapaah, Kwame, 109
Adis, Khalil, 156, 178
Adshead, S.A.M., 209
*Agrarian Justice* (Paine), 64–65
Aiyar, Swaminathan, 80–81
Akerlof, George, 43, 211, 225
Alaska Permanent Fund, 168
Alatas, Syed Hussein, 8
Alonso, William, 50, 51
Ambrose, Peter, 153
*American Journal of Economics and Sociology*, 67
Anan, Ganjanapan, 35
Anderson, Benedict, 40
Ang, Lilian, 126
Ang, Wan May, 126, 170
Ang, Yiying, 109
anti-segregation policies. *See* racial quota system
ARA Asset Management, 164

ARC report, 144
Arcasia Land, 138, 145
Arestis, Philip, 202
Arneil, Barbara, 37
Arrighi, Giovanni, 71
Ascendas, 138, 140t, 165t, 166, 217
Ascott Residence Trust, 165t
ASEAN (Association of Southeast Nations), 196, 214n
*Asian Cities* (McKinnon), 6
*Asian Development Outlook* (1998), 198
Asian Monetary Policy Forum, 208, 225–226
Ayutthaya (Thailand), 7

Bagli, Charles V., 212
Baker, Chris, 9, 199, 200–201, 202
Ball, Michael, 50, 152, 154
Balzac, Honore de, 42
Bandyopadhyay, Pradeep, 60
Bangkok (Thailand), 200–204
banking, 185, 192–195, 228
Barings Bank, 185, 192–195
Barker, E.W., 74, 75
Barlow, James, 116
Barrett, Wayne, 131